Group Work that Works

Promote cooperative learning more effectively by transforming your classroom into a learning community. Experienced K–12 educators Paul J. Vermette and Cynthia L. Kline offer their Dual Objective Model as a tool for improving your students' academic achievement and problem-solving skills, while encouraging their social and emotional development.

You'll discover how to:

◆ assign meaningful tasks that require students to rely on one another;
◆ build efficient teams, purposefully monitor group dynamics, and assess group projects effectively;
◆ engage students in schoolwork while developing crucial career and life skills;
◆ motivate students to see the importance of personal and group responsibility;
◆ maximize the benefits of student diversity in your classroom.

Emphasizing teamwork, persistence, communication, self-regulation, and empathy in a complex, diverse, and technological setting, these strategies can be easily incorporated into any curriculum. The book is filled with vignettes and sample exercises to help you apply the ideas to your own classroom. Each chapter includes a list of "Big Ideas," which invites you to consider how these strategies can evolve over time.

Paul J. Vermette has served as a teacher and supervisor of social studies in public and parochial schools in New York and New Jersey and has been a Professor of Education at Niagara University since 1985.

Cynthia L. Kline is an independent educational consultant and business professional serving both domestic and international K–20 settings.

Other Eye on Education Books
Available from Routledge

Group Work that Works

Student Collaboration for 21st Century Success

Paul J. Vermette and Cynthia L. Kline

Routledge
Taylor & Francis Group

NEW YORK AND LONDON

First published 2017
by Routledge
711 Third Avenue, New York, NY 10017

and by Routledge
2 Park Square, Milton Park, Abingdon, Oxon, OX14 4RN

Routledge is an imprint of the Taylor & Francis Group, an informa business

Library of Congress Cataloging-in-Publication Data
Names: Vermette, Paul J., author. | Kline, Cynthia L., author.
Title: Group work that works / by Paul J. Vermette and Cynthia L.
    Kline.
Description: New York : Routledge, 2017.
Identifiers: LCCN 2016047707 | ISBN 9781138668959 (hardback) | ISBN
    9781138668966 (pbk.)
Subjects: LCSH: Group work in education. | Team learning approach in
    education.
Classification: LCC LB1032 .V38 2017 | DDC 371.3/6—dc23
LC record available at https://lccn.loc.gov/2016047707

ISBN: 978-1-138-66895-9 (hbk)
ISBN: 978-1-138-66896-6 (pbk)
ISBN: 978-1-315-61836-4 (ebk)

Typeset in Palatino
by Apex CoVantage, LLC

This book is dedicated from Paul Vermette:
  To Kit, Matt, and Molly, a great team . . .
  To my many colleagues who work to educate the "whole child"
  24–7, 365 . . .
  And to "E Pluribus Unum," the spirit of respectful unity that
  lies in the heart of our pluralist democracy.

And from Cindy Kline:
  To Mom and Dad (my first teachers) for the inspiration
  to serve, enduring love, and for high expectations (they
  unfortunately didn't get to see this) . . .
  To my dearest educator friends and family (Mark, Steve,
  Kathy, Krista, Sarah, John and "the Drs. Jones") who
  consistently fight the good fight . . .
  To Emily Kaufman for her grit, patience, and attention to
  accuracy in editing . . .
  And lastly, to my son Khristian Cole, who's intellect AND affect
  will assuredly lead him to great things!

Contents

Meet the Authors

Paul J. Vermette

Paul Vermette has had a long history as a professional educator working with middle and secondary students as teacher, coach and, since 1985, as University Professor of Secondary Teacher Education at Niagara University. He has been driven by a deep-seated curiosity for discovering effective instructional strategies and a passion for helping teens develop cognitively and affectively. Two decades ago he discovered the power and promise of Cooperative Learning/ well-structured group work and began to focus his own research and experimentation on its implementation. In 2005, he teamed up with a graduate of the NU program, Cynthia L. Kline, to explore, design, and examine a set of classroom practices that aligned with what both field practitioners and scholarly researchers say is effective. Their collaboration continues today.

Paul has been an active scholar and has published over 90 articles and five books, his most recent title being *ENGAGING teens in their own learning*. He has been the honored recipient of numerous awards for his accomplishments, most notably as NY Teacher Educator of the Year and NY Outstanding Teacher Educator. He has served in a variety of capacities on educational boards and within NY State educational organizations, having powerful learning experiences in all of these endeavors. Many people have contributed to his growth and development, a wonderful result of this extensive teamwork and collaboration.

Finally, Paul has been very lucky in his many long years as an educator. His wife of 46 years, Kathleen, and son Dr. Matt Vermette (a teacher and coach himself) have given him the support to pursue his inquiries. Niagara University has provided a wonderful environment, dedicated colleagues, and a lengthy list of hard-working and compassionate students to work with, and grow from. Now in his twilight, Paul hopes to help educators see the utility of the Dual Objective as a vehicle to help every teenager develop his or her life potential while promoting the common good for this pluralist democratic nation.

Cynthia L. Kline

Cynthia L. Kline, having worked for an International Fortune 500 company for nearly two decades in sales, quality improvement, and training management, became enamored with the study of personal abilities that enable success. In 2003, she left the private sector for the public, becoming a secondary teacher and educational consultant, and soon encountered the work of Daniel Goleman (emotional intelligence) and the Collaborative for Academic Social and Emotional Learning who termed these abilities "key competencies." Fueled by the desire to guide youth in the development of these social and emotional skills, she taught for nearly a decade, focusing her classroom and consultation efforts on instruction through collaborative learning and fostering awareness of the foundational role that social and emotional learning plays in academic and life success. Today she has returned to the world of learning management where she brings her unique combination of talents to bear in improving education K-20.

Cynthia has presented extensively both nationally and internationally, has served on various boards during her tenure and as author, she has most recently published on the KVA model, which she helped develop to assist university professors with terminal degrees to develop strong instructional pedagogy.

Inspired by the many skilled educators with whom she has had the great pleasure of working, improving education to elevate student achievement is her passion and she appreciates every opportunity to discuss such with respected colleagues. She enjoys a contented life in western New York with family and friends, who bring meaning, challenge, and happiness to the art of living.

Prologue

The Real Question: "Why Should *You* Read this Book?"

Introduction and Welcome

From our outside perspective, we (the authors) think we have written a good book, an interesting book, and a powerful book that can help teachers change their practice to become more effective with their adolescent students. However, we also understand that the learning (and the reading, thinking, and reflecting) will have to be done by the reader, so we begin by asking about your motivations, intentions, strategies, and prior experiences.

So, because you are actually reading this sentence (as you indeed are), there are plausible answers to the title question, and they are important.

TASK: Why This Book?

Check the following that are true about why you are reading this book:

☐ 1.   An authority figure is forcing me to read it against my will.
☐ 2.   I am interested in developing new and useful instructional strategies.
☐ 3.   The cover illustration piqued my curiosity.
☐ 4.   I know that the authors are good teachers and I want to hear what they say.
☐ 5.   I hate group work and want to actively challenge the author's ideas.
☐ 6.   I am part of a PLC that chose this book and recruited me to join them.
☐ 7.   I coach sports and know that teamwork is good, but I don't use it in my content classroom.
☐ 8.   My students need more motivation to learn and they need to develop a satisfactory work ethic.
☐ 9.   I have experienced good teamwork and now want to know how to structure it as a leader.
☐ 10. I have experienced poor teamwork and want to know how to avoid the problems I expect.
☐ 11. Students in classrooms where Cooperative Learning is used seem to enjoy their educational experiences, and I want to know what those teachers know.
☐ 12. The Every Student Succeeds Act (ESSA) regulations call for a whole-child approach to learning, and I'm looking for ways to modify my practice.
☐ 13. Well-structured teamwork may help students become the people they need to become.
☐ 14. I want to be able to talk to parents and community leaders more effectively about the real skills that adolescents need to develop for life success.

Before we proceed any further, please note four things: (1) this book was written to you individually; (2) the authors expect you to engage deeply with activities and questions embedded in the narrative; (3) you should realize that we (the authors) are theorists and practitioners who hope that you implement and examine our suggestions and assess their impact on the learning and development of your students. Therefore, we should mention that, (4) while your purposes for reading this book may change as you read it, how you start will be very important. We hope your answers to the quiz above indicate a positive motivation and, if so, we will fulfill our promise to improve your practice. If they show your negativity toward this reading experience, we ask you to be fully aware of this bias, monitor how it affects your reading (metacognition), and give the evidence we offer a chance to convince you of its value. Self-awareness and self-regulation are key competencies and will affect how you process the ideas being promoted; your professional development will be a result of the two-way interaction this book seeks to promote.

We have created a text that conveys information about a powerful instructional strategy formal education now has, Cooperative Learning (CL), and about our version, called the Dual Objective Model. As you learn about the Dual Objective from the text, you will realize that you must actively translate ideas into practices and this "process of understanding" is controlled by thoughtful completion of our activities and your experimentation with the ideas in real classes.

You cannot get much out of this book if you skim it or peruse it; you must "work" your way through it to realize its benefits. This expectation makes it analogous to being a teenage student in your classroom; he or she will gain from your class the benefits commensurate with the effort put into it.

We start by trying to persuade you to give CL a try and we realize that there may be a hesitation to use teams in secondary education, a reluctance that defies the evidence. For example, in a widely publicized article for teachers, Tom Bennett (2015) criticizes Cooperative Learning, but as we read the article, we got the impression that he did not have a very accurate understanding of how to set up the structure, what to expect from the students at the outset, what researchers have found about implementation, and under what conditions to use it. We hope that he reads our text, reworks his plans to use CL, and writes to teachers again about an improved experience.

We know that teachers are good people, have good intentions, are too busy to carefully process many new challenges, often go on what they call "instinct," and have to work in the present. Here, at the outset, we ask you to plan to think deeply, to thoughtfully experiment, to keep fidelity to the model, to trust that every piece of advice we give you has been field-tested with real teenagers, and to share your journey through the book with somebody else.

Kline (author) has created a mantra that applies to the book's promise to help improve your students' cognitive knowledge and skills as well as their affective interactions and competencies. She wishes to take you from "well-meaning and intuitive" to "systematic and intentional" in your use of the Dual Objective Model of Cooperative Learning. We also hope that both you and Mr. Bennett give this book, and CL, a chance to make a difference.

Why Do We Promote Cooperative Learning and the Dual Objective?

TASK: Why Use Cooperative Learning?

As you probably know, today's adolescents are becoming citizens in a time of great change. Below is a short but impactful list of societal changes impacting the potential success of our youth. Please take a moment to clarify your own perspective by rank ordering how important each of these challenges are to your students' success from 1 (high) to 5 (low).

_____ a. Increased cognitive demands in school and in work.
_____ b. Increased social and cultural changes that affect communication patterns.
_____ c. Rapidly changing technological capabilities that require continuous knowledge upgrades.
_____ d. More frequent complex social interactions across multiple diversities and contexts.
_____ e. Increased frustration as traditional patterns (for success) no longer seem to apply.

Preparing teens to handle the pressures of these changes in their current and future lives makes the job of secondary teaching incredibly difficult in the modern age. However, we recognize the robust and respected research base that suggests that Cooperative Learning should be a regular tool for all teachers and, yet, it is a largely untapped resource. We also think that the Dual Objective Model, which stresses (1) **mastery of content and improved problem-solving abilities** while (2) **assisting social and emotional development and powerful interaction skills**, can play a huge role in answering the question of how to help teens handle each of the various changes mentioned above. We also humbly suggest that the structure of the book will likely challenge your ideas, your current practices, and your insights about school as you connect its applications to your own educational setting. We hope that you accept the challenge and make a commitment to push yourself to think deeply and keep an open mind about your classroom practice.

Three Important Concepts + One Model

We also suggest that there are three + one critically important instructional concepts that should guide our work with you and your work with your students. These can be seen as the collective lens though which we view effective learning for adults and adolescents. These three + one notions have guided our decision-making and will play a role in the construction of your version of the Dual Objective.

Growth Mindset

For over a decade, Stanford's Carol Dweck has been promoting her concept of *Mindset* (2006), of which there are two types. The *fixed mindset*, built along the never-changing model of IQ, suggests that cognitive ability is a stable and permanent feature of an individual human being, a quality that does not respond well to external practices. One can add learned items to memory but a person's overall potential, capacity, and ability are fixed. Students and teachers who hold this mindset are quick to protect their egos and accomplishments by ignoring challenges, basking in past glories (or banking on past failures), and coasting on quick and easy tasks in an attempt to maintain a familiar interpretation of themselves. They are what they are and that is that (i.e. "I am smart at math but bad at poetry; I make friends easily, have never been able to golf, cannot swim, don't like to read, and don't like to work in groups." Comments like these reflect a belief in permanent abilities for those with fixed mindsets.)

On the other hand, the *growth mindset*, which is much more conducive to accepting innovation, expanding abilities, facing challenges and the threats they bring, broadening experiences and recognizing change as normal, is the converse. People with this growth mindset may say, "I cannot do this," but it comes out this way when they say it: "I cannot do this . . . yet," suggesting that they think that they can change their abilities and potential, they can learn, they can develop, and they can succeed. They see their abilities as variated, temporal, and malleable; they see life as full of opportunity and their brains as developing.

A simple test can quickly demonstrate these two polar opposite responses to this one situation. If you were offered a reward, would you rather experiment with something brand new that may help you grow as a person or perform an old familiar routine that is sure to be acceptable? The growth mindset calls for risk and innovation and a chance to become something more; the fixed mindset suggests that staying in one's comfort zone is "good enough" and a safe choice.

Obviously, education should be built on a growth mindset and its very nature is to challenge a student's current capabilities. Educators want students to see the world with optimistic eyes and a hopeful heart, but can get bogged down in the perceived permanence of past failures and successes, the seemingly stable level of ability, and the fixed, maybe even genetically programmed, nature of character traits. Just as people can learn new cognitive and psychomotor skills and can raise their IQs, character traits are not necessarily in-born and forever; they can develop, improve, and be honed. Adolescents are in the *process* of becoming responsible, productive, and reasoning adults and teachers should be a positive force in this work in progress.

We note that teachers can continuously improve their instructional practice and students can learn new content, gain insights from new relationships, and develop new communication patterns. We see these things happening to you as you read on and give serious thought to transferring the book's suggestions to your own classroom.

Grit

In a now-famous work by Angela Duckworth (2016) of the University of Pennsylvania, the concept of grit—described as persistence and effort across a lengthy period of time on an important task—was shown to be a predictor of all kinds of successes by young people. The notion that one should not quit when faced with failure, difficulty, disappointment, or exhaustion is well known in the American ideological tradition but not practiced often enough in real-life situations. Overcoming failure through a long-term commitment, a deep work ethic, and a belief in improving ability (growth mindset) combine to predict eventual meaningful success (see Perkins-Gough's 2013 article in *Educational Leadership* for an interesting interview with Duckworth).

We suggest that you invest in mastering the ideas in this book and actually *expect* them to improve your practice. We also suggest that you commit to staying with your experimentation so that the initial learning dip dissipates, so you can develop familiarity with complex procedures, and experience increasing success. A noteworthy recent critic of Cooperative Learning (Bennett, 2015) has bashed it because he tried it and it doesn't work like its advocates/cheerleaders say; however, there is little indication that he has attempted to keep fidelity to its components and it seems as if he has given up on its value without extensive experience with it. We assure you that using it **once is not enough** for you to realize the potential of the Dual Objective. Teaching is incredibly complex, and thoughtful reflection over time, is necessary to teacher development. Plan to show grit as you proceed.

Deliberate Practice

The third concept we like to focus on is Anders Ericsson's deliberate practice (Ericsson & Pool, 2016) and it serves as the logical link between the first two concepts described above. If you believe you can improve (growth mindset), and you are in it for the long term (grit), what do you need to make effective change? The answer is concentrated effort on mastering the *really important* things. This sounds simple, but it is far rarer than we want to believe it is not easy to do. Deliberate practice is hard work; concentrated, elaborate, and lengthy efforts at attaining specific goals (or objectives) will consume time, focus, and energy. Ericsson's genius was not in discovering that practice makes better, but in understanding that much more practice was required than was usually expected and that the practice must be focused, meaningful, assessed, and altered according to feedback. In other words, practice must be useful, lengthy, and appropriate if it is going to help improve performance.

For an instant and superficial culture like ours, this may be asking a lot. A great book by Daniel Kahneman (2011) suggests that humans are composed of two thinking systems: first, a fast one that seeks quick and easy answers and protects itself by ignoring aspects of a situation that are troubling or confusing. For example, if you had difficulty grasping the paragraph above, you could just skip it and tell yourself that it is not that important right now or you could have cursed the authors and given yourself an excuse to give up *or* you could laboriously go back and carefully re-read it, examining it closely to try to discover meaning. If you did choose the re-examine option, then you have used the second thinking system—the slow one—and are moving toward deliberate practice. It is that second, slow system that is really the intellectual one that formal education seeks to enhance. Students find such think-work tedious, difficult, and confusing, even when it has great pay off. Deliberate practice, or what David Perkins (2009) calls "practicing the hard parts," is needed to maximize understanding and to change attitudes and beliefs through reason and evidence. Self-regulation of attention, meta-cognitive awareness, and concentrated examination lead to conceptual growth and, not surprisingly, fatigue (Baumeister & Tierney, 2011)!

As an opportunity to practice at "deliberate practice," re-write that last sentence in your own words.

Re-writing requires a concentrated effort and doing so helps build understanding. If you do similar tasks often, it will also increase your reading time and tire you out faster. Learning is not always simple and not always fun, but it is always meaningful.

+ One Model

To help integrate the three concepts above, we offer an approach that might help you get a deeper understanding of how thinking and learning create cognitive change. The model we wish to share with you is a version of how learning happens within the mind as it works, adapted from the work of Daniel Willingham (2009). Briefly skim over the visual provided in the space below and try to question how the parts interact to "cause" learning:

Figure P.1 Model of the Mind

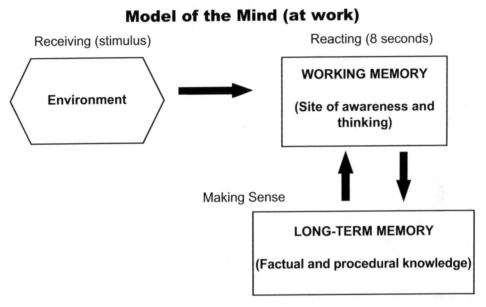

Model of the Mind (at work)

Receiving (stimulus)   Reacting (8 seconds)

Environment

WORKING MEMORY

(Site of awareness and thinking)

Making Sense

LONG-TERM MEMORY

(Factual and procedural knowledge)

Source: Adapted from "Why Don't Student's Like School?" (Willingham, 2009) by Vermette & Kline (2012)

Notice that having been exposed to a stimulus is just the beginning of the learning process. Looking at this page of words, sitting in a classroom during a class, or running a TED Talk on your computer are not enough to *cause* learning—learning is an active, not passive process. To get into short-term memory (STM), the external idea must be attended to and interpreted through the lens of an individual's unique personal cognitive network and must happen within a few seconds. This initial reaction, the focusing on something, begins the bridging between stimulus and understanding. Unattended stimuli are permanently lost. What we don't attend to is gone and it seems like it never was there.

To get a stimulus from STM into long-term memory (LTM), where it can be stored and strengthened, there must be *engagement* (i.e. thinking) that reciprocally and intentionally connects the new information with what is already stored. Learning activities, like those in Cooperative Learning, engage thought processes that deepen new ideas and integrate them into LTM. Deeper conceptual understanding results from many sessions of integrating STM with LTM in varied contexts. Positive learning experiences spark intentional processes that allow the new construct, (i.e. idea, piece of knowledge, insight) to be embedded in LTM and become part of one's personalized network of knowledge. (By the way, this process exemplifies the Piagetian notions of assimilation and accommodation and the Vygotskian ideas that conversation engages in clarification and advancement of thought.)

These last few comments may be confusing to some. To promote clarity, we offer an example drawn from secondary math content, which we hope you do not know already:

TASK: STM vs. LTM

Read the following sentence:

"Dividing by ½ is *not* the same as dividing by 2, even though many adults cannot explain the difference."

If you did not try to focus on the sentence, it is gone from STM already. If you *did* focus and understood the words, you had connected the stimulus with knowledge networks in your LTM; you may not yet be able to apply or explain the principle, but you did attend and interpret the information. You have made a superficial and quick attempt to grasp meaning. Many poor attempts at learning by teens stops at this level of commitment: simple reaction. More effort and varied experience is needed for real conceptual understanding.

If you went ahead and tried to analyze the connection between dividing by ½ or by 2, you were doing "deep processing," which is the necessary cognitive step for developing meaningful understanding. Deliberate practice is forcing oneself to do this deep processing until comprehension and application are possible. For many of us (depending on the context and our prior knowledge), this can be exhausting work.

We know that Cooperative Learning provides the motivational and conceptual context for frequent deep and meaningful processing of ideas by adolescents, thus increasing learning. You will see later that research supports this insight.

Let's abandon math for a moment as we ask you to try another example.

TASK: Making Meaning

Try your hand at remembering these points:

1. Two piles usually do it and people don't want to overdo it!
2. This must be done over and over again, even if it was done correctly the last time.
3. Many of us can do it right at home, but for some, they must pack up and travel first.
4. No matter where it happens, one must be prepared.
5. One has to be careful to NOT do too much at one time.

We hope you are asking yourself, "What . . .?" We wonder if you got bored, tuned out, and/or skimmed the last several sentences.

If you tried to memorize the sentences, it would have taken a while and many of you would not have been successful. If you tried to integrate the five of them and understand the "gist" as a whole, you would be doing what the mind does: it stores meanings generated from personal cognitive effort, not the specifics from the stimulus! Try it again and begin with the notion that all five items are connected to the practice called "washing clothes" (Bransford & Johnson, 1972). Was it easier this time? If so, it is because you activated prior knowledge from your LTM, which helped you focus on the new information. The sentences then made more sense. Note that if you had originally worked with a partner, your interactions may have led to seeing the organizing structure earlier and perhaps made the task more enjoyable—that is part of what CL offers to those who are used to thinking alone. Cooperative Learning makes problem-solving and meaningful understanding a shared experience.

We maintain that using team activities leads to real student–student interactions and conversations that promote, and work as the setting for, deliberate practice. "Talking to learn" with others is a process that activates prior knowledge, promotes deep processing, and entices feedback. It encourages integration of ideas and offers new ways to connect ideas. In truth, reading (and studying) this text by yourself, which most of you will be doing, is more difficult than sharing your ideas in a book club or a small group. You must attend to the ideas we present, engage in thinking and meaning-making that connects those ideas to ones you already have available (in your LTM), and then make decisions about further elaboration or experimentation with them. If you have others to talk to about the book the ideas will get clearer faster and be more deeply connected in personal and social contexts.

In Closing

As we head into the first chapter of this journey, we wish you to be clear on your personal approach to reading this book. In effect, we are asking you to set your own goals for the experience.

If you are to become a highly effective 21st-century educator, you almost certainly have to show grit, maintain a growth mindset, and be ready to engage in thoughtful and deliberate practice (either alone or in community). If you do these things as you read, you will be doing the deep processing (labeled as meaningful understanding) that is called for by Willingham's Model of the Mind from Figure P.1. You will be refining and extending old ideas, creating new ideas, seeing new relationships between ideas, and developing new skills. We are confident that you will be most pleased with your investment of time and energy and most satisfied with the resulting changes you make in your professional practice.

In order to facilitate ongoing benefit from this text after initial reading, we offer a listing of "Big Ideas" from each chapter for your reference. We encourage you to return to these to consider how they can impact your journey through change. Perhaps a discussion with colleagues, selecting a specific idea for emphasis in your practice, assessing your own performance (or that of a mentee), or for the very brave, asking your students to offer their insights on the elements that they can assess. There are endless options limited only by your goals and creativity, but we hope you do return (and often) to these ideas for your own personal benefit as well as that of your students.

We hope that you are moved to talk about the ideas in this book with others. Furthermore, your students will benefit from your professional growth and your use of the Dual Objective Model and they will bask in the successes of their improved affective abilities and cognitive achievements. Your gains in mastering successful Cooperative Learning have unlimited power to influence the success of your students: Relish the journey!

Prologue Big Ideas

1. Teacher change is incremental in nature and requires intention, thought, experimentation, and reflection on practice.
2. Change and reform is a pervasive theme in education and reflects social, economic, and political transformations in the nation and in the world.
3. Well-structured Cooperative Learning (using the Dual Objective Model) offers promises of deeper understanding and improved social and personal skills of students.

4. There are three critically important theoretical notions that promote educational improvement: grit, growth mindset, and thoughtful/ deliberate practice.
5. Conceptual learning follows an established model: attending to information/ideas from a source, recognizing it in short-term memory, and then consolidating it through an active interaction between short- and long-term memory. Multiple applications to new examples from varied contexts (retrieval practice) re-consolidate and deepen understanding, increasing the ease of future transfer.
6. The purpose of reading a book and/or thoughtfully engaging in a class is to spark new meaning, deepen understanding, and thus to change minds.

References

Baumeister, R.F., & Tierney, J. (2011). *Willpower: Rediscovering the greatest human strength*. New York, NY: Penguin Books.

Bennett, T. (2015). Group work for the good: Unpacking the research behind one popular classroom strategy. *American Educator*, Spring, 32–44.

Bransford, J.D., & Johnson, M.K. (1972). Contextual prerequisites for understanding: Some investigations of comprehension and recall. *Journal of Verbal Learning and Verbal Behavior, 11*, 717–726.

Duckworth, A.L. (2016). *Grit: The power of passion and perseverance*. New York, NY: Scribner.

Dweck, C. (2006). *Mindset: The new psychology of success*. New York, NY: Random House.

Ericsson, A., & Pool, R. (2016). *Peak: Secrets from the new science of expertise*. New York, NY: Houghton-Mifflin Harcourt.

Kahneman, D. (2011). *Thinking, fast and slow*. New York, NY: Farrar, Straus and Giroux.

Perkins, D. (2009). *Making learning whole: How seven principles of teaching can transform education*. San Francisco, CA: Jossey-Bass.

Perkins-Gough, D. (2013). The significance of grit: A conversation with Angela Duckworth. *Educational Leadership, 71*(1), 4–20.

Willingham, D. (2009). *Why don't students like school? A cognitive scientist answers questions about how the mind works and what it means for the classroom*. San Francisco, CA: Jossey-Bass.

1

Well-Structured Cooperative Learning

What? So What?

In this very short chapter, we intend for you to accomplish three goals. You should:

1. Be able to explain what effective Cooperative Learning looks like, and be able to spot commonalities across its various implementations;
2. Be able to describe the importance of fidelity to implementation protocols;
3. Be able to identify research-supported outcomes promised by the use of well-structured Cooperative Learning.

What is Cooperative Learning?

Despite the fact that much has been written about "group work," "collaboration," and "Cooperative Learning," the major thinkers (Johnson & Johnson, 1987, 2009; Slavin, 1983; Davidson & Major, 2014; Cohen 1994; Kagan, 1992; Vermette, 1998; Myers, Bardsley, Vermette, & Kline, 2017) on this topic seem to agree on some basics of well-structured CL:

- Students work in face-to-face small groups (five individuals or smaller) to **solve problems, create projects, master conceptual content, or analyze data and/or situations**.
- The structure of, and the feelings within, the heterogeneous group must be geared toward an ethos of **positive interdependence**, a

situation that demands that no one person can be successful without others being so as well.

◆ The **teams are usually arranged by the teacher**, and must be stable or what is perceived as **"relatively permanent"**; that is, they are not short-term groupings of mixed individuals to complete a temporary task but rather a unit that must work through numerous differentiated interactions over time.

◆ The **effectiveness** of the group's internal interaction must be **monitored and assessed** and **feedback must be offered** by team members and the teacher.

◆ **Assessment for, and of, learning** must include individual and group accountability, so that success or failure is earned by the individuals and the team.

TASK: Is This an Example of CL?

Please read the following classroom vignettes carefully and decide, by categorizing them as YES or NO, whether they are, in fact, well-structured Cooperative Learning exemplars according to the conceptualization offered above.

_____ 1. On Thursdays, Ms. Jenkins lets her 21 7th-grade FACS students work together on the week's assignment if they wish to do so. From bell to bell, she "works the room" (Konkoski-Bates & Vermette, 2004), offering them feedback on their work and encouraging them to share their ideas.

_____ 2. In Social Studies 11, Mr. Bautista (also Varsity Football Coach) has students assigned to their "base teams" of three or four. Every day that the class meets, the teams gather and share their ideas and make sure that everyone is learning the material for the Friday test. Each group that has every member score at 70 percent or better on that test gets a bonus: ten points for each member. He also gives out "interaction" awards, a five-point bonus to everyone on teams that he judges have worked well together as a "unit" all week. An additional point is given to everyone on teams with perfect attendance.

_____ 3. Dr. Smith uses a lot of short activities during his 8th-grade science class. Today there were five such learning activities and he used a random number generator to create and vary the small group memberships that completed each of these tasks. After each brief activity, Smith asks one student from the entire class to tell what happened and thus inform everyone about his or her group's procedures and results.

_____ 4. Dividing the class into boys vs. girls, Miss Jones sets her 9th-grade ELA class up for a debate about gender and how it affects fiction. Each of the two groups (12 boys and 11 girls) will pick one representative and use the first 20 minutes of class to prepare him and her for the two-person debate that will occur during the last 20 minutes. These representatives then debate in front of the whole room, with much cheering and shouting from the two

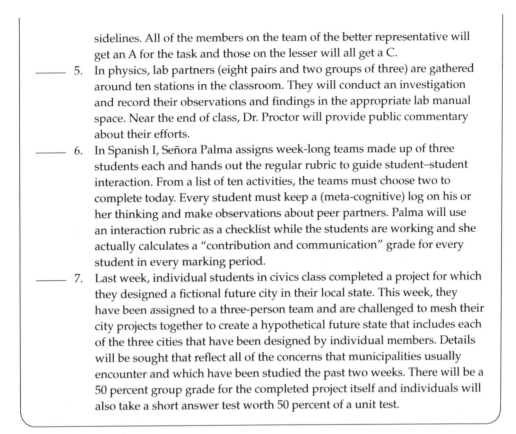

sidelines. All of the members on the team of the better representative will get an A for the task and those on the lesser will all get a C.

_____ 5. In physics, lab partners (eight pairs and two groups of three) are gathered around ten stations in the classroom. They will conduct an investigation and record their observations and findings in the appropriate lab manual space. Near the end of class, Dr. Proctor will provide public commentary about their efforts.

_____ 6. In Spanish I, Señora Palma assigns week-long teams made up of three students each and hands out the regular rubric to guide student–student interaction. From a list of ten activities, the teams must choose two to complete today. Every student must keep a (meta-cognitive) log on his or her thinking and make observations about peer partners. Palma will use an interaction rubric as a checklist while the students are working and she actually calculates a "contribution and communication" grade for every student in every marking period.

_____ 7. Last week, individual students in civics class completed a project for which they designed a fictional future city in their local state. This week, they have been assigned to a three-person team and are challenged to mesh their city projects together to create a hypothetical future state that includes each of the three cities that have been designed by individual members. Details will be sought that reflect all of the concerns that municipalities usually encounter and which have been studied the past two weeks. There will be a 50 percent group grade for the completed project itself and individuals will also take a short answer test worth 50 percent of a unit test.

The yes/no categorization task that you just completed is built along the lines of suggestions from Bruner, Goodenow, and Austin (1986) about student *mastery of concepts*, a critically important learning task. Notice that the definition/description of Cooperative Learning was offered and then learners were asked to actively analyze new examples for "goodness of fit." The use of non-exemplars (i.e. the items that were classified as "not CL" or "NO") may have forced readers to think deeply and precisely and therefore helped clarify the attributes of the concept of Cooperative Learning.

Such analysis and reflection makes communication—or in this case, an understanding of the definition—more productive. This *concept attainment* process is very powerful in secondary schooling as mastering key concepts goes way beyond simple vocabulary building, because secondary education is (1) built around the content disciplines and their carefully constructed concepts and because (2) most of these important concepts are abstract in nature, classification activities such as this one are powerful team learning opportunities. (Try this yourself: ask a colleague to do the task we offer below and then compare his or her results with yours and discuss the results. That discussion will deepen the understanding of both parties.)

TASK: Concept Attainment

In attempt to further reinforce the importance of concept clarification in secondary education and to influence you in your attempts at effectively teaching content vocabulary, we offer several statements (a–f) for you to ponder and evaluate:

a. In geometry, if a student thinks all triangles are "right triangles" and that, therefore, the Pythagorean theorem holds for every triangle, he or she is plain wrong.

b. In global studies, if a student does not distinguish between the economic patterns of capitalism, socialism, and communism, he or she will be very confused by historical and modern events.

c. In science, there is a difference between mass and weight that many students don't grasp and it hurts their understanding of scientific inquiry.

d. In science, teachers talk of bacteria and viruses: students need to distinguish them from each other and grasp the significance of their differences in matters of health.

e. In ELA, students frequently think that any word that ends in "-ing" is a verb, which is not true.

f. Many students use the term "novel" to refer to any book that they are reading or talking about; some books are non-fiction and, therefore, are not novels.

Note that these are very common misconceptions. Please do not underestimate how important it is to help students master the conceptualizations that are critical in the subject you teach. Misconceptions damage understanding—severely. To that effect, we should closely examine teaching that would fall under the concept label "Cooperative Learning" and return to debriefing the original task we asked you to complete.

Some teachers might think that all seven examples described previously *are* equivalent instances of Cooperative Learning, a result which might damage their ability to generate effective classroom structures in their own settings because they are *not* all CL.

Using the description of CL that was offered, we think that examples #2, 6, and 7 are clearly positive examples of CL: they meet *each* of the criteria listed in the description. We think that the other examples (#1, 3, 4, and 5) cannot be considered CL unless some changes are made in reference to the following concerns:

◆ In #1, students can choose *not* to work together and therefore can have no experience with teamwork or communication with more diverse people.

◆ In #3, there seems to be no individual accountability; students are not responsible for their own individual learning and conceptual growth (they must only complete a group project). Moreover, the creation of the teams seems randomized and very chaotic.

◆ In #4, the teacher has created a mess. The presumed classroom organization of "boys vs. girls" results in massive teams and reveals that there is little possibility of any meaningful learning for most students. Most students will be bystanders in the second half of class (or cheerleaders, not thinkers). Two huge groups segregated by gender with no structured interaction and a vague focus is a waste of everyone's time. This will also probably entice youngsters into behavioral problems; this is a classroom management nightmare about to start.

◆ In #5, there is a possibility that CL will surface in this situation. Students are working together, but we do not know if the tasks they are completing are routine and scripted or actually constructivist and integrative in nature. The end-of-class assessment is not very productive unless the teacher has a useful system to gather and provide feedback to individuals. Science classes have used lab partners since the dawn of the discipline, but we are not sure how well-structured they are to maximize gain for both parties. Slight adjustments, like those offered in the next two chapters, would help this teacher experience a far greater level of success.

A Concept Test on the Application of Cooperative Learning

TASK: Mr. Vee

We wish to close this section by offering one more example and ask that you now apply (transfer) your prior experience with the ideas in the chapter to answer the following question:

How does the following example meet the criteria for well-structured CL?

In Mr. Vee's class, students are placed into new three- or four-person teams on the first day of every month. Mr. Vee informs the students of his expectations for cooperation, communication, and respectfulness in their conversations and for thoroughness, accuracy, and reasoning in their end products. He describes team-based bonuses that are available to individual group members. He will be asking them to work in their teams in every class and he will be giving feedback on their performance in those settings. There will be weekly group projects, but no completely group-graded marks. Every student will produce a 50-word reflection about class every day and students are asked to produce a meaningful team name and icon that will be added to everything they create and design during the month.

We think that Mr. Vee demonstrates a thorough and effective use of Cooperative Learning in a secondary classroom. In fact, his methods foreshadow the Dual Objective Model for implementation as well. There is "high fidelity" in his design; that is, it aligns with all five CL criteria provided at the beginning of the chapter. This teacher has a tremendous opportunity to realize all the benefits that have been promised by the last 30 years of effective CL practice.

So how did Mr. Vee decide to structure his class as he did? How does he operationalize the process of carrying out Cooperative Learning effectively? What else might we want to know about his planning or execution as we try to plan for ourselves? Each of these questions is addressed in the next chapter as we begin to look at "how" CL takes shape in the classroom, and we introduce the Dual Objective Model as your guide.

Fidelity to CL criteria and following an effective execution protocol increases the likelihood that students will experience positive outcomes in their learning attempts. Not unlike any new undertaking, consistency and practice are key for both the teacher and learners, especially in the initial stages of employing CL. Some in fact, might question, "Why bother?" To that end, we acknowledge that the major reason a secondary teacher might take the time and effort to revise teaching practice is if doing so promises to deliver desirable cognitive outcomes (and/or readies their students for life beyond schooling). We hope to convince you of both as we continue.

In truth, the research base is chock-full of studies that show repeated academic or intellectual gains with the use of CL, most of it in the deep meaning type of learning that twenty-first century schooling expects from our students. (Interestingly, if the goal is just *memorization* by students, the gains generated by the use of CL are no worse than those of traditional teaching.) The excellence of Cooperative Learning for adolescents lies in its **meaningful conceptual learning and deep understanding**. Our own efforts, combined with those scholars that have preceded us, give us an expectation that the version of CL we have personally studied for a decade, the Dual Objective Model, will also systematically improve affective outcomes leading to more productive, skilled, and effective high-school graduates.

So now that you've encountered the "what" behind CL, let's turn to the reasoning for "why?"

Cooperative Learning Outcomes

For each of the following outcomes, we will explain a bit about why the findings support the use of well-structured CL, and we will offer a sampling of research that supports that notion. This is not an exhaustive research review (for that type of analysis, check into an article by Johnson & Johnson, 2009), but one that does faithfully represent existing scholarship and justifies our efforts to modify practice.

TASK: Cooperative Learning Outcomes Ranking

How important are each of these research outcomes to secondary school teachers? Please rate them HIGH, MEDIUM, or LOW. Perhaps, more importantly, think about how you personally feel regarding each.

_____ 1. Cooperative Learning makes teens see diversities more as strengths than as problems.

_____ 2. Cooperative Learning deepens conceptual understanding and increases achievement.

_____ 3. Cooperative Learning is beneficial to troubled students without hurting successful ones.

_____ 4. Cooperative Learning eases the transitions of students who have traditionally been "left behind" in regular classrooms.

_____ 5. Cooperative Learning extends the potential of effective computer use and/ or technology for instructional purposes.

_____ 6. Cooperative Learning develops experience-based respectfulness for, and communication skills with, a wide range of people in a wide range of situations.

Your rankings provide a window into your personal philosophy of education. They also should help you decide on your goals, objectives, practices, and assessments.

The good news for educators is that Cooperative Learning usage is linked directly to _all six_ of the outcomes listed above. To us, each of these is critically important to adolescent growth and development. Teenagers need to develop a work ethic, social skills, positive attitudes, a content-knowledge base, tech skills, communication skills, and an ability to solve problems with others, and the six outcomes listed above promote the abilities of every individual while promising to "raise test scores" as a byproduct of this kind of good teaching.

Let's take the six outcomes and place them into two groups: those that improve traditional academic learning (#2 and #5) and those that improve 21st-century work, life, career, and citizenship skills (#1, #3, #4 and #6).

Outcomes that Improve Traditional Academic Learning

Cooperative Learning increases student conceptual understanding and increases an individual's knowledge base for several reasons; these reasons apply whether the learning involved is discipline-based content, academic skills, or about effective use of technology. Constructivist theory tells us that frequent analytical processing of ideas across multiple settings deepens meaning for learners, especially for abstractions such as those taught in schools (Willingham, 2009; Flynn, Mesibov, Vermette & Smith, 2004; also see Vygotsky, 1962). Advocates of *deliberate/thoughtful practice* (Ericsson, Tesch-Romer, & Krampe, 1993; Hattie, 2012) call for many more opportunities for "applied practice" than are usually produced in traditional classrooms, but which can easily be realized in the CL classroom.

There is far more real student analysis and application of content in the conversations in the cooperative classroom than in the patterns found in the traditional one. For example, an 11th-grade student learning the concept of "nationalism" in global history will focus more on its meanings, its applications, and its nuances in actual discussion with classmates than he or she would from listening to a lecture, reading a text, or watching a video. The same would be true of ELA students who are attempting to distinguish "mood" from "tone" in small-group work. Their questions would be asked, the confusions would be spotted, their weak attempts at meaning would be validated and examined, and their learning would be publicly reinforced. In the traditional classroom, a student would often sit *quietly* and wait for the next class to start and hope to learn enough from home study to pass a test. Worse yet, in the competitive classroom, his or her comments and attempts to learn might be ridiculed, at least until she learned to keep them private.

Furthermore, although powerful, "talking to learn" (Myers et al., 2017) is still somewhat suspect in modern schools. Intuitively, we know that people learn by talking, yet secondary school people seem to think of student talking and interacting as a waste of time or they worry about the exchange of incorrect ideas. They also fear hearing wrong or incomplete answers from students' mouths. Studies (exemplified by Lampert, 2001) on ambitious teaching suggest that many teachers have not developed the skills to draw ideas from, and force reasoning out of, students and challenge them productively in large-group settings; our experiences suggest that these types of challenges and comments come out far more naturally in settings in which teenagers are having real discussions about real questions and when they are having genuine conversations. Finally, educators know that one-on-one tutoring is the most powerful instructional system (Bloom, 1984) *because* it often feels like discussion, focuses on the ideas of the learner, and is patient in its pacing. The closest thing that 25-student classes have to tutoring is Cooperative Learning, where the giving and the receiving of ideas and clarifications is more customized, timely, and supportive (Webb & Farivar, 1994) through interactions with others.

Let us illustrate this latter point about conversations that are similar to tutoring by examining a sample of hypothetical comments overheard from intra-team dialogue in 12 different classes over a few days of 9th-grade CL work. Student comments like these influence the team conversation in a positive way.

1. In ELA: (BOBBY) Chandra, why do you think that this is a scary description?

2. In Math: (MANNY) Lucinda, why do you think these two lines are really equal?

3. In Sci: (SALLY) We always take the first answer—why don't we get several before we decide?

4. In ELA: (MONROE) You guys know I got that idea from the reading. Why do you think he isn't sure what year it is?

5. In Sci: (DON) That wasn't rude; I just meant . . . Well then, what should I have said?

6. In SS: (CARLINE) Old people never say stuff like that. Around my house, that'd get a quick reaction. How about at your house?

7. In SS: (SANDY) What about women? They didn't get to vote 'til later! And why did it take so long for 18-year-olds?

8. In Sci: (WINNIE) It doesn't make sense—everybody knows that heavier things drop faster than the light ones. Right?

9. In Sci: (JACE) My mother always says that what doesn't kill you is good for you.

10. In Math: (MIKE) I don't get it. There are so many 2s in this equation, but they are all different things.

11. In Math: (PAUL) Oh, don't make me explain my thinking. I just want the answer.

12. In ELA: (DANI) The author uses the word "thunderous." How often do you hear that? Why not just "loud"?

As far as we are concerned, we would be happy to know that these various thoughts (all plausibly conjured up by real students in real situations) would be shared with "trusted" associates/friends in the team setting so they could be dealt with honestly, pointedly, and safely. (Try to imagine the reply to

each of these by a caring teammate, as would happen in a tutoring experience or in an effective CL team.) We doubt that these public statements
would be handled well in front of the whole class, but in small, secure teams,
they could lead to productive conversations about everything from the history of suffrage, to personalized sociology, to attempts at defending one's
ego, to group processing, to interpretation of writing style, and to basic flaws
in math knowledge. As in real life, real discussions open doors to conversations about meanings, about self, and about productive interactions, and
they do so for everyone's benefit.

These kinds of exchanges and discussions are good things that could
happen in school. Cooperative Learning, and our Dual Objective Model,
make them routine occurrences and hold the promise of great affective and
cognitive engagement.

Relevant Research Studies on Cognitive Gain from CL

We often get asked, "Why do you put so much trust in CL?" We often answer
by citing the research base and now we offer some of that base to you. The
studies and articles mentioned below provide support for conceptual growth
using CL and offer more detail on specific examples of its varied implementation formats:

1. Roseth, Johnson, and Johnson (2008) conducted a review of 148
    previous studies on the effects of CL on middle-level student
    learning across 17,000 students from 11 nations and across school
    subjects. In short, they found that CL increased achievement in
    every discipline, and they discovered that the quality of the peer
    relationships mattered greatly in that achievement. (The statistical
    approach they used is called meta-analysis and is a format that pools
    together many studies on a topic and examines the overall impact
    of the variables in the set of studies. Such "studies of studies" are
    valuable and seriously considered by scholars because they seek
    overall tendencies from varied contexts and do not rely on the
    results of a single specific investigation.)
2. By the turn of the 21st century, the cognitive achievement power
    of CL had been established, so we choose carefully from the huge
    set of specific studies available between 1980 and 2000. One that
    we thought should be mentioned was done by Lazarowitz, Hertz-
    Lazarowitz, Baird, and Bowlden way back in 1988. They taught two
    units in high-school biology in two different ways: individual mas-
    tery vs. Jigsaw investigation (a form of CL in which different parts of
    a topic are subdivided to group members, who then study their part

and teach it to team members). They discovered that the inquiry unit on cells taught with CL produced higher achievement and promoted the skills required for transfer and long-term conceptual gain. The other unit, on plants, required more information/fact learning for the test and was predisposed to assessing lower-level outcomes. In the case of fact learning, there was equal gain for the use of CL. This is a study that makes us keenly aware of our purpose as educators: Conceptual gain, transfer, social skills, and affective development are what we seek and CL is the best path to that end.

3. In another meta-analysis of many studies, this one on tech-assisted instruction, Lou, Abrami, and d'Apollonia (2001) determined that CL facilitated the increased ability of individuals to handle ill-structured problems (like those in real life) as compared to other types of instruction.

4. Nichols and Miller (1994) found that high school students in algebra learned more in CL groups than did their fellow students working in a more traditional setting.

5. Johnson, Johnson, and Stanne (1985) discovered that 8th-graders working in teams to study computers learned more and solved problems more effectively than did fellow students who worked alone.

6. In a Nigerian high-school science study, Okebukola (1986) combined CL with *concept mapping* and controlled for students' preferences to work together or alone. The results showed that preference didn't matter—students in all groups performed better after being taught with CL. This allays contemporary concerns over shy and quiet students "getting lost" or feeling excluded in active and collaborative classrooms (an opinion that does not hold up to the scrutiny of research). Stylistic preferences did not lower learning or damage these youngsters and they learned more in cooperative groupings.

7. In a study of 120 secondary math students, Jebson (2012) found that Cooperative Learning produced higher gains than did conventional methods and found no difference for the gains of males and females.

8. In one of a set of studies on math achievement from Cooperative Learning, Zakaria, Solfitri, Daud, and Abidin (2013) found supportive evidence that students learned more from Jigsaw CL than in a traditional approach. Also, like Okebukola above, they concluded that "preferences for instructional style" by teachers or students did not influence the higher achievement.

9. In 1987, Mesch, Johnson, and Johnson compared the use of CL with traditional classroom structures over a 24-week period in 10th-grade social studies with the larger cognitive gain on teacher-made tests

being shown by the CL group. This study is also noteworthy for it demonstrated that heterogeneous groups worked very well in the typical high school.

10. In a retrospective and comprehensive piece on their successes with CL, Johnson and Johnson published a great article in 2009 that listed hundreds of studies that showed a positive cognitive impact from well-structured CL implementation. In consultancies and workshops, we like to use this single article as a summary of all that has gone before; it is accurate, comprehensive, well-reasoned, coherent, and persuasive. It also makes a convincing case that CL works!

Outcomes that Improve 21st Century Life and Career Skills

The second batch of outcomes (#1, #3, #4 and #6) represent 21st-century life and career skills and are what Heckman (in Tough, 2012) calls **non-cognitive outcomes**. Heckman, a prize-winning economist, flat out says that these skills are **more important to life success than are the traditional cognitive ones** that have been the focus of recent educational policy efforts in the U.S. Whether they are called SEL, Habits of Mind, Life and Career Skills, Character Traits, non-cognitive skills, or dispositions (Kamenetz, 2015), the ability to get along with, and feel empathy for, others, recognize individual strengths, persevere, self-regulate, communicate across boundaries, and team up to complete a task, are at the heart of successful financial endeavors and they are central to happiness, fulfilment, and success. Business leaders overwhelmingly want these to be regular outcomes of schooling. Traditional schooling may have been reinforcing these kinds of actions through the years but has only done it in "hit or miss" ways. Sports teams, extracurricular activities, and school organizations pride themselves on teamwork, hard work, passion, and effort, and students volunteer for these activities knowing that they are expected to become better people for the experience. We ask, "Why can't those things be explicitly targeted (and accomplished) in the content classroom?" Our answer is that they can, and will be accomplished, applying the Dual Objective Model of Cooperative Learning

Why does CL produce such positive gains in "non-academic skills"? The answer to that question has two parts. First, feelings of respect, acceptance, and contribution need opportunities to grow and they need feedback to develop. Students who never interact with each other directly on relevant issues will rarely develop a meaningful understanding of others and their ideas and will probably be poor communicators as a result. Those who never have to take responsibility for somebody else will rarely develop an attitude of community. Those who only take pride in individual accomplishments will be at a loss after high school, where the reward structures in business, family, the military, and college are often tied to group-based success.

Many teachers say they cannot do CL because the "kids cannot work together"; this is a deeply flawed perspective. These teachers think that positive student attitudes toward group work and other teenagers are a required *input* into the CL equation: of course, this would be a nice thing to have, but we are realistic. We see **diverse teens working effectively together** as a desired goal, an **output** of careful instruction, high expectations, and an effective assessment system. We don't expect students to come to physics knowing physics: their learning during the course is an outcome. We should take the same approach with social skills and Habits of Mind; the affective skills are learned in classes in which they are taught, required, reinforced, examined, and practiced.

Second, aside from the sheer number of structured opportunities to develop non-academic skills, the CL classroom almost always requires learning activities that both demand and profit from high-quality student-to-student interaction. This is difficult for some students to grasp; when teamed, they often resort to having one student do all the work, and adding three names. They often don't understand that building effective personal competencies is a huge part of their formal education, and best developed through repeated trials involving social interaction. When the design of the activity requires the contributions of diverse others (for example, those advocated by Cohen, 1994, and Johnson & Johnson, 2009) and respectfulness fuels its effectiveness, students eventually will learn to work well together given the chance.

We offer the following universal classroom example to try to show this rather complex point. On the first day of any course, students are randomly paired for what the teacher calls an "icebreaker." Students typically have a few minutes to interview their partners; we suggest that the teacher *explicitly* ask students to be respectful and polite. We also strongly suggest that the teacher has these interview questions, including some subject-specific ones, printed and distributed. Examples from an ELA class could include: (1) How did you get your name? (2) What do you read? (3) What are some of your favorite movies? Why do you like them? (4) How do you and your family celebrate holidays? (5) What is the worst thing about school? (6) Are there places you'd like to visit? (7) Are you planning to graduate—and then what will you do?

Students are encouraged to make notes on the conversation and then are expected to write a brief essay about the other person and the experience of interviewing. (Note: We think that interviewing, which we conceptualize as "getting information from a person who has it," is a vastly important skill in the modern world and should be taught as such.) When ready, each essay is reviewed by the partner who has been the subject of the interview (peer editing). We urge teachers to mark these as a formal grade (usually a high one) and allow 50 percent of the grade to be decided by the two partners. This suggests strong positive interdependence.

This activity demonstrates that students will be expected to work together, that student experiences and thoughts are central to the course, that the teacher has thoughtfully designed effective learning activities, that student self-regulation leads to success, and that conversation will be the medium though which learning and growth will happen.

Research of Affective Gains from Well-Structured CL Implementation

Cooperative Learning research includes measures of non-cognitive skills, but it has not been a central feature of most of the literature. We hope this situation changes as a research base develops on the Dual Objective Model. Moreover, a 2015 article by Duckworth and Yaeger, whose notion of *grit* has been shown to be critically important, provides ideas about how to measure such non-cognitive outcomes. However, below are listed several studies that show "improved attitudes" (social and personal competencies such as caring about each other, building relationships, and providing useful help to others) as a result of CL implementation. Please note that the dates of these studies suggest that we have known for a long time about CL's power to "bring people together" and "develop the whole person," but schools have done little to formally advance those notions since the onset of NCLB and the standardized testing emphasis it spawned. Today there is renewed promise for a more balanced approach to developing the whole student, as central to national ESSA legislation, and CL may prove to be the most effective means to do so.

1. Gillies (2004) found that middle school students learned to care about each other in CL groups.
2. Webb and Farivar (1994) discovered that students could learn to help and appreciate each other in CL groups.
3. Cohen (1994) found that CL helped overcome bias, broke down "status" roles and helped students see each other as more equal.
4. Johnson, Johnson, Buckman, and Richards (1986) showed that students working in CL teams recognized diversity as a strength (not a weakness).
5. Slavin and Oickle (1981) used a large-scale CL study to discover that white students created far more cross-race friendships when they worked in racially-integrated teams than when they worked alone, and importantly, showed that there was no loss of achievement caused by the use of the team structure.
6. Johnson, Johnson, and Rynders (1981) found that self-esteem measures of students with disabilities rose when they worked in heterogeneous CL teams.

7. Slavin and Karweit (1981) discovered that working in CL teams induced students to like school and themselves better, and to increase friendships.

8. Johnson and Johnson's (1981) study showed that increased liking and helping of others, as well as more diversely integrated free-time interactions, were the result of a well-structured CL experience.

9. DeVries, Edwards, and Slavin (1978) revealed that working in CL teams caused a large increase in cross-race friendships in both black and white teens.

10. Gagne and Parks (2013) did an intensive study into the workings of 6th-grade ESL students. Their major finding was that students learned and used scaffolding and peer-assisted actions when taught to do so as a regular component of their class activities. Their collaboration taught them to be helpful and collaborative. Powerful student-to-student skills developed as an outcome of well-structured and intentional instruction.

In Closing

This chapter sought to accomplish three things. First, it offered a description of Cooperative Learning, synthesized from experienced practitioners and important scholars, which resulted in five attributes across a variety of implementations. To realize the benefits of Cooperative Learning, we remind teachers to design their group practices with these five factors in mind:

◆ Use **small work groups** of three or four students working face to face on desirable learning tasks.

◆ Place emphasis on **positive interdependence**, a feeling of mutual reliance on every member.

◆ Create **stable, heterogeneous teams**.

◆ Provide **feedback to individuals** about the quality of their **interpersonal interactions** during group work **and on the products of their work** effort.

◆ **Assessment** of and for learning must be given to **both group and individual**.

Second, we raised the challenge that fidelity to both CL criteria and an effective implementation model to aid classroom application (we suggest the Dual Objective Model) are crucial to creating successful CL learning experiences. More about the "how" is given in Chapter 2.

Lastly, we presented plausible reasons for the positive outcomes found by formal investigations into CL. Furthermore, we provided examples of these research studies.

To reiterate:

1. There is a promise of cognitive gain. The engagement within the groups as the students master content, or solve problems, or create original products, will produce meaningful conceptual thinking, sharing and assessment of many ideas, clarification and analysis of options, and validation of understanding. This is a formula for deep learning.

2. Moreover, there is also a promise of affective gain. Respectful exchanges of ideas, the monitoring of one's self in interaction, the offering of caring, timely, and useful feedback, the concern for the inclusion and contributions of each member, the recognition that diverse skills are necessary for complex tasks, and the notion that collaborative processes are culturally valued, all work to help shape individual social and emotional competence.

These twin outcomes—cognition and affect—are at the heart of the Dual Objective Model, our focus in the next chapter.

Chapter 1 Big Ideas

1. While there are numerous established models available, well-structured Cooperative Learning (CL) has several common features: (a) face-to-face small groups work on solving problems or designing products or mastering conceptual content; (b) within the group is a feeling of positive interdependence; (c) the teacher-built teams are stable across a period of time; (d) the teacher assesses and monitors student thinking and action and provides helpful feedback in a timely fashion; (e) both formative and summative assessment of individuals and groups are essential.

2. Misconceptions (the wrongful identification of concepts) are a massive problem in education. Often students are conceptually confused by abstract and complex subject matter and the same holds true for teachers. Not all group work is the well-structured Cooperative Learning that has great power for learning, and the importance of creating a meaningful personal model is imperative.

3. Teachers may have different priorities and different learning goals for various classes and individuals. However, each of the commonly acknowledged and important goals are met by the use of CL.

4. There are numerous research studies that support the power of CL for affective and cognitive outcomes and therefore support the use of the Dual Objective Model.

References

Bloom, B. (1984). The 2 sigma problem: The search for methods of instruction as effective as one-on-one tutoring. *Educational Leadership, 13*(6), 4–17.

Bruner, J., Goodenow, S., & Austin, G. (1986). *A study of thinking* (2nd ed.). London: Transaction Publishers.

Cohen, E. (1994). *Designing groupwork.* New York, NY: Teachers College Press.

Davidson, N., & Major, C.H. (2014). Boundary crossings: Cooperative learning, collaborative learning and problem-based learning. *Journal on Excellence in College Teaching, 25*(3–4), 7–55.

DeVries, D.L., Edwards, K.J., & Slavin, R.E. (1978). Biracial learning teams and race relations in the classroom: Four field experiments using teams-games-tournaments. *Journal of Educational Psychology, 70*(3), 356–362.

Duckworth, A.L., & Yaeger, D.S. (2015). Measurement matters: Assessing personal qualities other than cognitive abilities for educational purposes. *Educational Researcher, 44*(4), 237–251.

Ericsson, K.A., Tesch-Romer, C., & Krampe, R. (1993). The role of deliberate practice in the acquisition of expert performance. *Psychological Review, 100*(3), 363–406.

Flynn, P., Mesibov, D., Vermette, P., & Smith, R.M. (2004). *Applying standards-based constructivism: A two-step guide for motivating middle and high school students.* Larchmont, NY: Eye-on-Education.

Gagne, N., & Parks, S. (2013). Cooperative learning tasks in a grade 6 intensive ESL class: Role of scaffolding. *Language Teaching Research, 17*(2), 188–209.

Gillies, R. (2004). The effects of cooperative learning on junior high students during small group learning. *Learning and Instruction, 14*(2), 197–213.

Hattie, J. (2012). *Visible learning for teachers: Maximizing impact on learning.* New York, NY: Routledge.

Jebson, S.R. (2012). Impact of cooperative learning approach on senior secondary school students' performance in mathematics. *Ife Psychologia, 20*(2), 107–112.

Johnson, D.W., & Johnson, R.W. (1981). Effects of cooperative and individualistic learning experiences on interethnic education. *Journal of Educational Psychology, 73*(3), 444–449.

Johnson, D.W., & Johnson, R.W. (1987). *Learning together and alone.* Englewood Cliffs, NJ: Prentice-Hall.

Johnson, D.W, & Johnson, R.W. (2009). An educational psychology success story: Social interdependence theory and cooperative learning. *Educational Researcher, 38*(5), 365–379.

Johnson, D.W., Johnson, R.W., Buckman, L.A., & Richards, P.S. (1986). The effect of prolonged implementation of cooperative learning on social support within the classroom. *Journal of Psychology, 119*(5), 405–411.

Johnson, R.T., Johnson, D.W., & Rynders, J. (1981). Effects of cooperative, competitive and individualistic experiences on self-esteem of handicapped and non-handicapped students. *The Journal of Psychology, 108,* 31–34.

Johnson, R.T., Johnson, D.W., & Stanne, M.B. (1985). Effects of cooperative, competitive and individualistic goal structures on computer assisted instruction. *Journal of Educational Psychology, 77*(6), 668–677.

Kagan, S. (1992). *Cooperative learning: Resources for teachers.* Riverside, CA: University of California Press.

Kamenetz, A. (2015, May 28). Non-academic skills are key to success: But what should we call them? *National Public Radio.* Retrieved from http://www.npr.org/sections/ed/2015/05/28/404684712/non-academic-skills-are-key-to-success-but-what-should-we-call-them (retrieved 10/3/16).

Konkoski-Bates, E., & Vermette, P. (2004). Working the room: The key to cooperative learning success. Presented at the Great Lakes Association for Cooperation in Education, Toronto, Ontario.

Lampert, M. (2001). *Teaching problems and the problems of teaching.* New Haven, CT: Yale University Press.

Lazarowitz, R., Hertz-Lazarowitz, R., Baird, J.H., & Bowlden, V. (1988). Academic achievement and on-task behavior of high school biology students instructed in a cooperative investigative small group. *Science Education, 72*(4), 475–487.

Lou, Y., Abrami, P., & d'Apollonia, S. (2001). Small group and individual learning with technology: A meta-analysis. *Review of Educational Research, 71*(3), 449–521.

Mesch, D., Johnson, D.W., & Johnson, R.T. (1987). Impact of positive interdependence and academic group contingencies on achievement. *Journal of Social Psychology, 128*(3), 345–352.

Myers, J., Bardsley, M., Vermette, P., & Kline, C. (2017). *Cooperative learning for the 21st century* (in press).

Nichols, J.D., & Miller, R.B. (1994). Cooperative learning and student motivation. *Contemporary Educational Psychology, 19*(2), 167–168.

Okebukola, P.A. (1986). The problem of large classes in science: An experiment in cooperative learning. *Journal of Science Education, 8*(1), 73–77.

Roseth, C.J., Johnson, D.W., & Johnson, R.T. (2008). Promoting early adolescents' achievement and peer relationships: The effects of cooperative, competitive, and individualistic goal structures. *Psychological Bulletin, 134*(2), 223–246.

Slavin, R.E. (1983). *Cooperative learning.* New York, NY: Longman.

Slavin, R., & Karweit, N. (1981). Cognitive and affective outcomes of an intensive team learning experience. *Journal of Experimental Education, 50*(1), 29–35.

Slavin, R., & Oickle, E. (1981). Effects of cooperative learning teams on student achievement and race relations: Treatment by race interaction. *Sociology of Education, 54*(3), 174–180.

Tough, P. (2012). *How children succeed: Grit, curiosity and the hidden power of character.* Boston, MA: Houghton-Mifflin.

Vermette, P. (1998). *Making cooperative learning work: Student teams in K-12 classrooms.* Upper Saddle River, NJ: Merrill/Prentice-Hall.

Vygotsky, L.S. (1962). *Thought and language.* Cambridge, MA: MIT Press.

Webb, N.M., & Farivar, S. (1994). Promoting helping behaviors in cooperative small school groups in middle school mathematics. *American Educational Research Journal, 31*(2), 369–395.

Willingham, D. (2009). *Why don't students like school? A cognitive scientist answers questions about how the mind works and what it means for the classroom.* San Francisco, CA: Jossey-Bass.

Zakaria, E., Sofitri, T., Daud, Y., & Abidin, Z.Z. (2013). Effect of cooperative learning on secondary school students' math achievement. *Creative Education, 4*(1), 98–100.

2

The Dual Objective Model

How Do We Implement Well-Structured CL?

Introduction

Many educators are becoming intrigued by the potential benefits of using CL, but they question how to do so effectively within the classrooms they manage. Increasingly cognizant of the importance that non-cognitive skills play in successfully negotiating everyday life, they seek an effective classroom model that addresses both cognitive and affective development in an efficient manner. To these passionate practitioners we offer the Dual Objective Model as both a planning and execution tool for enacting 21st century Cooperative Learning. This chapter offers a detailed description of the Dual Objective Model of Cooperative Learning, it introduces the reader to several cases of teachers experimenting with its implementation, and offers a culminating question and answer session built on our personal teaching experience coupled with the experiences of colleagues who have implemented the model in their practice.

TASK: Ms. Johnson's Science Class

Please read this vignette of an 8th-grade science classroom somewhere in northern Florida and annotate components that you find favorable and/or productive:

Ms. Johnson starts class promptly as the bell rings: 27 students are seated and one manages to sneak into hers as the ringing stops. "Good morning," the 17-year veteran says, flashing a sincere smile. "Today we have much to do, and I need to see how our projects and our relationships are developing. Please take out your green folders, reassemble with your base groups, and pick up the green sheet from in front. OK?"

It takes about a minute of animated talk and laughter and milling around before everyone is settled in. Ms. Johnson has time to quietly address one student, Margaret, who had been slow to move. As everyone quiets, she addresses the whole group again: "OK, today we will be working on the plant projects in our teams. We have three things to keep in mind and these will be checked when I get to your group: (1) How is the booklet coming along and how does it explain the results of your experiments? (2) How well are we recording our observations and insights? (3) How well is our team working together? Have I told you that 95 percent of all science research is done in teams?" A loud groan ("UHHH-HHH!") suggests that she has told them that before; perhaps a few times.

The next 30 minutes is marked by the student group work and by Ms. Johnson attending to each station, where she talks to students, listens, and directs them to materials *and* writes comments on some individual logs. She passes by the front board several times and places a few check marks next to an item stating, "We will listen to each other and work together respectfully."

With five minutes to go, she calls the class to order. "First, we saw some nice progress today. The booklets are comprehensive, coherent, creative, and in good English. They will be shared Friday, and at parents' night; they will make us proud! Tomorrow we will make sure that the rubric is being used effectively. Second, most of you have really understood some of the principles of growth that we had outlined last week and can find them at work in the plants we're studying. Remember that 50 percent of the quiz will be done individually, so where some of us are a bit confused, we can help each other tomorrow. You have the objectives for the test in your handouts. Finally, you worked together very well again today: so many jobs today require adults to work like that, and you can do it now. I need at least one of you to read from your notes about the team process today—Margaret?"

Having digested and analyzed that piece of teaching, you are ready to compare your insights with ours. We are using this exploratory exercise to introduce you to our CL model, called the Dual Objective, as it plays out in a middle-school classroom. We hope you noticed some or all of the following factors and anticipate that this chapter will provide an overview of their alignment with the model's components:

- ◆ The teacher has a clear structure to the team interaction that the students will be doing that day.
- ◆ The students are in existing, stable, and internally diverse teams.
- ◆ The teacher is assessing and providing feedback on both the academic growth (as shown by the project) and the affective growth (as shown by the behavioral expectations and the feedback at the stations).
- ◆ The academic task being completed appears to be complex, aligned with standards, ill-structured, and challenging. Moreover, there appears to be individual accountability for each individual's learning.

Figure 2.1 The Dual Objective Model

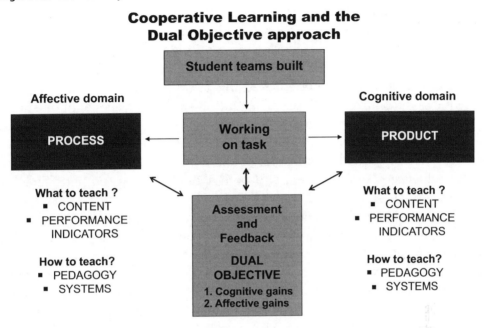

If you saw those items (or can see them now) you are identifying the structure and "flow" of our Dual Objective Model (see Figure 2.1). Simply put, the Dual Objective has been designed for teachers who seek to help teenagers develop their ability to show desirable life skills, demonstrate social-emotional competence, and/or utilize powerful Habits of Mind and simultaneously help them master the complex conceptual content of the discipline.

The research is clear, compelling, and supportive of the concept that cognition and affect are intimately interwoven within the process of learning (Costa & Kallick, 2014). Whether we are aware of this connection as we struggle to make meaning, or learn with ease and it goes unnoticed, evidence shows us that cognition almost universally occurs through an affective lens. The Dual Objective Model is a powerful planning and implementation tool which addresses these twin influencers of success. Although the model can be applied in a non-collaborative environment, we find it most powerful when used to facilitate well-structured Cooperative Learning.

The Dual Objective at Work

Let's first turn our attention to the central flow in the Dual Objective graphic. The three fundamental components—**building teams, working on task**, and **assessment and feedback—demonstrate a sequential progression essential to *executing* an effective CL learning experience**. In the *planning* stages, one would reverse the sequence, determining the expected content outcomes, designing tasks that will best achieve those goals, and then building the appropriate teams. We elaborate thoroughly in Chapters 4 and 5 regarding the building of groups and assessing for growth, but the heart of the model, *working on task*, drives our focus as we continue in this chapter.

The proficient teacher employing the Dual Objective Model plans and executes CL learning experiences using a *process/product framework*. This orientation recognizes that the *product* (i.e. evidence of essential understandings, discipline-specific content objectives or performance indicators) and the *process* (how the students get there) are interdependent indicators of success, and are equally important. Both are present in any learning activity, both influence overall success, and both should be assessed and feedback provided to those involved.

The focus on *product* is not new, as we are accustomed to assigning work to students to show mastery of a specific concept, grading it, and providing feedback regarding how well the student achieved the academic (cognitive) goal. However, the idea of addressing the *process* used by students to learn as a means of developing 21st-century competencies is *very* new. Our model addresses these in the same way. Within the cognitive domain, we ask the teacher to consider what to teach (the discipline-specific content) as well as how to best teach it (pedagogical methods/activities/tasks). The affective domain is treated in the same fashion. We challenge the teacher to consider affective outcomes and content that match well with the cognitive, and to carefully attend to the methodologies, activities, and tasks that will allow students to develop these foundational competencies within the given learning experience.

For example, in a math unit on polynomials (or other particularly challenging content), the teacher may choose to tackle the affective skill of "persistence." In a social studies lesson on discrimination, the skills of "perspective-taking" and "building empathy" pair very naturally. The FACS and technology teachers may find "striving for accuracy" as a highly appropriate fit for their disciplines as a whole, and those teachers assigning presentations in their classes may find "thinking and communicating with clarity and precision" a worthy affective goal. In these instances, the affective and cognitive content align tightly, as one facilitates the other. In other instances, specific affective skills may be part of a school- or district-wide initiative, and the teacher can actively attend to their development in the classroom by employing the Dual Objective Model. In these cases, the teacher would simply start with the affective content and outcomes, and search for the best places throughout the curriculum where they could be practiced in concert with the cognitive content.

Determining disciplinary content is relatively straightforward, typically guided by standards, curricula, resource materials, etc., but on the affective side of the model, the content is far less well defined. To assist efforts in locating options, we recommend several sources to examine, compare, and choose from. We suggest that teachers look closely at the lists of competencies offered in Appendix 1, including: the Life and Career Skills and Learning and Innovation Skills of the 21st Century Partnership, the 49 Character Qualities from Character First, CASEL's Five Social and Emotional Learning Core Competencies, Covey's Seven Habits of Highly Effective People, Wagner's Seven Survival Skills, and the 16 Habits of Mind offered by Costa and Kallick (2008). All of these examples are plausible choices for those educators seeking a well-developed taxonomy of affective skills for developing their students' personal competencies.

In our consulting work, we have come to favor Costa and Kallick's *Habits of mind* for its brevity, breadth, and ease of use. More recently, the 21st Century Partnership's P21 Framework Skills have caught our attention as part of an overall process for creating life-ready youth. An abbreviated listing of both is offered in Figure 2.2. We believe that either would provide a great affective "curriculum" for any secondary program. We urge educators to spiral affective competencies in their totality across disciplines and throughout all secondary years as age-appropriate. Doing so (with any of the taxonomies) as part of the school mission allows students to develop a

Figure 2.2 Habits of Mind and P21 Framework Skills

The Habits of Mind (Costa & Kallick)	P21 Framework Skills (21st Century Partnership)
1. Persisting 2. Managing impulsivity 3. Listening with understanding and empathy 4. Thinking flexibly 5. Thinking about your thinking 6. Striving for accuracy 7. Questioning and problem-posing 8. Applying past knowledge to new situations 9. Thinking and communicating with clarity and precision 10. Gathering data through all your senses 11. Creating, imagining, and innovating 12. Responding with wonderment and awe 13. Taking responsible risks 14. Finding humor 15. Thinking interdependently 16. Remaining open to continuous learning	1. Think creatively 2. Work creatively with others 3. Implement innovations 4. Reason effectively 5. Use systems thinking 6. Make judgements and decisions 7. Solve problems 8. Communicate clearly 9. Collaborate with others 10. Adapt to change 11. Be flexible 12. Manage goals and time 13. Work independently 14. Be self-directed learners 15. Interact effectively with others 16. Work effectively in diverse teams 17. Manage projects 18. Produce results 19. Guide and lead others 20. Be responsible to others

deeper understanding of their power to promote personal readiness for life; thus, school would actually "teach the whole child," a popular but often difficult practice to implement.

So how does the teacher effectively translate the Dual Objective Model into action in a Cooperative Learning environment? Most **critical to success is fidelity to the components of the model, aided by thorough planning**. In the planning stages, the teacher has to think deeply about the three fundamental components of the model and answer these questions:

1. What is the disciplinary content to be learned? What are the expected outcomes (the cognitive objective/s)?
2. What affective skills (content and outcomes) will be utilized and developed during the *process* of collaboration (the affective objective/s)?
3. What *product(s)* will the students generate or create as a result of working together?
4. What learning activities (tasks) will facilitate both cognitive and affective gains?
5. What assessments (formal and informal) will be used?
6. How will groups be built?
7. What will the teacher do while the students are working?
8. How will feedback on product and process be provided to individuals and their groups to target areas for growth?
9. What technologies might assist your effort?

Looking back at Ms. Johnson, we see that she has her students making a booklet (on plant growth), conducting an experiment, preparing for a quiz *and* "listening with understanding and empathy" (Costa & Kallick, 2014). The groups are teacher-made and stable. Finally, she spends almost the whole period listening and talking with students, assessing their effort and outcome, keeping them on track, and giving them feedback and advice. This is an example of the Dual Objective in operation.

CASE: Ms. Nicola's Drama Class

Let's re-examine the model one more time with an example drawn from the 12th-grade Honors Drama class of Ms. Nicola. She wants to use the Dual Objective and is planning accordingly. The students will be studying the six elements found in most successful plays and will work in teams every day. They will complete the two-week unit by creating their own play.

These are the *key questions* (a condensed version of the earlier list) that she will consider during the planning stage:

1. What are the cognitive and affective objectives and products? (What tasks have to be completed?)
2. How will the groups be built?
3. How will she assess and provide feedback regarding the students' work and their interactive efforts during the classes?

Our Take

As we will do throughout the book, and as was done in the previous case, we prefer to have you work through classroom vignettes, giving you the chance to analyze a situation or scenario, and compare it to your existing practice or knowledge base, as well as offering our insights and comments. Here is what we think about this developing plan:

◆ The tasks we envision for the students would be simple: The students must adapt a script (for a scene) based on a commonly known movie, novel, or play and decide the complexity of their production. They would envision the scenery, the dialogue, and the set changes and must find roles for each member of their group. They must also attend to the performance (product) rubric that Ms. Nicola has created *and* to their daily demonstration of affective skills, namely (a) creating, imagining, and innovating, and (b) thinking interdependently. (The teacher has created these objectives.)

◆ The teams would be teacher-built with an eye for balancing *talent, background, experience, gender, passion, attendance/availability, tolerance* and *existing relationships.* They would vary in size from three to four students each, and Ms. Nicola might allow two or three groups to perform different scenes from the same play (so they can talk across teams during class).

◆ She should provide a rubric for the performance, which will be used to guide student work efforts. The elements for the production might include: (a) coherence, or fidelity to the development of the scene; (b) level of engagement by audience; (c) use of vocabulary and word choice; and (d) "stage presence" of each member. Students would also benefit from posting a checklist for the process, the actual interactive work students engage in, for referral during class. Students would do daily reflections (as outslips) by selecting and completing two or three of the stems presented below. (We suggest that these be filled out and turned in before class is dismissed.)

1. Today our team created . . .
2. I was innovative today when . . .
3. An example of my thinking through an issue with a teammate today was . . .
4. Our work was made better today by . . .
5. I contributed to the development of a scene by . . .
6. I contributed to engaging our audience by . . .
7. I worked on my stage presence by . . .
8. One thing that might help our group is . . .

◆ Ms. Nicola will be "teaching" the affective skills by having students reflect on their application of the skills they actually use during the project. The daily outslips accompanied by a start-of-class discussion (where feedback is shared, implications are pondered, and connections to the "drama of life" are considered) and an end-of-project group analysis will provide the needed structure.

The **fundamental elements of the Dual Objective Model** are not negotiable:

1. There must be a **worthy and relevant task to complete**, project to create, problem to solve, or content to be mastered.
2. **Groups must be assembled that will be functional** and which will allow developmental growth by individuals.
3. **Work time must be given in class and the teacher must observe**, discuss, assess, and comment on the quality of the interaction and the completion of the task.

These are a rather simple set of directions, yet there are an infinite number of ways that any single teacher can implement them (Kline & Vermette, 2014). We hope to use the next few chapters to provoke your thought and provide some options so that you can comfortably utilize the necessary elements to engage your students conceptually, socially, and emotionally in ways that best prepare them for the realities of their post-secondary school lives.

In the context of discussing the Dual Objective Model and its component parts, we wish to acknowledge briefly the potential challenge to application in an environment of predetermined curricula. Today teachers are often barraged with teaching resources focusing on specific disciplinary content. State curriculum frameworks, national standards, local scope and sequence and curriculum guides, textbook tables of contents, or seemingly endless online resources. These may direct decisions regarding content choices for units and lessons, they *may* be collaborative, but seldom if ever, do they address the affective domain for learners. In these cases, the teachers borrowing material may find themselves faced with adequate cognitive content, but challenged to adapt the affective element.

CASE: Mrs. Phillips Holocaust Unit

Consider Janis Phillips, a 10th-grade social studies teacher who knows she must teach the Holocaust. This is a starting point for backward planning of both the course and the unit (Wiggins & McTighe, 2005). We ask, "What will be assessed and, therefore, what will be taught?"

Let's say that Mrs. Phillips chooses these two questions from state assessment archives to frame her unit:

1. Hitler's plan, called the "Final Solution," required which of the following?

    a. A majority rule referendum of the non-Jewish people over age 18
    b. A massive outlay of resources and manpower
    c. Financial assistance from other Axis partners
    d. Cooperation by Jewish leaders in neighboring countries

2. Which groups were persecuted in the Holocaust along with the Jewish people?

    a. Gypsies
    b. Homosexuals
    c. People with serious emotional disabilities
    d. All of the above

With those items in mind, Mrs. Phillips can plan her lessons, starting with these two objectives that are aligned with the two sample questions:

1. Describe the factors that allowed Hitler and the Nazis to begin the Holocaust.
2. Identify the various groups in Germany that were directly harmed by the Holocaust, and its influence on each.

There is nothing earth-shattering about what we have just described: determining cognitive content and creating cognitive objectives. Now Mrs. Phillips must select complementary affective skills for the lessons. Since we anticipate good constructivist instruction in the unit, we expect disagreement, insight, insensitivity, impatience, reconsiderations, and controversial statements to occur as students interact with ideas and each other. Given this likelihood, we suggest the addition of listening with empathy and/or managing impulsivity as affective objectives. Students prepared to show their skills of empathy and to exhibit self-regulation will make deeper meaning of the content than they typically would had they not been groomed to do so; they may also have insights about their demonstration of these two affective skills. We urge Phillips to be explicit about her expectations for students to show these competencies and to provide feedback on their abilities to do so. This would be the Dual Objective Model in operation.

Frequently Asked Questions (Q&A) About the Dual Objective Model

To close this section, we will draw on a tactic that we use at our workshops: a few minutes of Q&A. We have chosen eight very common questions that we are asked when we explain, and teachers examine, the Dual Objective and offer answers that should deepen your developing understanding of the model.

Moreover, before we enter the Q&A, we reiterate that in order to employ the Dual Objective Model effectively, there are several fundamental realizations to which a teacher must subscribe:

1. The teacher as facilitator of learning.
2. The art of teaching involves providing students opportunities for cognitive and affective growth.
3. Learning occurs when students actively engage in experiences that cause their current understanding (or lack thereof) to change/develop.
4. Teachers own the process of teaching, and students own the process of learning.

1. Why does the Dual Objective Model approach belong to the Cooperative Learning family?

People we talk to argue about this often. In truth, students use affective skills all the time when they are working alone and the Dual Objective applies there as well. However, because of the greater cognitive gain associated with CL and because many affective skills demand a collaborative structure (such as "listening with empathy") the Dual Objective fits perfectly as a variant of the CL approach.

Also, notice that the choice of affective skills is important and there are many taxonomies that can be utilized. In some schools, though, the focus on certain items may have already been decided for you; and you should concentrate on those. Lockport, NY, has selected kindness, humility, honesty, respectfulness, and responsibility as their "virtues" and they are explicitly stated in the school (and district) statements. The Ontario Ministry has six abilities that must be "graded" on every K–12 student's grade report: responsibility, organization, independence, collaboration, initiative, and self-regulation. The Collaborative for Academic, Social, and Emotional Learning (CASEL) lists five that they recommend: self-awareness, self-management, social awareness, relationship skills, and responsible decision-making. Many school districts subscribe to character programs that target the development of select "traits" on a monthly basis, etc., while others are committed to Covey's "Leader in Me" program, and its seven principles. Regardless of entry point, the teacher must be explicit in his or her affective objective and know ahead of time what s/he will be looking for as evidence.

2. So I teach both the cognitive objective, "describe four causes of the war," and I also teach something like "managing impulsivity," but isn't this a lot for one lesson?

Nope. You already have a very solid plan to teach the content, and you have an assessment of it planned for the end of class. For the affective component, think about the skills (competencies) that the students will need to do well in the lesson and the assessment, and then plan to integrate those—including your feedback—into the lesson. Since the students will be working in Cooperative Learning teams, make sure they know what "managing impulsivity" (or other choices) means in that context, and then observe and give feedback. One more idea may help; if you use an exit slip as a reflection or as an assessment measure, make sure that at least one of the items deals directly with the affective skill being utilized:

a. The most important cause of the war was . . . because . . .
b. One way I showed self-regulation (called "managing impulsivity") was when . . .

If you look back at the model, you will see that use of the second item would be "teaching" the concept of impulse control and concentrating on its actual application and transfer to the situation at hand.

3. Doesn't this mean that teachers will be teaching values and morals and philosophical principles? Can we do that?

The words "morals" and "values" in today's society can be very controversial. The authors recognize that their tone is often one of a religious nature, rather than of secular society. Affective skills should **not** to be confused with one's belief systems involving morals and values. They are instead concrete skills that we must foster to prepare our youth for their place in contemporary life. Given that, schools have traditionally taught societal norms, and rightly so, but only recently has our society recognized how critically important it is to do it intentionally. Paul Tough's 2012 book, *How children succeed*, put the importance of non-cognitive skills in the spotlight. For example, if you require students to arrive to class promptly, you assess timeliness of assignments, and have consequences for cutting class, aren't you focusing attention on punctuality or responsibility by promoting a desirable way to do things? Yes you are, and you are inducing a particular behavior and attitude. Also, if you expect students to always do their best work and persist when challenged, aren't you promoting a strong work ethic? Yes, and the Common Core actually states that persistence is formally part of the standards in math! People who complain that schools don't teach students how to be good people and effective workers are wrong; it just isn't done very intentionally or systematically. The need is clear, but the choices are many for the teachers seeking resources from which to choose affective skills. We have looked at many taxonomies; those that we believe present the best options are *Habits of mind* by Costa and Kallick (2008) and the Learning and Innovation and Life and Career Skills (part of the P21 Framework) of the 21st Century Partnership (see Appendix 1). As teens work toward developing these, they become far better able to navigate the complex life and work environments they will encounter as they move on to higher education and the world of work.

4. How do I manage all the documentation needed/generated by using the model?

Although there is often some type of documentation required when building and assigning groups (see Chapter 4), we assume this question is about the process of working on task and documenting quality therein. Assuming that you already employ methods to assess and grade cognitive growth in the form of student products, our attention here will be to the affective side of the model. The amount and type of documentation needed to capture useful data and provide beneficial feedback for affective growth depends entirely upon how often your students work cooperatively and the goals that you have for them: Chapter 5 offers specific solutions that we believe you will find helpful.

One issue that we believe is imperative to address here, however, is the notion that **it is unfair to assess students on something that you do not teach**. Please re-read the previous sentence. Now this may seem like a "no-brainer" when it comes to cognitive achievement, but when you evaluate the *process* used for learning *and its related affective competencies*, you must think in the same way. Have you given adequate practice for the targeted competence/ies? What evidence of mastery do you have to show for the individual? (Can you fairly use the word "mastery" when referring to affective competence?) What evidence of progress do you have to show for the group? Have you collected enough data to make a fair assessment?

You must find a method of gathering, analyzing, and reporting data on affective skills in such a way as to facilitate feedback that causes student growth. Although many of us are used to providing scores on grade reports for "participation," "effort," or the like, seldom do we actually have objective evidence to back our "opinions." The Dual Objective is not founded on subjective opinion but on educational research applied intentionally and systematically, resulting in objective substantiation of student progress in both domains. This is one of a very few methodologies today that can be employed actively in the classroom to develop (teach) the "whole child."

When doing Cooperative Learning through the Dual Objective Model, you need evidence of growth (or lack thereof) for both the cognitive and affective objectives. You can think of them in the same manner. If you use rubrics for outlining expectations for a product, why not also create a rubric for process (affective expectations)? If you use outslips to check cognitive grasp of material on a daily basis, why not add questions that target affective progress? Students could keep a journal—a place where they could document how they are doing on the affective competencies, a process that will help them build metacognition and self-awareness as well as actually helping them to learn the meaning and application of the targeted skills. There are as many methods and resources for capturing and managing this data as there are for cognitive data, and there is no one right way to do it. Adapt what you use currently, use ideas from this book, investigate technologies, ask your colleagues, and ask your students. Find what works for you and your students through trial and error if need be. In an age of data-informed instruction, the better the data, the better the results. If this requires you to change practice, do so boldly: it works.

5. It sounds like you think we should do this every day and in every lesson: Is that right?

Every lesson that you teach should promote deep conceptual thinking and reinforce Habits of Mind, 21st Century Partnership skills, or the like. Why would you not? Systematically planning and teaching to make students more effective problem-solvers, better people and citizens, and more experienced collaborators sounds like a good plan to us. In addition, making a commitment on a department, grade, building, or district level, across disciplines, and throughout secondary schooling, will yield *far* better results than those of the individual teacher; but **if you must be an island, be so**.

We are starting to see these more "global" aspects of developing the whole child making their way into state *academic* standards, acknowledging their necessity and importance. In New York State for instance, math and social studies have "practices" within their disciplines while college- and career-ready standards have recently been added to ELA. A sampling includes:

◆ Show respect in issues involving difference and conflict.
◆ Make sense of problems and persevere in solving them.

- ◆ Critique the reasoning of others.
- ◆ Use technology to interact and communicate with others.
- ◆ Gather information from multiple sources and assess its credibility.
- ◆ Ask questions.
- ◆ Attend to precision.
- ◆ Demonstrate respect for the rights of others.

These skills are universally transferrable from discipline to discipline and from academic to everyday life. These, and others like them, form the foundation for success beyond the classroom, and are widely regarded as universally expected by employers and higher education alike. Can we spend our classroom time devoted to anything better?

6. The model shows that we should have a clear objective for both the affective and the cognitive domains, but it also says that we should plan "how to teach" the affective skill. What does that mean exactly? In brief, we simply mean that the teacher has to have an explicit plan for the strategies/tasks/learning activities that will teach the chosen concepts. For example, if today your students are being "taught" to deepen their ability to "listen with empathy," we ask several questions:

- ◆ Have you had a conversation with them about the meaning of those words?
- ◆ Have you shown them a model of the skill and discussed with them how to do it?
- ◆ For today, when you "work the room" and observe their teamwork, how will you *judge* how well they "listen with empathy" and how will you give them feedback for improvement from the data you collect?
- ◆ Is there a time allotted to discuss these skills and their connection to life beyond the classroom?

Doing those things *is* "teaching" the affective competency "listening with empathy." We know that a lot of teachers do this intuitively when an opportunity appears: this is the famous "teachable moment." What we ask is that you **plan those teachable moments and intentionally integrate them** into your everyday plans.

7. I teach courses where my students are expected to complete high-stakes tests and I am responsible for getting them ready for those exams. What I've been doing (drilling for recall) seems to work, as I have a good pass rate, so why change?

Unfortunately, "drilling" students to prepare them for contemporary standardized tests is a far cry from a real education and while we understand that political pressures might be the root cause of such a decision, any teacher who goes that route is abdicating his or her responsibilities as an educator. We will make two suggestions here, and add that we'd like you to go back and look at the Johnson and Nicola classes described earlier. In each of them, students are *not* just mastering material (i.e. regurgitating facts or vocabulary lists); they are solving problems, creating new interpretations, or generating products that show integration of concepts and deep understanding. These students are better equipped to take this learning and apply it in new and different situations as called for later in their education or lives. This is the result and goal of true learning.

There are two additional points we'd like to make on this matter. First, adolescents learn deeply when they are fully engaged in their efforts to learn over a period of time. This almost always puts us on the side of projects and small projects called "learning activities." Dewey's famous dictum, "We do not learn from experience; we learn from doing and from reflecting on experience," comes into play when worthwhile projects are assigned and completed thoughtfully. The research on formal Project-Based Learning (PBL) is mixed, but suggests that its use has many positive outcomes and does not harm learning, as measured by exams (see Chapter 6). Combined with the research on Cooperative Learning, we see teams planning and completing complex, interesting, and self-regulated projects as the avenue for great cognitive and affective gain. If such work can be completed in a 20-minute time frame *within* a specific class, we call them "learning tasks" and we expect positive benefits for all who contribute. ("Projects" obviously take more time and are usually not done in one class period.)

Second, expectations in future careers will *never* require preparation for multiple-guess tests. Knowledge that an adult individual has constructed will not be passively tapped by simplistic queries: Real life is not a game of Jeopardy. Knowledge is only useful as it transfers to help in an authentic context. By the time they are adolescents, learners should be aggressively learning and using new ideas in varied and multiple contexts, not guessing at answers to arbitrary questions that are purported to be aligned with real skills. When a student's team is actually doing a project, real cognitive and affective skills can be observed, assessed, and improved through the Dual Objective.

8. **All this change feels a bit like overload. Didn't one of you already write about the ENGAGING framework? Should we do ENGAGING or the Dual Objective?**

This is an interesting question to answer and we could summarize that whole book, but we will give you a very short version of the ENGAGING framework in the context of the Dual Objective.

Simply put, ENGAGING is a memory device to help people remember eight factors that increase adolescents' engagement and their deep understanding of conceptual material. Actually, each of the eight is easily integrated into the context of the Dual Objective Model.

Figure 2.3 The ENGAGING Framework for Cooperative Learning

E	**ENTICE EFFORT AND BUILD COMMUNITY** Enticing effort by building community stresses the motivational aspects of students working together and being supported by their peers.
N	**NEGOTIATE MEANING** Negotiating meaning stands for the thinking done by an individual as she works through her own notions of new information in the safety of the group setting. Almost all CL learning activities are constructivist not behaviorist in nature. Therefore, students analyze, examine, assess, create, and construct their ideas, not simply replicate them.
G	**GROUP FOR COLLABORATION** Grouping for collaboration is central to CL. In truth, the Dual Objective Model extends this aspect of the ENGAGING framework in much more detail.
A	**ACTIVE LEARNING AND AUTHENTIC ASSESSMENT** Active learning is what is needed to integrate new ideas into long-term memory. This thinking can be done alone, but groups offer more ideas, feedback, challenge, discussion (conversation), stimulation, and enjoyment than does solitary study. Moreover, the Dual Objective requires participation and thus allows for authentic assessment of the affective side of the model.
G	**GRAPHIC ORGANIZERS** Graphic Organizers are often used in CL activities. They can be used as part of a Think–Pair–Share, as a product of a group session, or as an assessment. They are almost always conceptual, customized, and creative ways of structuring the learning of material in any discipline.
I	**INTELLIGENCE INTERVENTIONS** Intelligence interventions suggest that there are multiple modalities (intelligences) (Gardner, 1983) and strengths at play during cooperative work. Since people are neither all the same, nor are they all good or all bad (at everything), groups provide a richer mixture of strengths than does a person working alone. You will find that this increases appreciation for diversities in a way that cannot be easily approached by other means. Elizabeth Cohen (1994) knew this truth.
N	**NOTE-MAKING** Note-making is a universally applicable learning activity, but in a CL setting there are several opportunities that are not available otherwise. Students can compare their interpretations, reflections, or constructions; students can jointly construct meaning; and students can synthesize their various renderings into a cohesive whole. Note-making is not just to keep a record: it is a "place" to experiment, evaluate, and design meanings.
G	**GRADE WISELY** Grade wisely is the final part of ENGAGING. In essence, it means shaping the environment to challenge teens and provide opportunities for them to shine and be acknowledged as well as receive corrective feedback. Literally, the Dual Objective Model doubles the opportunities for success by stressing both the cognitive and affective aspects of the learning experiences in class. Everyone can "win" every day!

Source: Modified from Vermette (2009)

In Closing

This chapter clearly details how to set up and use the Dual Objective Model of Cooperative Learning. In offering the cases of secondary teachers Johnson, Nicola, and Phillips, we gave the reader a chance to see various types of implementation and planning that go into its use. Moreover, the explanation of the Dual Objective Model (Figure 2.1) allowed us to emphasize the twin foci of cognitive growth (product outcomes) and affective gain (from attending to the process of working on task) as well as the importance of having both affective and cognitive assessments and feedback in the same lesson. Finally, the use of the questions and answers provided a detailed way to answer anticipated reaction to the model. We suggest that the reader make a commitment to return to this chapter and re-read it sometime in the near future, after you have built an experience base of experimentation. It will make you better.

Chapter 2 Big Ideas

1. Research suggests that responding to challenges such as answering questions, hypothesizing about meaning, and sharing ideas *before formal instruction* actually increases learning.

2. The Dual Objective Model has several features: (a) building of student teams; (b) creating engaging learning activities; (c) monitoring the group work; and (d) providing useful feedback for cognitive gain and for affective development.

3. Models of teaching that are student-centered and require student voice result in deeper analysis, better teacher feedback, and a more positive classroom atmosphere.

4. Assessment for both cognitive gain and affective growth must be carefully planned and this includes student self-assessment.

5. Affective skills (sometimes called "soft skills," non-cognitive skills, dispositions, or competencies) such as empathy, meta-cognition, persistence, and teamwork are malleable and important to academic learning and to lifelong success. Career readiness demands the development of these affective skills and using the Dual Objective makes these skills explicitly featured and integrated.

6. For most teachers who are already using some form of CL, the shift toward the Dual Objective will mean focusing on the affective expectations of the model and the design of team worthy activities.

7. The Dual Objective requires some focused teacher change and is consistent with an existing approach called the ENGAGING framework.

References

Cohen, E. (1994). *Designing groupwork.* New York, NY: Teachers College Press.

Costa, A., & Kallick, B. (2008). *Habits of mind across the curriculum.* Alexandria, VA: ASCD.

Costa, A., & Kallick, B. (2014). *Dispositions.* Thousand Oaks, CA: Corwin Press.

Gardner, H. (1983). *Frames of mind: The theory of multiple intelligences.* Cambridge, MA: Harvard University Press.

Kline, C., & Vermette, P.J. (2013). Well-structured cooperative learning in all classrooms: Using the dual objective to maximize affective and cognitive gains. *International Journal of the Science of Education (Formazione & Insegnamento),* Volume 11, No. 4, 2013 pgs. 85–103.

Tough, P. (2012). *How children succeed: Grit, curiosity and the hidden power of character.* Boston, MA: Houghton-Mifflin.

Vermette, P.J. (2009). *Engaging teens in their own learning: Eight keys to student success.* Larchmont, NY: Eye-on-Education.

Wiggins, G., & McTighe, J. (2005). *Understanding by design.* Alexandria, VA: ASCD.

3

What Do the Students Do in CL Groups?

When we ask teachers about what they have students do when they are in groups, we hear a range of answers, including the following three common comments:

Teacher #1: "I just tell them to gather up some friends and then get together to go over the chapter."

Teacher #2: "I have them in assigned teams and they are working on specific tasks."

Teacher #3: "Half of every class is silent reading and completion of individual worksheets."

Obviously, the third teacher has not seriously considered the benefits of CL and is sticking to a traditional script about what counts as instructional practice. The first teacher is either very trusting of student wisdom or a bit lax in vision since there are many options the students could pursue, and many of them are not very beneficial for cognitive and affective growth. This chapter examines the well-structured nature of the second teacher's comments about specific tasks. The nature of the team task(s) is an important consideration for successful implementation of the Dual Objective Model.

Introduction

For many readers, this is the only really important chapter in this book: perhaps you don't care about theory or philosophy, research is not your thing, and you don't think that you have the time to invest in creating a well-structured system, or you just see yourself as very pragmatic. If so, you still might want to know the answer to the question: "What are some group-based activities that I can have the teens do in class (that will not cause discipline problems and actually help them learn the content)?" Others, who are interested in all those other "theoretical" things, may still be very curious about designing effective challenges (tasks/activities) and wonder about what other teachers are having students do during group work.

For both the analytical reader and the pragmatic reader, this chapter provides a description of many such activities and a host of suggestions for creating your own. Enjoy this chapter; it is at the heart of what students and teachers do every day of the year.

(Student) Talk: Why Do We Want it in Our Classrooms? Does How Much Matter?

Gone are the days of the Peanuts' Mrs. Donovan (wah, wah, wah, wah), or Ben Stein's "Bueller? . . . Bueller? . . . Bueller?" neat single rows, and the misconstrued belief that quiet classrooms mean quality learning! Enter the noise of productive talk. In the Dual Objective Model of CL, the *majority of the spoken utterances* are by thoughtful and emotionally engaged students. This focus on intentional student talk provides a distinction between traditional classrooms, where almost all the talk belongs to the teacher (see Goodlad, 1984; Cuban, 1993), and classrooms using well-structured CL.

This is a big difference; when we mention during consultancies that the *majority of (thoughtful) classroom utterances are by students*, we are often challenged. We suspect that you too may not quite believe us when we make that claim, particularly if you have never observed effective Cooperative Learning in action. We understand the potential concerns, so let's get a few out in the open that we have actually heard in our consulting work:

- ◆ Students will not talk about their tasks . . . they'll just socialize.
- ◆ I (the teacher) will "lose control" and class will become a "noisy mess."
- ◆ It takes too much time . . . How can I cover all the material if I give students time to talk?

Furthermore, many of the teachers we work with have seldom, if ever, seen colleagues teach, so the opportunity to see students "talking to learn" is limited to their own classroom approach.

In this chapter we will provide you numerous "glances" into typical and exemplar classrooms to allow you to see how student talk (or lack thereof) can and does impact understanding, and what this looks like in its most effective form. We expect that if you share any of the above concerns you will find comfort in your discoveries as you read. Ultimately, we hope that you will come to believe this truth: **Student talk matters greatly and when it occurs in well-structured cooperative groups, it is almost always beneficial.**

This can be a startling realization: Students talk more about content in the Dual Objective Model (and feel better about it) than they do in very powerful traditional lecture/teacher-centered systems. Moreover, it is difficult for students to have a meaningful conversation without paying attention and thinking about something (i.e. content). Thus, the Dual Objective version of CL may maximize *engaged learning time* (the "time on task" variable that correlates well to increased learning), while providing positive experiences and motivating the development of social-emotional skills and well-being.

A quick flip back to the prologue of this book and locating the model of how the mind works gives us a clue as to why talking about content (i.e. true conversation) *causes* learning: The back-and-forth information exchange and examination found in dialogue provides a continuous flow of stimuli which demands the frequent integration of prior knowledge held in long-term memory and embeds it with new information being attended to in short-term memory. This internal processing of information in the minds of *each* student, whose engagement is sparked by the conversation and mediated by the affective skill of attention and the cognitive work of intentional integration, changes their brains and their thinking. Real dialogue *causes* cognitive changes, a process that is often called "deepening learning," through the connecting of different people's ideas in meaningful ways.

To exemplify, listen to the voices of these students as they engage in an interesting and powerful conversation during an ELA class. The students have read and annotated Bryan Walls Jr.'s great book, *The road that led to somewhere* (1983), a novel that tells the true story of an enslaved family who journeyed from 1846 North Carolina to freedom in Essex County, Canada. The team of students (Selena, Marcia, and Darryl) has been charged with: (a) creating titles for 6 of the 45 "miles" (chapters); (b) explaining their decisions; while (c) being empathetic and supportive of each other. As you read the dialogue, you may note that the students are paying attention and listening to each other (thus showing respect), examining a variety of ideas (from multiple sources), and responding logically, thus sparking another round of examination and synthesis. They are also apparently concerned about others' contributions and their individual emotional connections to the situation. Whew! This all seems to be a lot of feeling-thinking-working and collaboration in a very short time; again, we may be confident that brains are being changed (incrementally and continually) as this classroom event proceeds.

CASE: Mr. White's 10th-Grade ELA Class in Northern Virginia

Selena: OK, come on—listen up. Here is what I think we are supposed to do. We have to write new titles for six of the chapters in Walls' book about slavery and freedom.

Darryl: Great . . . that's a lot of work. I read the thing and have just a few notes, but I think White wants our chapter titles to actually mean something important—UGH!

Marcia: Darryl, it won't be so bad. We've already discussed all this stuff and we have the illustrations everybody drew. Yours were great—mine were . . .

Selena: Good point, but we gotta move—we only have 20 minutes. Remember that each of us has to be ready to explain *why* we used the new title we dream up. I don't know why Walls called them "miles" in the first place: then we wouldn't have to do this title thing. Anyway, Darryl, I bet he calls on you to represent us, so get your pen out.

Darryl: (*Grumbling*) OK.

Marcia: We all read #12—what happened in there?

Darryl: (*Looking at his notes and grimacing*) Oh. Remember Caesar getting eaten by the dogs and the slave catchers?

Marcia: Oh yeah. When I read that—well, I felt sick. I couldn't draw that part. He—he gave himself up for the others.

Darryl: What kind of people would. . .?

Selena: People back then thought that the runaway slaves were—not human. They didn't think of him as a man.

Darryl: (*Shaking his head softly*) Yeah right—they knew. They knew they were hunting men—and kids too! They were just lying to each other about it being OK, then those ____ could steal the slaves' lives. I also thought those Southern white people were all Christian folks—like my aunt in Atlanta. She could never think Jesus would think killing people was OK.

Marcia: Wait, what about "The Ultimate Sacrifice" because he dies for family—his people.

(*Darryl and Selena both smile and nod.*)

Marcia: OK, we got that one. Brutal. Darryl, if he calls on you to explain, what you will say?

Darryl: I'm black (*laughter*) so I don't think he will call on me for this chapter title, but we all agree: Caesar died so the others could escape, right?

Selena: Hmm, I wonder if he would be sensitive to call on you about that chapter. I wonder if it is easier for non-black kids to talk about this stuff. If White does call on you, are you OK to do it?

Darryl: Well, this whole slavery thing ain't personal like Caesar was my own family, but I did feel different—angry—when I read that part. You felt sick, I felt mad. You know Walls is black too and he wrote it!

Marcia: Are we OK on this? Let's look at another—time is running out. How about #7?

Selena:	OK. Funny you suggested that one. I loved it. There was all that singing old spiritual songs and thinking about ancient African nations—like nostalgia for their roots.
Marcia:	Hey! Roots, that's good—like the movie we saw part of last week!
Darryl:	They made a new one now. Nobody watched except my aunt—did you?
Marcia:	In another part, there was a lot about not being free yet, that they had to get to Canada to be truly free human beings—maybe the title could be something like "Roots and Freedom"?
Darryl:	Well, they don't actually get to Canada in the chapter, but I like the "roots" thing—so something about being on the way and roots? Hmm, how about "Uprooted, but Not Yet Free?"
Marcia:	I like it. That's two down, right? Selena, what else do you have?

Our Take

◆ We think that the students benefited greatly from the conversation, more than if they had used that time reading, listening to a lecture, or watching a video. Synthesizing the events of the chapter allowed the students to review Dr. Walls' book and reconsider very important notions of slavery and of African-American lives in another time.

◆ They also developed deeper awareness of the emotional impact of slavery on real people.

◆ Every student contributed, personal connections were made to both content and to fellow students, and emotions/feelings were mediated by peer acceptance and peer interaction. In this short time, these young people are getting a real education and they are doing it by sharing their prior experiences and their own cognitive networks within the bounds of 21st-century teamwork.

◆ There is also a good chance that they may be aware of the value of their own sense of community or sense of belonging and its benefits in a diverse democratic society. Motivation theorists (Farrington et al., 2012; Glasser, 1999) stress this point to teachers of adolescents as often as they can.

Student Talk in Learning Activities: How Do Different Types Matter?

We begin the rest of the chapter explaining the life work of a dear colleague of ours, John Myers of OISE, on "talking to learn" and then will proceed to show you a variety of examples and structures that you can adapt, apply, modify, reject, or simulate in your own classrooms. We also wish to mention that we anticipate that in order for student talk to spark deep thinking, it is usually driven by a task given by the teacher and mediated by expectations of exchange, respectfulness, persistence, and integrity. If you look closely, you will see that students doing collaborative talking to learn are also forced/enticed into experiencing the positive affective growth that is promised by the Dual Objective.

Myers, Bardsley, Vermette, and Kline (2017) detail seven kinds of purposeful talk that students can engage in. Many of these verbal interactions appear to be conversations, while some are more directed attempts to transmit knowledge or offer feedback. We focus here on four of the seven categories as they comprise the structure of the most productive Dual Objective tasks we advocate:

1. Tasks that ask students to do "exploratory" thinking (**exploration**).
2. Tasks that ask students to solve complex problems and/or make decisions for the common good (**problem-solving**).
3. Tasks that ask students to design a new entity that demands a variety of skills, experiences, and perspectives (**product construction**).
4. Tasks that simply ask students to help another student review, rehearse, or reflect on his or her work (**feedback and validation**).

Let's play for a few minutes with some class tasks/activities and try to use the four-part schema above to categorize them.

TASK: Identifying Student Talk

As you examine these examples, consider the purpose of student talk and classify them as (a) exploration, (b) problem-solving, (c) creation of a new entity, or (d) to provide reinforcing feedback.

_____ 1. In Chinese I, paired students are using flashcards to test each other on a set of 20 new nouns.

_____ 2. In History 9, groups of four are creating museum displays that compare Islamic culture in the years 1550 and 2016.

_____ 3. In Entrepreneurship 11, groups of three are making a list of 25 advertising jingles that they can actually sing from memory.

_____ 4. In sociology, teams of four are working on a solution to the problem of obscene graffiti on the walls of local elementary schools. They will draft a proposal to take to the city council.

_____ 5. Individuals in English 8 have been blogging in teams of four (two students from both classes) with another school's sister class. Each team of four has come up with ten sentences about a mythical being that they created and

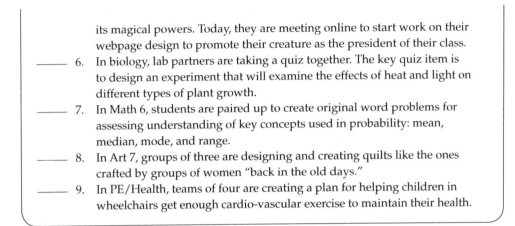

its magical powers. Today, they are meeting online to start work on their webpage design to promote their creature as the president of their class.

_____ 6. In biology, lab partners are taking a quiz together. The key quiz item is to design an experiment that will examine the effects of heat and light on different types of plant growth.

_____ 7. In Math 6, students are paired up to create original word problems for assessing understanding of key concepts used in probability: mean, median, mode, and range.

_____ 8. In Art 7, groups of three are designing and creating quilts like the ones crafted by groups of women "back in the old days."

_____ 9. In PE/Health, teams of four are creating a plan for helping children in wheelchairs get enough cardio-vascular exercise to maintain their health.

If you have read the nine vignettes slowly, you may have envisioned each of these classes in operation. You may have attempted to get a sense of what the student talk would look like, what would be said, by whom and to whom; what would be produced as a result; and maybe, what the discussion would "feel" like as it took place. Each of these is an important consideration and with experience and reflective practice, you will be able to shape student conversations to become more productive and more inclusive, while maintaining the positive nature of the interactions. (By the way, this concept categorization activity, built on important work by Bruner, Goodenow & Austin (1986) is a problem-solving activity that you likely completed alone but which could be done *with* others.)

With that said, we want to note that all student talk is not equal. Some interactions can be divisive and intrusive, some periods of quiet may be positively productive, and some insights can be plain wrong. Nevertheless, most of the time, what students actually say is what they are actually thinking, so getting them to talk about important content in important ways will be a boon to learning. Simply put, making learning audible and visible is almost always a good idea (Ritchhart & Perkins, 2008; Hattie, 2009).

Our Take

Next, we'd like to share our insights about the four categories in relation to the nine vignettes.

◆ The first type of talk, "exploratory," is mostly about motivating students to share insights and knowledge related to a topic or a challenge. The Entrepreneurship 11 groups are simply rehashing old familiar memories from their lives. These types of tasks are often very open-ended "rambles" that reveal both prior knowledge and prior knowledge gaps; by all accounts, they are personal and idiosyncratic, and they can draw every student's attention toward the *content* the teacher wishes them to work with.

◆ There are aspects of *exploration* in the categories c) and d) as well, usually when students are starting to think about solving a challenging problem or creating a new product. However, in these cases, that exploratory talk soon gives way to the actually far more demanding work of analysis and synthesis, the solving or the constructing that is done as students are completing the task. These two steps of student talk are aligned with the Two-Step teaching model of Flynn, Mesibov, Vermette, and Smith (2004), who call the two steps "exploratory" and "discovery."

◆ The history students creating the museum display in vignette #2, the solving of the graffiti issue in vignette #4, the creation of the promotional webpage in vignette #5, the construction of an original experiment in vignette #6, and the designing of the health plan in vignette #9 are examples of a much more complex use of talk. (They also have been judged the most interesting, most demanding, most engaging, and most powerful by the teachers who have assessed this set.)

◆ The final type of talk, what we think of as "simple practice," and which we call *feedback and validation*, is found in two types of group work. The first is reflected in Frank Lyman's (1981) powerful think–pair–share, in which students think briefly alone and then exchange ideas with a partner. Moreover, many of Spencer Kagan's famous structures (1992) are built around simple, quick exchanges of information in various short-term formats that he calls "structures." The second type of *feedback and validation* is demonstrated by the flashcard use in vignette #1, in which students rehearse each other's knowledge of nouns. This use of student talk as validation on low-level memory tasks is common, but should be used sparingly. We accept constructivism's basic tenet that remembering is a byproduct of understanding and we hope that this flashcard exercise is used as a quick review, *not* as a way to introduce new content.

(We will expand our discussion of "exploratory talk" in Chapter 5, with an eye for how the teacher helps structure and assess the potentially elaborative nature of such student–student interaction. Moreover, more about Kagan's structures is available in Appendix 2.)

Introducing the Affective Component

Let's return to Myers' four categories of student talk and this time ask a few questions about how affective skills are integrated into the activity. For example, focus for a minute on these five 21st-century affective competencies and be ready to re-examine the four categories of talk *and* the nine vignettes:

◆ Persistence
◆ Teamwork (collaboration)
◆ Listening with understanding and empathy
◆ Self-awareness
◆ Managing impulsivity (self-regulation).

Returning to the model of the Dual Objective, you might have noticed that you most often think of schoolwork in terms of a student-generated product: a paper, a project, a tangible creation to show student understanding. Students doing these projects are not "learning a concept" as much as they are "having a learning experience" (see Dewey, 1938, for more about the importance of experience in education). However, the Dual Objective Model recognizes the equal partnership of the *process* used by students as the product/task is completed. The social-emotional (affective) skills brought into play by students in making the product are not the so-called "hidden curriculum" of the 1960s, they are, rather, one-half of the *explicit curriculum* of the Dual Objective, and they are expected, visible, audible, re-enforceable, and improvable.

By the way, **all school lessons have connections to the "non-cognitive domain"** (Tough, 2012), **but only in the Dual Objective are they integrated, taught, and assessed** on a regular basis.

The tasks that require complex thinking, varied experiences, and a range of skills, such as those found in solving the graffiti problem (#4), designing an exercise plan in health (#9), and the creating of the promotional webpage in ELA (#5), also provide great opportunities for the students to practice intentionally each of the five skills bulleted above. Persistence develops from the long-term nature of the project completion; teamwork is central to the quality of the final product; empathetic communication allows for each to contribute and for all ideas to be vetted as they surface; self-awareness influences how each student chooses to participate and build off others' ideas; and self-regulation helps the individual place herself in the context of a respectful exchange of ideas.

Most readers think the types of projects just mentioned are all good activities but might not fully recognize that all of them call for complex social-emotional contributions from each student to be effectively completed. The Dual Objective stresses that the teacher is teaching *both* the cognitive *and* the affective sides of the group task, and therefore, the benefits are to both domains. Thus, the types of talk called for in categories b) and c) **(problem-solving and product construction), are the ones we advocate for teachers to use frequently and with great intention**.

The tasks in categories a) and d) are often far less productive. For one thing, the actual talk may not be all that beneficial to the learners. Conversations can be reduced to single word responses ("good," "you got it," and "OK") or simply take the form of a recitation ("I remember the Nestle song, the McDonalds' song, and the Ram Truck song"). Feedback from rehearsal (category d) and exchanging brainstormed ideas (category a) *may* result in new thinking, create a feeling of validation (or enjoyment), and make class lively, loud, and inspiring, thus having a positive impact. But, these types of discourse don't regularly provoke deep thinking, generate reasoned arguments, force reconciliation of diverse opinions, or spark fresh insights, and thus don't call for nearly as much affective or cognitive skill development as do more complex tasks (Webb et al., 2009).

In our experience, we see the need for all four types of student talk over the course of an entire school year, but tend to rely on the types of verbal exchanges enticed in problem-solving or product-design learning activities. Because we see classroom practice as moving through a variety of shorter and longer segments of student talk during any one classroom period, we suggest that you begin with quicker, exploratory student–student interactions that build toward a longer problem-solving challenge later in the class.

Student Talk: What Are 100 Products Which Students Can Create Together?

As teachers become comfortable with this new student-centered classroom, they will continue to search for new and intriguing learning activities. To that end, we offer the chart (Figure 3.1) called the "100 Products." For teachers seeking a tangible product to capture the essence of the outcome of the student–student collaboration, we suggest you consider using (some of) these.

To digress for a moment: Some of the products listed are provocatively possible and worthy of future experimentation. Some of these you've already done and judged. Some don't seem to fit your current unit of content. There are some you wouldn't "touch with a 10-foot pole" (puppet shows in algebra, anyone?). Your own experiences, your perceptions of your students' tolerance for change and creativity, and your own willingness to innovate will help you narrow/expand this list.

Figure 3.1 100 Products

1. Acts of kindness	35. Games (with rules)	68. Puppet shows
2. Ads (for magazines, newspapers, web)	36. Graffiti	69. Puzzles
	37. Good news–bad news	70. Questionnaires
3. Announcements	38. Graphic organizers	71. Questions
4. Autobiographies	39. Grocery lists	72. Quizzes
5. Awards	40. Headlines	73. Quotations
6. Bedtime stories	41. Infographics	74. Real estate notices
7. Billboards	42. Interviews	75. Recipes
8. Blogs	43. Job applications	76. Reenactments
9. Book jackets	44. Journals	77. Reports
10. Book reviews	45. Laboratory reports	78. Resumes
11. Brochures	46. Letters	79. Reviews
12. Bulletins	47. Lists	80. Rubrics
13. Bumper stickers	48. Lyrics	81. Sales pitches
14. Campaign speeches	49. Menus	82. Schedules
15. Captions	50. Mobiles	83. Self-descriptions
16. Cartoons	51. Myths	84. Skype interviews
17. Certificates	52. Newscasts	85. Slogans
18. Character sketches	53. Newspapers	86. Social media profiles
19. Collages	54. Obituaries	87. Speeches
20. Comic strips	55. Observational notes	88. Scrapbooks
21. Community service activities	56. Pamphlets	89. TV commercials
	57. Parodies	90. Telegrams
22. Contracts	58. PechaKuchas (20/20 Presentations)	91. Travel flyers
23. Conversations		92. Tributes
24. Critiques	59. Persuasive letters	93. Tweets
25. Debates	60. Placards	94. Videos
26. Definitions	61. Plays	95. Vokis (voice-over avatars)
27. Diaries	62. Podcasts	96. Want ads
28. Directions	63. Poems	97. Wanted posters
29. Dramas	64. Portfolios	98. Web pages (Facebook, Google Docs, etc.)
30. Editorials	65. Posters	
31. Epitaphs	66. PowerPoint/Prezi presentations	99. Wikipedia entries
32. Essays		100. Wills
33. Fables	67. Propaganda sheets	
34. Field trips (virtual/live)		

Source: Modified from Vermette (1998). Adapted by C. Kline (personal communication, 2014).

TASK: Choosing Products

Let's analyze further possibilities of integration. We ask you to imagine some grade 6–12 teachers wanting students to think deeply about the following pieces of content:

- ◆ Explain the sequence of the five steps to a political revolution.
- ◆ Describe the differences between compounds and mixtures.
- ◆ Add fractions with unlike denominators.
- ◆ Demonstrate the importance of a thesis statement.
- ◆ Analyze the effects of poverty on young children.
- ◆ Explain the seasonal changes on Earth.

Now please search through the 100 Products and assess the utility of coupling the stated objective with the products listed. Can you find a preferred product or two for each?

Notice that there are many, many options and alternatives. If you find a couple of good ones for a particular objective, you may also invite the students to *choose* from that subset, thereby giving them team ownership over their own work. This practice of choice is often a highly motivating tactic (Glasser, 1999; Pink, 2006). We could spend hours giving you many more examples of the process just described, but prefer to suggest that you take a hard look at your own course objectives, then look at the 100 Products and make some reasoned decisions.

We offer two examples from the list above: the first is to add fractions with unlike denominators.

Possible group products for this objective include: (a) creating an infographic including the steps to do this operation successfully; (b) creating a song that sings the steps to solution; (c) creating a batch of word problems that show what unlike denominators "look like" in real life, then illustrating the addition of those quantities; (d) creating a cartoon storyboard telling the stories of various examples of two fractions being added; and (e) creating a handout with incorrect solutions and explanations of why they don't work.

The second example is from science: "explain seasonal changes on Earth." Possible team products that could be created for this task include: (a) building a paper mache model that allows manipulation of the Earth and the Sun and a partner video describing the effects of movement; (b) designing a five-page booklet showing the differences for each season and gearing it to middle-level students; (c) writing lyrics, performing and recording a song that describes the causes of seasonal changes; and (d) modifying an existing diagram of these changes by re-writing the captions and written explanations.

Since neither of the authors is extraordinarily creative, we are always talking to other teachers about the products they ask their groups to create. We borrow freely, as should you. Moreover, we frequently refer back to this list for inspiration. In truth, there is no limit to the number of good learning activities that spark deep conversation in which group members talk and think and feel and learn.

We wish to present you with a hypothetical case study of a student to embed you deeply into the work of recognizing and appreciating teamed activities in the secondary classroom.

Examining Lee's Day: Shadowing a Student to "See" Her Talk

CASE: Lee's Day

Lee is a junior at Gardener High School in a small city in southern Idaho. On a particular day in mid-November, a visitor (a high-school principal from Indiana) doing a "shadow study" (Lounsbury & Clark, 1990), finds himself watching her closely throughout the day. Among his notes are the following:

◆ She started the day in Spanish 3. They did whole-class recitation, in which she appeared to participate half-heartedly. The class then watched an eight-minute movie on the significance of being able to function in a globalized society and the importance of bilingualism. For ten minutes at the end of class, she sat with Peter and they created a brief Spanish song (to the tune of "Twinkle, Twinkle") with information based on a paragraph about Maria, an immigrant from Mexico to NYC. She smiled, chatted, sang a bit out loud during this stretch and actually frowned when the bell rang, ending the period. The teacher did not pay attention to her efforts.

◆ In second-period physics, Lee read the chapter for 20 minutes and then listened while the teacher explained the key points in the chapter. Her eyes were fixed on the teacher and she wrote in her notebook twice. There was a PowerPoint that aligned with his comments (actually, many were his verbatim words). The homework was posted on the board.

◆ She spent third period in the library with a classmate named Arim, tutoring 5th-graders on reading skills. I did not observe this event, which she was doing for a specialized service leadership project.

◆ In AP Global, she was in a very mixed team (with wheelchair-bound Anthony, Kim, Sasha, and Salam) which worked almost the whole time on their project: creating a graphic novel of what the U.S. will be like in 100 years. She argued with the others a lot, mostly because she thought they were "just guessing," not extrapolating from the evidence of present trends, as per the directions. There were several interesting moments, ending in laughter and fist-bumps all around as the team continued. Her body language was all over the place, but when she talked she made eye contact and *always* smiled. I listened as well as I could: she used each of the others' names, she asked for their input or opinion, and twice she asked the somewhat quiet Anthony what he was thinking. Three separate times during class she mentioned that she thought that their plan was "coming together nicely."

◆ Fifth period was PE and was focused on team basketball. An old practice of having two good players serving as captains for picking teams was used and she was last pick of all 17 students. She trudged over among her teammates and sat on the bench until there were two minutes to go, when she went into the game. She never touched the ball.

◆ This was lunch and my chance to debrief the day with her. The first thing she did was thank me and wondered if I thought she was a good student and would succeed at college. After we chatted a bit, she urged me not to leave but to stay and watch her in ELA, which she loved. She went on to tell me about her accomplishments there: writing a story, crafting poems, putting on a play, teaching the 5th-graders, reading books she liked and sharing her insights, making a video clip for the school show, and Skyping and blogging with 11th-graders in Buffalo and Mexico. As we examined these accomplishments, she mentioned that almost all of them had been with classmates in a team, although she was particularly proud of her journal entries on these varied experiences.

◆ I did go to ELA and it was a lively and a bit chaotic: It looked and felt far more like a work room in a business advertising firm than a classroom in southern

Idaho. Groups of three and four were working on laptops and tablets designing infographics for publicizing an upcoming school/community event. They were working on adjusting the base graphic to particular audiences (parents, the local Chamber of Commerce, elementary school children, etc.) and were making sure everything looked good on computers and mobile devices, with one group working on a paper version to post around school. I asked Lee about how her classmates felt about it, and she said they all liked it a lot. Lee said that one of the introverted kids (Anthony from Global class) told her once that he liked this class because they were never put on the spot, everyone had help from their teammates, and although they had individual duties, they were not called on publicly with everyone watching and judging (something he really hated).

◆ I stayed and went to her math class last period. It was a very classic 1957 class. The teacher started by going over the homework: Lee was called on for #3, read from her paper, and then stared into space. After ten minutes, Mrs. Wyatt showed a new problem on the board, and then gave the class a chance to do a few by themselves. Lee had her head down as she worked. Next to her was Arim, who appeared agitated and then whispered something softly to Lee. Immediately, Mrs. Wyatt spun around, telling him to keep trying himself and not to bother others. Both Lee and Arim then kept very quiet and looked out the window. When it was time, Mrs. Wyatt asked for individual volunteers to answer the problems; they came to the board, wrote out some things, and then received her verbal praise. Lee appeared totally vacant, absent from the process. (At least in PE she watched others play the game and actually cheered when Marina scored.) As class ended, she grabbed me and said, "Thanks for coming to ELA, but I don't like math. Mrs. Wyatt told me that I wasn't 'math material' but that I should keep trying. I gotta run, I'm meeting my Global team at the computer lab to work on the graphic novel for a while before practice." Then she was gone.

Our Take

A long time ago, Mihaly Csikszentmihalyi coined the concept of "flow": it represents a period of total engagement in an activity. Not only is this state of flow a self-actualizing experience, it requires the integration of thinking, focus, and emotion, and results in the greatest growth in an individual. His most relevant study (Csikszentmihalyi & Larson, 1984), done with high school student subjects, revealed that rarely do teenagers fully engage and reach flow *during* the school day; however, extra-curricular activities frequently produce flow states (times in which students are maximizing their human potential). This study suggested that teens move through the day in a somewhat sluggish way, their energies ebbing and flowing and their attention a sporadic thing. However, under some conditions, they can focus, feel powerful and enthusiastic, and engage fully, often in those activities that (a) they have some control over, (b) have meaning to themselves and society, and (c) involve direct, systematic, and intentional interaction with peers. Although not examined by formal scholarship (yet), these three conditions very much mirror the conditions students might find themselves in during a well-structured Dual Objective lesson; we would predict the same high level of engagement in subject matter classes as Csikszentmihalyi found in extra-curricular ones.

Now we don't expect students to come to school 180 days a year and become transfixed by the events of all of their classes that day; however, it could and should happen once in a while. It seems to us that Lee, a fine person with good intentions and moderate skills, may have been in (or approaching) flow regularly in ELA class, where she plays an important role, and on this day, in Global, where the team was committed to creating a quality product and following a respectful process. It was clear that she neither focused well nor worked hard in any of the other classes. Moreover, several of the classes singled her out for her limitations, a practice that is toxic for many students. Further, some instructional events invited humiliation by peers, a truly damaging state for teenagers.

Notice that her role varied in different classes. If she was an important figure in class, and her effort influenced others and contributed ideas, she responded well. If she was an object in the background, a receptacle for information, she became passive; worse, if she was not a recognized part of the class, she felt emotionally invisible and became "zoned out."

Interestingly, the shadow studies done long ago by NASSP had shown that students rarely contributed to the development of the class (even in discussions!) and that they sat and were asked to listen and respond or record information. In a fine book, Larry Cuban (2002) wrote about how computers were supposed to change this passive student role, but didn't really (and this was in Silicon Valley!).

Some might say that one of the reasons students were more engaged in Lee's ELA class was the natural integration of technology. While we applaud effective technology integration, it is not the tools themselves that create success, but the classroom protocols and systems established for their use. In support of such, review again the comments that Anthony made (each of which had nothing to do with technology, but rather validation, support and safety) about why he liked ELA class. The Dual Objective is alive and well in this class. The use of Cooperative Learning (with assumed affective objectives) provides the security and safety for students to maximize their learning experience (potentially reaching "flow"), by shifting students from passive recipients to active contributors to class (and in this example, the school/ community). What has made students the centerpiece of classroom cognitive activity here has been the adoption of well-structured Cooperative Learning and the intentional integration of valuable affective skills: sharing this perspective is why we wrote this book!

Leaving the consideration of flow aside, let's think about the variable called "engaged time on task." Sitting in class, staring at a textbook, and watching a teacher talk are all passive activities. No doubt these can become active, and productive, if the student can fight the boredom and force herself to be actively engaged with ideas (if *not* with other students). This is the reason we have some "winners" in the school competition: It is possible to profit from this type of education but to do so takes enormous will power and self-motivation. (Frankly, many people who have become secondary teachers were good at this kind of learning both in high school and in their major courses in college; they now believe that every teen should be able to do so as well, in every class.) However, it is much easier for most teens to be actively engaged when the role of student is seen as an important cog in the lesson, as it is in the Dual Objective.

We joke that if a teacher can teach a class without any students present, then he shouldn't bother. You cannot use a CL structure *without* students. Student thinking, student feeling, and student talking are at the center of a high-quality class, and at the heart of the Dual Objective experience.

Using Established Frameworks to Invent Team Activities

Having examined our take on the four categories of student talk and its importance in practice, let's broaden our scope and explore some more plausible secondary learning activities from the perspective of the Dual Objective.

Bloom Level

Benjamin Bloom is credited with having created taxonomy of cognitive experiences from low to high. Subsequent scholarship has always maintained that higher levels are better than lower: They are more demanding, more conceptual, and better able to be transferred and lead to deeper understanding. We anticipate that you have long experience with "Bloom levels" and will anticipate that we favor activities that entice upper level thinking. You would be right to expect that from us. Let's take a few minutes to examine several examples that differ in their cognitive tasks à la Bloom.

TASK: Comparing Classes

Please compare and contrast the following sets of class descriptions, and determine which you would be most apt to borrow in reference to its approach for enhancing student learning. Mark your choice with an "X." When complete, read the "Our Take" section below for how we see these comparisons.

Math 9

_____ 1. Mr. Favor collects homework at his desk as students enter. He then has the students work alone on examples in class for ten minutes immediately after he explains the sample problem to open class. He later calls on students to come to the board and show their work and then gives them feedback on their answers. The new homework is then assigned.

_____ 2. Mrs. Favor starts class by showing the students the type of problem they will be learning how to solve that day. They have two minutes to try a problem, and then they share their work for five minutes with a lab partner. She then does a demo at the board, calling on several class members to explain their conjectures. The last part of class involves pairs solving similar problems while she "works the room."

French 1

_____ 1. Mme Finch asks the students to work in their three-person groups. She gives them a list of five nouns and six verbs and asks them to construct a brief story using as many of the vocabulary offerings as possible. She mentions that one person from each group will be randomly selected to report to the entire class.

_____ 2. M. Robyn gives the students several French sentences that construct a dialogue and use new vocabulary. The students are given 12 minutes to help their peer partner memorize the dialogue to act out in front of the class.

Marketing

_____ 1. Ms. Capital is having her students complete a worksheet which asks for the definition of six new words and which has a fill-in-the blank reading guide to the text (pages 184–188, a section on advertising). They can work together if they wish, but will be turning in their own work for a grade.

_____ 2. Working in triads, Ms. Labore's students are doing three things: they are translating the definitions of six new terms into their own words; they are writing explanations of how each new term would connect to an advertising campaign for selling a new type of car; and they are examining how the students are integrating their own sense of perspective while interacting. They can turn in one report for the three _if_ each attests to having contributed.

Social Studies 11

——— 1. In Mr. New's class, students are spending the entire period designing their five-minute TV news story on a historical event from the 1920s (which will be videotaped the next day).
They have guidelines to follow and the four-person teams are checked regularly while working in class.

——— 2. In Mr. Alden's class, the students have a 20-item quiz on the 1920s tomorrow. Today, they are allowed to read and study the chapter by themselves and are encouraged to take notes if they wish. Any such notes will be collected at the end of class so they cannot be shared. The quiet room is seen as promoting deep thought and Mr. Alden reads at his desk during the period as well.

Our Take

Compare and contrast activities (Bloom level of analysis) are powerful in and of themselves. However, in the task above, when we asked you to identify which you might "borrow," we moved your work from analysis to evaluation, a bit more complex. (The difference between evaluation and analysis does not matter to us as they are both higher-order skills.) Both of these Bloom levels build deep understanding, improve the likelihood of remembering, and increase the ability to transfer.

Now, let's examine our take on each set of classroom experiences, and how well each of the teachers employs Bloom's taxonomy for the benefit of their students.

◆ Math 9: We clearly think that Mrs. Favor is having her students working at the analysis level, where they have to solve and defend their decisions. Mr. Favor, however, is having students do simple comprehension-level work and occasionally seeking application from some students.

◆ French 1: We see that Madame Finch is trying to have her students create an original story while incorporating specific content. This is synthesis, or the construction of a new product using knowledge. The whole point of secondary schooling is to help teens combine and transfer ideas to new situations. She hopes they learn by using the content, which is a very Piagetian notion (and one that we hold dear). Monsieur Robyn's attempt at having them memorize scripts in the French language, even though fueled by peer interaction, is not as rigorous and is a far more boring activity for most teens.

◆ Marketing: We have little use for traditional worksheets (filling in blanks in a narrative) as a substitute for instruction that requires actual thought. Ms. Capital is mostly filling time and, by making peer interaction an option, she is not promoting affective growth either. Meanwhile, Ms. Labore has her teams doing several things: they are translating, which we see as creating their own meaning, and thus synthesis; they are using evidence to defend a proposition which is most likely an analysis-level action; and they are assessing their actual practice (evaluation). These students, if they are actually doing the tasks, will be learning a lot today.

◆ Social Studies 11: Frankly, we are not at all clear about what Mr. Alden wishes the students to do: "Study the chapter" is language that is extraordinarily vague and can mean almost anything. Our guess is that there are many students wasting their time in this 45-minute part of their day. His emphasis on quiet and orderliness has a long history, but as Benedict Carey's (2014) book suggests, much of what we used to think was right about how to learn has been shown to be incorrect, including the value of sustained quiet. Those students who *do* take high-quality notes are probably learning and will be able to get enough answers right on the test to allow a nice bell-curve of scores; which will enable Mr. Alden to blame the "loser" students on their inability and lack of effort, rather than acknowledge his own poor instruction. Mr. New's project, which is multi-dimensional and results in synthesis, does allow smart students to flourish but challenges each member of the class to explore and contribute. There is no evidence in research that such a system hurts the brighter kids, and much that suggests that it helps the lower achievers a great deal.

To close this section: Upper-level Bloom activities are more productive than lower level ones, and the Dual Objective Model of CL encourages such interactions.

Gardner's Multiple Intelligences

Back in 1983, Howard Gardner hoisted a banner that proclaimed that intelligence, the human capacity to understand and use ideas, was not a simple entity. By that time, people had reduced smartness into a number. Intelligence was whatever was measured by an IQ test, and one's score (100, 160, 94) was seen as a good indicator of ability and a predictor of one's future. This, of course, has turned out to be a clearly false idea.

Gardner had, in fact, discovered and posited a multiple intelligence entity. Indeed, he has identified eight such intelligences, distinguished them from personal preferences called learning styles, and worked for 30 years to get schools to think seriously about using, promoting, and assessing with these eight categories of smartness. We are confident that you have been exposed to them already and probably encouraged to adapt them for classroom use. Perhaps you know them so well that you saw them jump off the page as you examined the 100 Products a few pages back. Perhaps you thought about MI theory when Lee was "benched" in PE (it is hard to learn a skill like dribbling the basketball without deliberately practicing it). Finally, some of you have been "taking notes" as you read the book—these notes can be visual diagrams or drawings as well as verbal statements. Mind maps and graphic organizers are visual-spatial representations of knowledge. If you are annotating this book, you are using your *intelligences* of choice.

We accept Gardner's conjecture that intelligences are a bunch of things and that a person's profile is differentiated by strengths and weaknesses in each one. We think regularly with his typology and we plan with it in mind:

1. Verbal-Linguistic: the ability to use and interpret written and spoken words.
2. Logical-Mathematical: the ability to discern patterns, use logical structures, and/or a fluency with numbers.
3. Musical: the talent to produce and appreciate sounds and their patterns.
4. Body-Kinesthetic: the ability to utilize body movement or gestures to find or express meaning.
5. Visual-Spatial: the capacity to think in pictorial form and to visualize accurately.
6. Naturalist: the ability to recognize and categorize objects in nature.

(And the two affective ones):

7. Intra-personal: the abilities to recognize one's inner states and emotional states and to regulate meta-cognitive factors.
8. Inter-personal: the capacity to interpret others' actions and to work effectively with all types of people.

We suggest that, as you prepare to assign a task, you think a bit about how the demand of the task aligns with these eight intelligences. No one is or has ever been *great* in every one of them (although he may have had fine motor skills, there is no record that Leonardo da Vinci was a dancer or an athlete). So, varying the tasks over time, while keeping the teams intact, allows different strengths to come to the fore and creates opportunities for each student to work from strengths and from weaknesses, while allowing those who excel to help the collective.

Three Suggestions about Multiple Intelligence Applications

1. As we said, keep the teams together for a period of time so that you can have them complete several tasks with different MI expectations. If you talk to colleagues in other disciplines, you could even coordinate efforts and keep the teams intact. One day, the teams can create new illustrations for the chapter on photosynthesis (visual-spatial); in another class, the team may find themselves selecting music for an upcoming presentation; in another class, the team could be comparing their emotional reactions to various front pages of newspapers of September 12, 2001 (the identification is intrapersonal and the sharing is interpersonal).

2. Keep in mind that Gardner called intrapersonal and interpersonal *intelligences*; this means that they are much more than just "qualities" or "talents." The value he places on people who excel at these competencies is comparable to those who are "really good at math." Even though there are no standardized tests for these talents (yet), there are folks, like the College Board, who intend to create them (Kyllonen, 2012). While grit levels (persistence) better predict success at West Point than do science scores (Duckworth, 2016), and KIPP schools now teach non-cognitive skills (Tough, 2012), these practices are not in the mainstream curriculum in most schools. We think that they should be. When they do become valued outcomes of schooling, teachers who are familiar with the Dual Objective will already be implementing a system that is aligned with 21st-century goals.

3. Not every lesson can possibly tap into each of the eight intelligences, but being aware of them allows you to record your own patterns of expectations. One of the authors, being fond of artistic activities (visual-spatial), often heard one of her top-achieving students lament these activities, with the explanation that "I just don't like this stuff," but always completed the work, often with better quality than students with a stronger artistic ability. Students, especially high achievers, often don't like to take such risks (working from outside of their self-declared strengths), because they fear both the potential negative impact on their grades and "losing face" by being seen as struggling.

   This is a severely limiting situation, and requires wise and direct handling from the teacher. We must be prepared to discuss issues like community vs. individual, preference vs. ability, how to work from one's weaknesses, and facing the fact that when we don't get to choose in life, we must still achieve. Having high academic achievers work from weakness enables their overall development, which they may not even recognize in themselves or acknowledge as a need. High academic achievers need as much attention to developing empathy for others less able, contributing to community, and appreciating other's perspectives as any students.

Preparing all students for a globalized 21st-century environment should challenge them frequently and in varying ways where high effort on difficult tasks should be honored. Dweck's growth mindset (see Prologue) encourages us to get students out of their comfort zone, whether by challenging them with new types of tasks or by working with unfamiliar classmates.

Vermette's (2009) concept of "grading wisely" is at work here: Do not underestimate how big a factor grading is in getting teens to try to do different things. The 20 years of the so-called school reform movement has taught them to be strategic learners *not* curious, flexible, and open investigators of the world around them. Curiosity and creativity need to be reinforced by curriculum and demanded by teachers if formal education is to reach its potential, preparing youth for the unknown.

A Concern for Motivation: Glasser's Four Motivators

We embrace an appetite to understand adolescents and their motivations and to utilize our insights to plan effective instruction. Such giants as Steinberg (2014) and Siegel (2014) have helped us see the experiences, the lives, and the perspectives of teens in a new light, and books like Michie's *Holler if you hear me* (2009) provide case histories for us to examine. Moreover, many secondary teachers are outstanding in their abilities to understand and relate to teens. However, this is not a book about adolescent lives or even about motivation to learn, so we will provide a simplified approach to the motivational aspects of task construction and hope that it is sufficient to help you plan more effective CL experiences.

If our guru, Glasser is correct, teens want four things in life, four things that will motivate them toward their best effort. Students flourish in structures that provide the following:

1. **Fun**: Students are more motivated if they find what they are doing to be pleasant and enjoyable and if there is humor involved. We ask you: How will the individuals enjoy the collaborative experience? Will it be fun or tedious? Will it spark smiles or induce frowns and frustrations? Will the teamed work period be something that the student will share with friends and others or will it be forgotten immediately afterward?

2. **Freedom**: Students are more motivated if they can choose from alternatives and can make decisions that matter. We ask you: How much choice is involved in the students' work as they plan and complete a task? Is everything set in stone or can different groups produce different products while experiencing different processes?

3. **Sense of belonging**: Students are more motivated if they think that they are in a group that cares about them as individuals and if they carry a sense that they belong. We ask: How does the work in today's class build relationships between students and how does a student *feel* when entering the room? Is this *his* class, *her* team, *their* project or is this third-period class just an obligation to fulfill?

4. **Power**: Students are motivated if they feel they are competent in the work and if they play an important role in the classroom interaction. Power is the toughest motivator for teachers to deal with as they work with teenagers. Teens are at a time when they most seek power to control themselves and others and to feel needed. Many of us wrongly think that competition feeds motivation, when in truth, almost all competitions result in *dozens* of losers and few winners. A great deal of classroom competition usually results in a great deal of "giving up." Influence, however, is limitless and is a staple in group work.

Collaboration allows *power* to manifest itself in the two meanings that Glasser has for the concept: (1) the students feel *mastery* when they achieve something, learn something, or are a contributing part of a team that succeeds. (2) They also need to be an *influence*, to demonstrate to themselves (and peers) that they matter. When Allen scores touchdowns, he matters; when Lee works on her Global project, she matters; when your students do things in class that change the lesson or help classmates, they matter.

In traditional classrooms, only a handful of students usually matter. Most don't overtly participate, don't ask questions, or make enlightened insights. Moreover, sometimes mattering is a negative thing, like coming in late, or talking under their breath, or tapping a pencil that annoys. Class clowns matter, but they are usually disruptive in the whole-class setting. In any case, your attention to the situation means that the student matters.

We think it is much better to have individuals working directly with each other so that their efforts can matter to peers on a regular basis. The Dual Objective approach does just that and, when followed with fidelity, has built-in controls to help the interaction be a positive experience. Teenagers who experience fun, freedom, a sense of community, and power are likely to value their schooling experience and work diligently, deliberately, and democratically on their teamed tasks.

Team Self-Assessment (Group Processing)

Finally, as we close this chapter about what students do while they are engaged in team-based learning activities in the secondary classroom, we must mention an aspect of Cooperative Learning that is often ignored, yet is one that research suggests is a critically important factor, what Johnson and Johnson (1987, 2009) call "group processing." In short, a regular feature of effective Cooperative Learning is a discussion by the team itself about its effectiveness and its process.

In the Dual Objective, we stress the importance of the teacher knowing what is happening in the groups *and* providing powerful feedback to both affective (process) and cognitive (product) outcomes. (Again, see Chapter 5 for more on this point.) However, we do not mean to downplay the power of self-assessments done by the team at the conclusion of their learning efforts.

Here is an example: After spending 25 minutes working on their projects in their three-person teams, the students in Mr. Jackson's 10th-grade math class have been given the last 7 minutes of a 50-minute class to discuss the following prompts and to record their collective ideas in writing for his overnight formal review (assessment *for* teaching). The class has been working on applications of geometry to the real world (cognitive outcome) and two Habits of Mind, "striving for accuracy" and "questioning and problem posing" (affective outcomes). These are some of the possible prompts they must complete before class ends today:

1. We worked toward accuracy today by . . .
2. Evidence that everyone has contributed is found in . . .
3. A question we struggled with today was . . .
4. One example of how we tried to solve a problem was . . .
5. The geometrical concept that is most difficult for us to use is . . . because . . .
6. An example of how we built off of each other's ideas was when . . .
7. We still want to know about . . .

Mr. Jackson sometimes uses the same group-processing sheet on consecutive days, allowing him to make comparisons across multiple days. He always reads these overnight and returns them the next class. Often, it is the best information he can get about his students' growth, and if it is used, students feel empowered and important. Moreover, it is a flexible tool; he can make adjustments to the number of items based on what he has seen *during* the class work, and it may redirect his teaching efforts through informed interventions. We often have an outslip that is too long intentionally, so that we can cut it in this manner and leave the option of giving some *choice* to the team. So, hypothetically, today Mr. Jackson could say "OK, your team must complete #1, #4, #6 . . . and any one other, that gives you four, so get going please."

For projects spanning days or when more in-depth feedback is warranted, one may choose a summative assessment employing student reflection (self and outward). A suggestion here would be to collectively have the groups create a class rubric for successful interactions, and use it at the end of each learning experience to gather insights. Students could consider criteria they collectively deem important to being a good group, evaluate themselves (Likert scale), and their teammates, reporting results to the teacher. (There are many polling and survey apps out there which can assist.) The teacher could then facilitate discussion about the results for the benefit of both individual growth and team awareness, with potential to use such as evidence of progress when it comes to formal grade reporting.

As students become more skilled at the process of reflection, metacognition improves, and they can become independent in their feedback discussions, deepening their self-awareness. One might think this process of evaluating self may result in inflated "scores," and that there may be unfair assessments of others, but it actually happens very infrequently. One of the authors (Kline) has done this successfully for years, with extremely positive feedback from students, parents, and administrators alike. Students like the process, as the criteria give them direction, the evaluation voice, and the feedback, constructive guidance. They are fairly heard and valued, which, when done well, is highly motivating!

Kline introduces her formal Cooperative Learning unit at the beginning of 7th-grade for her students. Although she exposes 6th-graders to group work by occasionally working in cooperative groups, in grades 7 and 8 it is the norm. The Team Evaluation Rubric is designed as suggested in the paragraphs above by and with her students and serves as their measurement tool throughout their 7th- and 8th-grade years when working on projects in excess of two days. All of her students are familiar with the seven criteria, and can explain their interpretation fully. Upon completion of a given group project, the forms are completed by each student for self and all other group members and turned in for tabulation and analysis (Kline suggests digital resources be used for this process whenever possible). Once data are analyzed, Kline meets with each team for a group processing debrief session where feedback from all team members is shared. Comments written on the rubrics are offered in aggregate for each student, but anonymously, so no single team member feels unable to respond in truth. Many teams freely discuss their written comments, so each member has the opportunity to improve where needed to maximize their learning experiences. The tabulations are recorded for each student and included as part of a work habits "grade" during grade reporting, alongside

Figure 3.2 Team Evaluation Rubric

| **Team Evaluation Rubric** |
| Name _____ Date of evaluation_____ |
| Dates of work on the project _____ Class period_____ |
| Description of the project_____ |
| Name of the group_____ |
| Absences (who/when?) _____ |

Scale 2 = rarely/seldom 3 = sometimes 4 = usually					
Names of students in the group	*Myself*	*Student 1*	*Student 2*	*Student 3*	
Desirable behaviors					
1. Listened actively and openly to others.					
2. Worked collaboratively with others by sharing ideas and workload.					
3. Was prepared and stayed on task using time wisely.					
4. Encouraged others to offer ideas, give feedback and participate.					
5. Addressed differences of opinion in a constructive and productive way, keeping negative emotions and impulses under control.					
6. Helped others have fun, and / or enjoy the teamwork.					
7. Treated others respectfully.					
Totals					

Information gained from completing this form will be shared for the improvement of those involved. We learn best from candid, caring feedback based on thoughtful reflection.
Explain here why you gave any 2s above. **Provide specific examples**. Use back of sheet for further explanation, if needed.

_____
_____

Using the scale below, answer the following questions:
1 = not at all 2 = not very happy 3 = OK, but could have been better 4 = pleased 5 = thrilled

How pleased are you with the quality of the product produced by your team?	1	2	3	4	5
How pleased overall were you with this experience working with your team?	1	2	3	4	5
How pleased were you with your own contribution to the project?	1	2	3	4	5

Describe one thing that you learned by doing this activity:

_____
_____

Describe one thing you would do differently **yourself** to improve upon this experience.

_____
_____

Modified from "Making Cooperative Learning Work: Student Teams in K-12 Classrooms," Vermette (1998). Adapted by C. Kline (personal communication, 2012).

academic achievement. Kline is diligent in stressing the development of the whole child as a goal in her classroom. (See Figure 3.2 for the Team Evaluation Rubric.)

In sum, this group-processing aspect of the Dual Objective Model puts assessment on the team and can easily provoke it into more positive development of affective skill sets. Studies of effective teams in the business world frequently include team self-analysis, so not only will it improve teaching, but it will realistically help prepare students for the demands of the 21st-century workplace.

In Closing: A Checklist for Good Activities

We think that we have a made a strong case that students talking to each other on well-structured tasks can vastly increase the quantity *and* quality of student understanding and improve students' ability to work effectively across diverse groupings. We also think that we have offered you a host of very practical suggestions for designing or adapting possible tasks and activities, and tied those practical suggestions to theory and research. In addition, we have given you an opportunity to examine your own understanding of student perceptions of various teamed activities.

We would like to close by commenting on a handful of things we'd like you to consider as you ready yourself for tomorrow's group work activity. You can see these as a checklist of sorts and use it to help plan your own learning activities.

_____ 1. **Is there a plan for individual accountability and teamwork (do they need each other?)**

If a student can do an activity alone, the sense of needing others (positive interdependence) is diminished and so is the motivation to attend to each other. Teachers should make sure that everyone in the team is mastering the content, contributing to the product, and is being recognized for his or her role.

In the Dual Objective, activities using any of the four categories of student talk also require the learning and deeper application of interaction skills, which by their nature *requires* student–student contact. Whatever cognitive objective is assigned to the team, the teacher must also explicitly identify the affective skill being utilized (i.e. "Today we are solving quadratic equations *and* learning to be persistent!" or "Today, we are creating a family budget *and* developing the ability to ask questions respectfully").

_____ **2. Does the task require each team member to maximize success?**
As you invent the task, imagine the contributions that each student could make in the team work. If necessary, add a stipulation that taps into their skills or interests (i.e. "Make sure that your story board involves animals from the local geographical area" or "Remember that your video has to have a musical lead-in that captures the feeling"). This gets easier as you know your students and as you become comfortable with designing good tasks.

_____ **3. Do students know which affective competencies you will be expecting them to deploy? Do they know how they are supposed to interact with each other?**
While this is largely a topic for Chapter 5, here we wish to urge you to make clear what the *process* objectives are for the group work. Are students working on self-awareness, respectfulness, listening with empathy, clear communication, or their ability to be flexible? Whichever non-cognitive competencies are chosen, they should be made as explicit as the cognitive objectives. In effect, working in groups is practice in using non-cognitive collaborative skills on a daily basis.

_____ **4. Do students have a way of recognizing individual contributions?**
This is not complex: How does the teacher help every student become aware of the effort (or lack thereof) by every member of the team? We urge you to make this a standard requirement in every interaction and actually collect data on student perceptions of each other during the work.

_____ **5. Is there sufficient challenge in the activity to entice deep thinking: elaboration, examination, and/or exploration?**
Throughout this chapter, we have stressed the advantage given to learning activities that demand higher order thinking skills, yet we have known many teachers who only use "group work" to have students do simplistic sharing or vaguely worded tasks generally verbalized as "study together . . ." A quick review of the many examples from the chapter shows that when students are challenged, they tend to shift from *receivers* to *creators*, which is consistent with our adaptation of the model of how the mind works.

Rigor is a widely used term these days. Generally, it is thought of as an amount. To some, a rigorous course has a great deal of reading, long and detailed tests, and many writing assignments. However, we see rigor as challenge; it is more the quality of the work than the quantity. Are the students doing something original and worthwhile? Are they being asked to do something that integrates knowledge and concepts from the field? Are students asked to work effectively with diverse people who have different ideas, backgrounds, interests, and expectations? Are they asked to be accurate and use evidence about every part of their experience?

We hope that you create and implement rigorous and challenging tasks that diverse teen teams can engage in and emerge from successfully, and we hope you do this on a regular basis in all classes.

Chapter 3 Big Ideas

1. The design of the teamed-learning activity is a critically important part of the Dual Objective: the activity should be one that gets each student to contribute, one that is visible to the teacher's analysis, and which results in deeper understanding every member.
2. The model of how the mind works that we showed in the prologue calls for extended interaction between an individual's short-term and long-term memory: When students talk to each other as they collaboratively solve a problem or create a product, they deepen their understanding of content and practice their interpersonal skills.
3. The quantity and quality of (on-task) student talk relates to the amount of their individual learning.
4. A key teacher skill is to listen carefully to team talk and to assess the timing and content of their feedback/interventions.
5. There are four useful categories of student-student dialogue: (a) exploration, (b) problem-solving, (c) product construction, and (d) validation and feedback. Recognizing these categories while "working the room" will help a teacher decide on an intervention.
6. Student–student dialogue offers students the chance to improve their affective skills.
7. There are hundreds of possible products that students can create while collaborating in the classroom. Teachers do not have to be creative and invent their own activities and projects; they can borrow, modify, and adapt from existing options.
8. All classes are not equally engaging and students are rarely in "flow" during class. However, thoughtful lesson planning can improve this condition.
9. Design and modification of teamed learning activities can be assisted by several considerations: (a) integrating various Bloom levels, (b) utilizing Multiple Intelligences theory, and (c) intentionally applying Glasser's Four Motivators.

10. A possible checklist for assessing a team learning activity could involve the following factors: (a) Is there a place for individual accountability? (b) Is it likely that each member can contribute? (c) What are the explicitly stated affective skills to be used? (d) How are students going to assesses themselves and each other? (e) Does the learning activity present a real challenge that is going to demand deep thinking and spark student conversation?

References

Bruner, J., Goodenow, S., & Austin, G. (1986). *A study of thinking* (2nd ed.). London: Transaction Publishers.

Carey, B. (2014). *How we learn: The surprising truth about when, where and why it happens.* New York, NY: Random House.

Csikszentmihalyi, M., & Larson, R. (1984). *Being adolescent: Conflict and growth in the teenage years.* New York, NY: Basic Books.

Cuban, L. (1993). *How teachers taught: Constancy and change in American classrooms 1890–1990* (2nd ed.). New York, NY: Teachers College Press.

Cuban, L. (2002). *Oversold and underused: Computers in the classroom.* Cambridge, MA: Harvard University Press.

Dewey, J. (1938). *Experience and education.* New York, NY: Macmillan.

Duckworth, A.L. (2016). *GRIT: The power of passion and perseverance.* New York, NY: Scribner.

Dweck, C. (2006). *Mindset.* New York, NY: Random House.

Farrington, C.A., Roderick, E., Nagaoka, J., Keyes, T.S., Johnson, D.W., & Beechum, N. (2012). Teaching adolescents to become learners: The role of non-cognitive factors in shaping school performance. Chicago, IL: Consortium on Chicago School Research.

Flynn, P., Mesibov, D., Vermette, P., & Smith, R.M. (2004). *Applying standards-based constructivism: A two-step guide for motivating middle and high school students.* Larchmont, NY: Eye-on-Education.

Gardner, H. (1983). *Frames of mind: The theory of multiple intelligences.* Cambridge, MA: Harvard University Press.

Glasser, W. (1999). *Control theory in the classroom.* New York, NY: Harper & Row.

Goodlad, J.I. (1984). *A place called school: Prospects for the future.* New York, NY: McGraw-Hill.

Hattie, J. (2009). *Visible learning: A synthesis of over 800 meta-analyses relating to achievement.* London: Routledge.

Johnson, D.W., & Johnson, R.W. (1987). *Learning together and alone.* Englewood Cliffs, NJ: Prentice-Hall.

Johnson, D.W, & Johnson, R.W. (2009). An educational psychology success story: Social interdependence theory and cooperative learning. *Educational Researcher*, *38*(5), 365–379.

Kagan, S. (1992). *Cooperative learning: Resources for teachers*. Riverside, CA: University of California.

Kyllonen, P.C. (2012). *Measurement of 21st century skills within the Common Core State Standards*. Paper presented at the Invitational Research Symposium on Technology Enhanced Assessments, May 7–8.

Lounsbury, J.H., & Clark, D.C. (1990). *Inside grade eight: From apathy to excitement*. Reston: VA: National Association of Secondary School Principals.

Lyman, F.T. (1981). The responsive classroom discussion: The inclusion of all students. In A. Anderson (Ed.), *Mainstreaming Digest* (pp. 109–113). College Park, MD: University of Maryland Press.

Michie, G. (2009). *Holler if you hear me: The education of a teacher and his students*. New York, NY: Teachers College Press.

Myers, J., Bardsley, M., Vermette, P., & Kline, C. (2017). *Cooperative learning for the 21st century* (forthcoming).

Pink, D. (2006). *Drive: The surprising truth about what motivates us*. New York, NY: Riverhead Books.

Ritchhart, R., & Perkins, D. (2008). Making thinking visible. *Educational Leadership*, *65*(5), 57–61.

Siegel, D.J. (2014). *Brainstorm: The power and purpose of the teenage brain*. New York, NY: Tarcher Penguin.

Steinberg, L. (2014). *The age of opportunity: Lessons from the new science of adolescence*. New York, NY: Houghton-Mifflin.

Tough, P. (2012). *How children succeed: Grit, curiosity and the hidden power of character*. Boston, MA: Houghton-Mifflin.

Vermette, P. (1998). *Making cooperative learning work: Student teams in K-12 classrooms*. Upper Saddle River, NJ: Merrill/Prentice-Hall.

Vermette, P.J. (2009). *Engaging teens in their own learning: Eight keys to student success*. Larchmont, NY: Eye-on-Education.

Walls, B. (1983). *The road that led to somewhere*. Essex, Canada: Olive Publishing.

Webb, N., Franke, M., De, T., & Melkonian, D.K. (2009). Explain to your partner: Teachers' instructional practices and students' dialogue in small groups. *Cambridge Journal of Education*, *39*(1), 49–70.

4

How Does the Teacher Build Effective Teams?

Introduction

As a teacher begins to plan his or her implementation of the Dual Objective, there are a number of questions that should be answered thoughtfully and carefully. Maintaining fidelity to the fundamentals of the Dual Objective Model is essential to success and the construction and development of the student groups is one key factor. Other writings have explored this topic (Bennett & Cass, 1988; Gillies, 2006; Vermette, 1998), but most practitioners simply ignore its importance. Unfortunately, we know of attempts at using CL that have failed because the group composition process was neither thoughtful nor intentional. We use this chapter to provoke opportunities to reconsider the entire process and its implications and offer advice based on research, personal experience, and collaboration with many colleagues over the past decade.

We start this chapter with a simple request for the reader:

TASK: Building Teams

Please compare and contrast the three different approaches to creating teams taken in each of these 9th-grade Spanish I classrooms:

Señorita Hernandez: Typically, the students in this class work individually on tasks and on tests, and class activities are mostly individualized. However, occasionally, Señorita Hernandez will use a modified think–pair–share, and give the students a minute or two to compare their answers with others around them. She almost always allows them their choice of partners.

Señorita Blanco: Typically, at least one-third of each class is spent in teams that the teacher has created. In those teams, the students solve problems, create scripts, answer questions, create captions for visuals, and/or rehearse new vocabulary. She gives *each* student a daily grade composed of three factors: (1) effort, (2) contributions to each other, and (3) production.

Señorita Gomez: A couple of times a week, the students get in groups arranged by their achievement in the course—highs with highs and lows with lows—as determined by class rank. When they work in class together, it is mostly to edit others' work and/or review homework.

We hope that you found differences among these three teachers, all of whom claim to be using Cooperative Learning. We see differences in (a) the type of work being completed by teams, (b) the frequency of teamwork, and (c) the means of assembling the groups. Without belaboring the issue, we start out by making our suggestions and recommendations on this third point:

1. The teacher should build the teams, and point out why they will be successful (sharing criteria).
2. The students should spend enough time together in a team that they get to know and appreciate differences as they do work that requires a variety of skills, background experience, and knowledge.
3. The teams should be assessed frequently (as done by Srta. Blanco) and feedback should be given to individuals as well as to teams; students should not be solely "group graded" on projects, especially on ones that involve work outside of class!
4. The teams should gather as an entity nearly every day that class meets, so it is seen as a regular part of how the world operates.

From what we have just postulated, it is clear that we favor the approach taken by Srta. Blanco. She uses her teacher-created teams every day and for different purposes (and on different tasks). She monitors students' thinking and interactions closely and gives feedback on *both* cognitive and affective actions that she observes. Her vision of the future life of her students includes the following expectations:

◆ Students will be working in collaborative settings the rest of their lives.
◆ Students will be interacting *across* gender, social class, race, religion, culture, and ethnicity the rest of their lives.

- Students need to experience and embrace the practice of respecting others in a pluralist setting.
- Students working together generally produce better outcomes than each working alone.
- Students will need to transfer their collaboration skills in increasingly complex, ill-structured, and interdependent problematic situations *after* high school.

By the way, the students have heard these things frequently from Srta. Blanco: She tells them *why* she builds the group as she does, why they are expected to learn together and help each other, and what she is looking for as she "works the room" during team time. These are all very wise ideas.

The Basics of Team Composition

In the following section, we will elaborate on several factors that may help you create effective teams in your own situation.

Question #1: Who Works with Whom?

TASK: Student Roster

Here are brief descriptions of the 12 students in Mr. Piazza's 11th-grade chemistry class in a large, suburban high school in the Mid-West. Please take a few moments and answer this question: "How would you divide them into three four-person groups for a three-week unit?"

- **Josh** is a good-looking, sophisticated student-athlete. He is on the honor roll, is captain of swimming and tennis teams, and is Junior Class President. His hobbies include music and acting in local community theater. His family has moved around a lot, but they promised that he would graduate from this school. He has told people that he wants to become a scientist.
- **Aramis** is a good-natured, fun-loving young man. He is not a very good student and doesn't seem to care about academic achievement, but does seem to care about the girls and about his skills as a drummer. He is a bit of a rebel but comes from a very religious family and his sister is Senior Class President and Honor Society Secretary. He was removed from the school baseball team because of a prank.
- **Anwar** is slight of build and exceedingly quiet. His grades are good but teachers don't think he tries very hard. He enjoys gory teen movies and is a walking Wikipedia of film knowledge of all kinds. He is not very athletic but often dresses in "sports garb." His motorcycle makes him popular and unusual.

◆ **Jacinta** is an outgoing, highly energetic, dog-loving young lady. She and her friends spend lots of time at the local animal shelter, walking and attending to the dogs. She has very uneven grades: her academic achievement is highly unpredictable as is her attendance at school. Since September, she has been very concerned about her ailing mother, who can no longer work outside the home. Her father, a day laborer, is urging her to get an afternoon job to help bring money into the house.

◆ For her 16th birthday, **Ramona** got six piercings and a tattoo and now she is known all over school. Only reluctantly does she put away her expensive phone and is never without it after school hours. She used to play school sports, but not this year. Her grades are OK but she truly hates chemistry and this is reflected in her homework and attendance for class. She loves art class and is taking two courses this year.

◆ A close friend of Josh is **Lucia**, an Italian-born immigrant girl who came to the district this year. She is quiet, but is mastering English. She loves TV and mimics the accents and intonations of actors—which has made her popular. Since her grades stabilized, she has shown an interest in going to college for linguistics. She is taking English, Spanish 3 and Arabic 2 this year.

◆ **Yoon** is a recent immigrant from Korea, coming to the U.S. (and the district) two years ago. She has many friends, perhaps because she is friendly and outgoing and is always supplying students with Korean treats! She is well-known for her holiday excesses, and especially loves Halloween: She dressed up as Catwoman last year, and school had to send her home to "cover up" (after *way* too many photos were taken). She works on the school paper and is raising money to help ELL learners in the district.

◆ **Darby** is a super student (#1 in his class rank) and is very serious about receiving scholarship money for college. He organized a Black History Celebration last February and received state-wide attention for his efforts. He frequently challenges racial stereotypes and is sensitive to national issues involving discriminations of all kinds. (This includes weight and he is, himself, around 300 pounds.)

◆ **Christine** re-named herself Caitlyn after Bruce Jenner's gender change went public in summer 2015. She is a self-acclaimed champion of the oppressed and wishes to go to college to become an activist for social change. While some students say she goes "overboard" on some issues, teachers genuinely like her energy, determination, and quick mind. Her grades are very good in all subjects and she spends time tutoring middle school kids in the afterschool program. Many parents urge their children to stay away from her, but other students seem friendly and open to her. She is a strong and vocal Catholic in a heavily Protestant town.

◆ **Sabrina** is the daughter of the local (male and female) Muslim leadership and represents the religion and culture very openly and clearly. Her grades across all courses do not reflect her commitment to learning, but do show that she cares enough to handle academic challenges responsibly. She loves all kinds of contemporary music and plays several instruments well. She boasts that she will get 100 percent on the chemistry final exam.

◆ **Martina** wants to be a veterinarian but has poor grades in the sciences and math. She transferred to the district as a 9th-grader from a Southern state when her parents divorced and she has had a difficult time making friends. She still communicates often with old friends from back home. She has a short and almost nasty way of disagreeing that fellow students both dislike and mock behind her back. She is starting to miss school on a regular basis and no longer does any homework. She has a very strong relationship with Mr. Becker (the social studies teacher) who has brought her into his after-school United Nations club.

◆ When he gets off of his skateboard, **Max** is charming, funny, and "full of life." He is very smart and says things that make people laugh all the time. He is never harmful with his humor; he uses it to bond with others and has been that way since his mother passed away while he was in 7th grade. School is a necessary business to him and his achievement is in the middle of the group. The one thing that quiets him and makes him serious is the Holocaust—a topic that is studied across all disciplines at this school. His Jewish heritage is meaningful to him and he is an advocate for "all things Jewish."

Guidelines for Building Teams

While the science of composing groups can be seen as rather "soft," the size of the group (n = 4) and the recognition of balancing traits and experiences is widely supported by many advocates of CL (including Vermette, 1998; Myers, Bardsley, Vermette, & Kline, 2017). Basically, we urge several considerations:

1. Seek to balance gender (Webb & Farivar, 1994), social class, past achievement, interests and activities, and past experience. Early work by Vermette (1998) discovered that when building groups, teachers relied most heavily on what they thought of as "student personality" and sought to put students together with personalities that aligned (and, more importantly, would not conflict).

2. Envision the group actually working together and visualize it being a positive experience, but also be ready to troubleshoot anticipated difficulties: We call this approach the "theory of the team," and it helps us prepare to deal with events during group work. Another aspect of the theory of the team is anticipating individuals playing various roles within the group as it succeeds. (Assigning specific roles is an actual component of the Johnson and Johnson model.)

   Keep the following questions in mind while you seek "balance" in your teams: (a) Who will keep conversation going when the flow of ideas slows down? (b) Who will make sure that everyone contributes ideas and supports others? (c) Who will keep things positive in tone?

(d) Who will be there every day to keep the group intact? (e) Who will present a calming tone or a humorous moment when it is needed? Forming tentative answers based on the expectations of behavior built around the vision you have of a successful team interaction can be helpful in placing teens in productive teams. (Note: coaches in team sports often envision their players at various positions or in various roles built on individual strengths and the needs of the team. We urge this similar process in the classroom.)

3. Do not *publicly* explain attempts to ameliorate a serious defect of an individual student member. Do not speak publicly of an individual's weaknesses or of the problems she or he will pose for the team. (By the way, this happens much too often; such teacher comments are often seen as a form of sarcasm that almost always backfires. Sometimes this is unintentional, as in making comments about attendance, but nonetheless unwelcome and inappropriate.)

4. Do not *publicly* refer to a particular student as the "token in the group." Research by Miller and Harrington (1992) suggests that this damages self-esteem and limits his or her willingness to contribute. Whenever possible, have individual students recognize their own and others' strengths and their ability to achieve.

5. Realize that self-made groups will most often end up as friend groups that will be exclusionary in nature (Mitchell, Reilly, Bramwell, Lilly, & Solonsky, 2004). Moreover, random teams will not result in the desirable (criteria-based) matches that teacher-made teams would promote.

6. Trust yourself and your observation skills and keep studying, observing, assessing, and understanding the students. Know your students as well as possible and proceed with your insights about them clearly in mind. As the year wears on, your knowledge of students should deepen greatly and improve your decisions.

7. If a team appears to be dysfunctional and intervention has been attempted unsuccessfully, do not hesitate to switch groupings. Teams who understand and follow consensus protocols often learn to mediate disagreements and challenges productively, but if this does not occur you will need to remedy the situation.

8. Include student attendance in considerations as you determine group size. For classes that will have some groups larger than others (three vs. four), take care to place students with chronic absenteeism in one of the larger groups. If all groups are equal, place these students where their absence will be less likely felt—this is often with other students who can handle more responsibility. (The work requirements may need to be modified in these situations.)

Our Theory of the Team

Based on what we know about the youth in this class, we think that a good way to group them for the first time and one that reflects the criteria we have mentioned above is as follows:

Team #1: Josh, Lucia, Darby, and Martina
Team #2: Aramis, Yoon, Max, and Ramona
Team #3: Caitlyn, Jacinta, Anwar, and Sabrina

We would like to add four specific comments about our construction of the three teams listed above. This is our "theory of the team":

1. We put Josh and Lucia together in Team #1. They are already friends but not in a way that will exclude the others; we expect that the existing relationship will likely "invite others *in*," not isolate them.
2. Following the advice drawn from Webb and Farivar (1994), we were careful to balance gender as a demographic variable: Only Team #3 has a majority female group, and that was forced by the gender distribution (numbers) in this class.
3. Social class is a major factor in U.S. society. In this suburban school, there are "social rankings," but parental wealth and parental career patterns are not obvious (or the teacher doesn't know them yet). If these assigned groups do work well together, it will be a good thing for bridging the economic divides that may exist. If they don't succeed, social class differences may lie at the core of the problem and the teacher should recognize that factor. As time wears on, the teacher can learn about specific family situations and about family interaction patterns; these may become important factors when new teams are created.
4. School achievement (grades and marks) are important but that is mostly because of the *effort* a student gives, not because of raw ability (as in IQ score). Cooperative Learning should improve motivation and engagement; therefore, it should improve marks for Martina and Jacinta. Dweck's growth mindset (2006) comes into play here as well. Students who haven't done well before can get a fresh start, reject the idea that they are "just bad" or "dumb in this subject," and think about new opportunities and how they can work harder/differently and achieve more in the new environment. Parents think it helps their youngsters socially to be "on a sports team"; they will come to believe that it also good for their children academically to be "in a chem team" at school.

Question #2: What Should the Teacher Tell (and Not Tell) Students About the Groups?

In the case of Mr. Piazza, he could tell the students several of these things:

◆ When you work together to reach a group goal you'll each get better individual achievement results.

◆ When you get to know how different personalities approach work, you'll begin to more clearly articulate who you are and what is important to you. This is helpful as you investigate college and professional life after school.

◆ We are all members of the same community: This collaborative process will help unify us! (Out of many, one! In fact, "e pluribus unum" is a nationally accepted slogan in the U.S.)

◆ Each of you has different strengths and a contribution to make: That diversity is what assures that each of your groups can be successful in the work we will be doing.

◆ This is great practice for those who are more capable to learn to offer assistance, and for those who are not as strong, to learn how to advocate for yourselves (to ask for help).

◆ This isn't forever, it's for now, and it gives you a chance to work as people do outside school, where you don't get to choose your teammates. I want you to be successful there, so I am giving you practice here in a low-risk environment.

Each of these pronouncements sets a positive expectation and a positive tone to the group work. Each of these statements expresses confidence in the team, and its members, and is founded on sound social science scholarship. (This statement about scholarship presents a factor that many students, parents, and teachers may have never considered. While many of us teach the way we do because it reflects the way we were taught, many of us teach the way the science suggests will work. We expect doctors to know their research: We educators have ours, too, and we should attend to it.)

On the other hand, inspired by Miller and Harrington (1992), we would remind Mr. Piazza to *never* say any of these things:

◆ We need a girl in this group.

◆ I thought she would be disruptive, so I put her in that group because they are stronger.

◆ That group needed an Asian voice.

◆ Somebody in that group has to keep an eye on "that one" so he doesn't get too "bossy."

- ◆ I had to put him someplace.
- ◆ He seldom comes to school, so I put him in the bigger group.

Or, the worst one of all:

- ◆ We need to spread the "slackers" around.

The above comments all single out a student as a weak member, *or* as a token in the group, *or* as an undesirable member of the class community. Each statement denies and devalues individuality and uniqueness. Obviously, each of these perceptions is negative; both to the individual involved and to the group as a whole. Schooling is for every student and teachers are far better served when working from an honest but positive approach.

Question #3: What Are Some Other Important Factors that Should Be Considered When Building the Teams?

Previous Experience in Teams and Groups

A quick check of the research literature revealed no studies that used a variable called "previous experience with CL." This is a shame and should be rectified in the coming years, but in the meantime we speculate: Students who have had positive experiences working on/in teams and groups bring different expectations, experiences, and skills to the cooperative classroom than do students who have had no experience or negative experience when participating on/in teams and groups. This latter condition can bring heavy emotional baggage to your attempts to use CL: **Past experience matters.**

When initiating CL for the first time with students, some investigative work is required. Especially important in earlier grades is the need to draw the connection between working together for academic purpose, and other instances where students have worked as part of a group to complete a task or goal. For instance, one of the authors introduces CL in 7th grade to her students by starting with a brainstorming activity where they identify various occasions in their lives where they have worked with other people to achieve something. Drawing on participation in sports teams, musical groups, scouts, faith-affiliated groups, family events, service groups, *and* drawing on previous CL experience in classes, etc., students generate answers to the question, "What are some of the potential problems that can happen while working with others that could cause a group not to complete the task, or to end up with a bad experience?"

The brainstormed list is analyzed and consolidated by the class into a revised version identifying things *not* to do in a group. Students continue their work to convert each item from a negative into a positive to modify the list into actions that *should* occur to assure a successful group experience. Finally, the class clusters these actions into similar themes, and writes criteria for success based on each of the themes that surfaced. These criteria then govern group interactions, and become the basis for a process evaluation rubric that all teams will use to assess their work together. (Oddly enough, year after year the same basic issues arose, resulting in very similar goals and, ultimately, evaluation criteria. In addition, these ran closely parallel to a number of annual performance review criteria for a well-known Fortune 500 company. Who'd have thought that 7th-graders were so worldly?)

This activity manages negative experience from the start, getting it out in the open, and moves productively from negative to positive, approaching successful group process as a shared goal in which every student is therefore vested. When this activity is introduced at the beginning of the year, the rubric provides valuable data for subsequent CL experiences and for creating effective groupings.

Once the school year is into its second month, the students' prior experience with CL will include those experiences offered in your own class. For example, Mr. Piazza has limited information on each student who is described in the original list of 12, but if this is October 1st or later, he also has his own observations (and data) from their initial group work attempts on which to base his next set of groupings.

The earlier well-structured CL is used in the school year, the better these perceptions will be; the integration of solid theory, clear expectations and experience is necessary for the teacher to develop mastery of the technique. The best teachers explore this "new way of doing business" in tandem with their students, fully open to change, unafraid, hopeful for the gains it promises, and fully committed to success (for the sake of their students). Please note that many teachers who reject CL because "they hated group work in college" (and they are legion) are almost always referring to badly designed group projects done by badly designed groups outside of class: We suggest that before one condemns a procedure, one should try to do it correctly, as called for in the Dual Objective Model.

As we close this section, we thought we would mention a motivational theory developed for practitioners and shared admirably in Ambrose, Bridges, DiPietro, Lovett, and Norman (2010). Three factors make up how motivated a student will be during a specific learning segment: (E) *expectations of success* matter greatly as do (V) how much *value* a student places on success and (NE) the level of support (*nurturing environment*) the student feels in the classroom community: therefore, **E x V x NE = motivation**.

We suggest that prior successes (with CL) raise expectations (E), that enjoyable peer interaction across diverse types will increase the importance and value of success (V), and that a solid team structure will be seen as supportive to each individual (NE). In short, we see the construction of the team as a vital ingredient to each of the three motivating factors discussed by Ambrose.

Our experience suggests that, for most students, over time, the Dual Objective will create higher expectations of, and more avenues to, success; raise the importance and desirability of cognitive and/or affective achievement; and transform individual experiences into a "community-supported" effort. This should then increase motivation and engagement and positively affect educational outcomes. (Indeed, this seems to be what actually happens as CL becomes the norm in schooling practice.)

Students Who Transfer

One of our favorite school districts in the U.S. is Indian River, in northern New York, which is near a large military base and has a tremendous student turnover ever year. (As soldiers are deployed, their children's lives change, too.) Thus, the school culture is transformed on a regular basis and much student turnover is seen as the norm. School personnel have done a great job helping these students transition, and in planning for turnover. However, in most other places, students coming and going is a large disruption and has serious effects on classrooms built around cooperative structures. We have several pieces of advice for teachers facing this latter situation:

1. While groups are usually of very equal sizes within a single classroom, the addition of a new student should *not* be done to equalize size of groups; the new student should be placed with a group whose members are amenable to accepting and assisting his or her adjustment to the situation. This turns a potential adjustment problem into a positive opportunity to apply social skills, to leverage diversity, and to enrich the social environment of the class.

    Generally, teachers are faced with two temptations when new students are brought to their classroom doors. One is to have the student take an empty seat and try to figure out what is happening on his or her own. Private conferences may follow and sometimes a particular student is asked to be the new student's "buddy." The second approach is to single the new student out publicly: This involves putting him or her on the spot by saying something like, "Introduce yourself, please; tell us all about where you are coming from and why you are here with us now." While this may help ease transition, for many teenagers it is an awful experience, fraught with anxieties about not fitting in, revealing too much self without knowing others, and/or stumbling through the public sharing of self. (This experience is the setting for one great scene in the Hollywood movie, *Inside Out*, in which the main character freezes when asked to introduce herself to the class; that scene is worth watching again and again.) However, as all of us know, self-disclosure of this kind is much easier, even welcomed, in a setting that is much smaller, attentive to personalities, interactive in nature, and friendly. This latter description is much more likely to be found in a CL-structured classroom than in a traditional one. To reiterate, introductions should be done at the team level, not whole-class level.

2. As a regular practice, the Dual Objective setting obviously calls for assessment of interpersonal skills. As the new student discovers this routine and begins to participate, he or she will find that there are many measures of success in this class. This understanding creates more opportunities and higher expectations as well as a ready avenue to fit in. It is the rare student who doesn't wish to connect in a new setting and the vast majority of the time, successful integration into the entire class takes place this way: (a) first, fit into a four-person base group; (b) second, become part of the large group *along* with, and assisted by teammates.

To return to our example of Mr. Piazza for a moment, we suggest that he make comments about the potential for new students joining the class and the need for welcoming them in at the beginning of the year, and suggest that everyone's affective skills will come in to play when that does happen. We see school as real life, *not* simply as preparation for real life: Affective competencies operate "24–7, 365" and the classroom is a laboratory for practicing and examining applications.

We'd like to mention briefly that students who transfer out of Mr. Piazza's class might find leaving the comfort of a supportive environment with strong positive relationships a bit disturbing. This does not mean we favor cold, hard, emotion-free, and distant structures that are easy to leave; it suggests that some time should be used to say farewell to teammates (and classmates), which may soften the transition the individual is facing.

On a different note, the metaphor of school as prison is held by many teenagers: We are currently celebrating an 80 percent U.S. high-school graduation rate (an all-time high). Still, that means that 20 percent of students do not finish school, suggesting that the school experience is not meaningful, nor are the relationships there enough to keep a dangling teenager in attendance. Dropping out should be a difficult thing and while the research cannot say that extensive use of CL increases high school graduation rates, there is little reason to think that it will not do so. In fact, college-level research (Astin, 1993) does suggest that strong relationships do indeed keep college students in school.

English Language Learners

There is a tremendous amount of energy and attention being focused in modern North American schools on effectively assisting students whose first language is not English and who will have difficulty navigating the academic demands of high school. For secondary students, this frequently means that the ELL student is also an immigrant to the nation/community and, there-fore, also new to the cultural practices of the dominant group. In many ways, television is the "great socializer" as these teens try to create their identities, stay connected to past experiences, develop their educational abilities (cogni-tive and affective), and balance all this new information. (Spending hours watching TV may increase some English language, but it may have a down-side in terms of learning how to work with others, think critically, and com-municate well.)

Given that short sociological statement, we see that the adolescent ELL student most likely needs several things in his or her secondary experience:

- ◆ a chance to formally study and informally use English in the context of the native language;
- ◆ an opportunity to investigate subject matter content in the same way that all students are expected to;
- ◆ a chance to connect with other students in a supportive and **non-competitive** environment;
- ◆ a chance to have an adult mentor help monitor his or her social and emotional development in terms of the new culture;
- ◆ a realistic opportunity to be understood, accepted, respected, and valued by peers.

Simply put, we clearly believe that the Dual Objective approach to Coopera-tive Learning does all these things and does them well. Jane Echevarria's SIOP (Sheltered Instruction Observational Protocol) approach is a widely used and deeply respected strategy for helping ELL students and CL is an integral part of that approach (Vogt & Echevarria, 2007).

We'd like to add a personal note about this topic. One of the author's fathers (Vermette) was a native-born U.S. citizen whose mother tongue was not English. He heard no English until he was six and his family moved him 1500 miles (from Maine to Illinois) to be placed in a residential school with only English speakers. While he survived and flourished eventually, those were rough years for that little boy. Our national concern to assist youth in similar situations today is laudable and necessary. Thoughtful interventions such as the Dual Objective would help make the individual's transition to their new reality more enjoyable, more powerful, and more helpful to everyone involved.

Students with Disabilities

Of the four factors for which we have chosen to offer extended ideas, the record of CL success for students with disabilities is most notable and suggests that teachers should strive to use CL as often as possible for their benefit. The research has been clear on this for three decades: When included in intra-class teams, *all* individuals achieved more, were happier about life and school, and felt more connected to their peers than when they were in traditional classrooms.

Cooperative Learning has great capacity to "differentiate naturally," particularly when following the Dual Objective Model. Teachers charged with fulfilling the tenets of IDEA, must provide specially designed instruction that meets the unique needs of children with disabilities, be they mental, physical, behavioral, emotional, or learning-related. The use of CL offers practitioners a way to afford students with disabilities extra support and fosters compliance with the premise of Least Restrictive Environment. In fact, many IEPs and 504 plans have behavioral components that are directly assisted by the sustained and structured interactions afforded in well-structured Cooperative Learning as well as social-emotional goals that are specifically addressed in our Dual Objective Model.

We wish to share an anecdote from one of our graduate classes at Niagara University in 2015. A graduate student who became knowledgeable about CL shared with family members her take on what she was discovering about the social and emotional effects of the Dual Objective. One of those present at the family gathering was a 4th-grade teacher who listened carefully and then experimented with a classroom re-design that put an unpopular 4th-grader (with a condition we'll just call X) in a heterogeneous team for a week.

In a week's time, that student's mood and dispositions changed, as did his attendance, his classroom contributions, his grades/marks, and his public attitude. Moreover, his teammates now knew him as a person, not as that "problem kid," and they liked him: their lives were better, too. It may all sound too good (or a bit like a Hallmark movie), but there are no real surprises here. Cases like this are embedded in the research base that calls for the use of inclusive classrooms with cooperative team structures. Frankly, we didn't wish for it to happen; we expected it to happen.

By giving appropriate forethought, teachers can mitigate potential concerns by following a few general suggestions regarding grouping and governing of teams with special populations.

1. Group thoughtfully. Consider the needs within IEPs and 504s and place students with issues carefully with other students who have demonstrated empathy, patience, leadership, compassion, etc., as affective strengths. This balance offers stability and lessens potential for situations to arise.

2. Hold all students responsible for behavioral norms accepted by the class for successful group interactions. This may require separate discussions with students who have IEPs or 504s from the balance of the class to scaffold understanding and establish reasonable and positive expectations individually. In so doing, take care as to not overshadow team independence and interdependence.

3. Remember that academic skills do not equal affective skills. Do not confuse high academic achievement with ability to lead a diverse group to a shared team goal. Sometimes those with the "best grades" may not be able to comprehend the challenge faced by students with special needs in the process of learning. Look again for those affective markers referenced above.

4. Monitor teams with students who have special needs on a very regular basis, with focused attention to IEP goals. Provide plentiful feedback and celebrate achievements in the moment to reinforce positive accomplishments.

5. If students are open about their disabilities, have them discuss with their group how they best deal with their challenges, how this might impact their work (if so) and, if needed, draft modified rules of engagement that the group agrees to abide by.

6. If a student with special needs consistently impacts the groups they work with negatively (when expectations are understood and feedback has been provided), other pedagogy should be pursued. Although we are charged with differentiation, the greater good must prevail in cooperative classrooms.

These suggestions simply scratch the surface of what might work for your classroom. Read the literature, talk to special educators about strategies, employ sensitivity and high expectations, and remember your students will only develop the skills that they are encouraged to practice. All students need the opportunity to learn how to work with others effectively; it's a life skill.

As we leave this segment, you might want to know which student in Mr. Piazza's class has special needs. Ramona was in a car accident last year. It has left her in a wheelchair as she slowly recovers, and she processes information a bit more slowly now than she used to. She is just Ramona to her teammates and they always manage to figure out how to make it work.

Three Pieces of Wisdom

This chapter closes with several more pieces of advice that may help the teacher promote the growth of the teams as they work together.

Three Before Me

The Johnsons' technique called "three before me" is a useful tool to help students begin to rely on each other and *not* rely solely on the teacher. This is especially helpful for anxious high achievers who are "sort of perfection-ists" and who fear that relying on their classmates will take them off the desired track, as much as it is for the less confident student who needs constant reassurance. An example should help: As the students turn to each other to work on the assigned team task, they realize that they do not under-stand how to begin, or what is expected. Hands go up. But instead of clari-fying the task herself, the teacher reminds them to try to figure it out for themselves and says, "Please re-read the instructions, then ask your team-mates (the other three), before you ask me!"

Amazingly, this approach works in two ways (even though it will be found annoying by some students). First, the very discussion of what the task entails (build a model? create an artifact? write a story?) results in each student attempting to make meaning and to agree on what their *actual* goal is. When they do decide on "what they are doing," both the group and each individual hold more ownership in the end product and are more committed to its success. It has become their own project, *not* the teacher's.

Second, people generally find it incredible that the same thing can be interpreted in different ways by different people. This is a very common consequence of unintentional ambiguity. (For example: read this sentence: "He was headed for the gutter." We have to ask, is he bowling, fixing the roof, or maybe having his life go sour? Each of these is a plausible interpre-tation of the wording.) A group is more likely to come up with multiple interpretations than is any one single individual and these differences are very instructive over the long haul. They make us sensitive to individuality and cultural backgrounds, they slow our haste to judge (a very good thing according to Kahneman, 2011), and they broaden our appreciation for complexity, clarity, and empathy.

In truth, the authors occasionally violate the traditionally accepted suggestion that teachers "be as clear as possible" and intentionally create developmentally appropriate vague or ambiguous team tasks. We do this to make the process of establishing clarity and agreement (figuring it out) an integral part of the project. In the spirit of the Dual Objective, this provides students with an opportunity to exchange ideas and set goals respectfully and with purpose.

Leaving the Teams Intact

Teams should be constructed for a "relatively long time": that is clearly vague, isn't it? Often teachers design their day's activities and include group work of some kind, but far rarer is the experience of thoughtfully constructing the actual teams. However, if the teams are built carefully, they should be left intact for a while: at least a week, perhaps as long as a quarter/marking period. This long-term approach has several advantages:

1. While first impressions are important, generally the more time and interaction people have with others, the better they get to understand them and the better able they are to communicate well with them. A "team de jour" approach invites superficial interactions between students and focuses attention on simple completion of the task *and* discounts the value of the actual interaction.
2. Over time, a variety of tasks will be given to the teams. If care is taken in the design of the tasks, different students will display different strengths and, therefore, be seen differently by others in the group. (This, in fact, is at the essence of Elizabeth Cohen's 1994 equal status model of CL. Moreover, these talent differences also highlight the value of Gardner's MI theory.)
3. Since we don't advocate the assigning of specific roles to each member of a team, different people can take on the roles of leader, reporter, and encourager in a far more fluid manner over a long period of time. Successful teams need these roles to be played, and every student needs to develop his or her abilities in each of the roles. This is best done in a somewhat cohesive environment rather than in a sort of "slap dash" or "mix and match" structure.
4. Perhaps it doesn't have to be said, but school *does* reflect life and the modern business world that uses diverse teams on a regular basis and for long-term projects, *not* just "quick discussions." They use teams to balance strengths, bring different perspectives and experiences into play, and widen the experience base available for analysis.

Announcing Teams

Almost always, announcing the team memberships stirs up some people in class. A teacher should do everything he or she can to avoid student-generated public displays of disappointment or resistance that will be embarrassing to some students and damaging to attempts to build a sense of community. We offer several tips:

- ◆ The teacher should make it clear that there is damage done by negative outbursts and, in the spirit of developing necessary social skills, respectful acceptance of personal differences is expected to be part of the process. For younger students, this may require a reminder every time new groups are formed of how respectful behavior looks as teammates are announced, and seated. You might hear, "High-fives are great at sports events, but please not here. How would you feel if everyone on your team got a high five, but you did not? Please no grimacing (demonstrate), sighing, rolling of the eyes, tongue clicks, hip thrusts, etc., because all of these are hurtful, and we do not do that here. Everyone matters, everyone has value, and every-one *will* be shown that . . . Remember our cardinal rule? (I don't have to like you, but I do have to work with you and show you respect)."

- ◆ Adult groups rarely face such public outbursts, whether the announced groupings are in the army or college classes, or take place in the rearrangement of departments in an office or in the assigning of shifts at a factory. (Private grumbling may be common within the adult world; public grumbling, less so.)

- ◆ If the teacher begins with a small-sized group *and* a brief and clearly focused in-class task, the activity will be completed quickly, everyone will participate, complaints will be stifled, and successes will be enjoyed. The teacher then has that positive experience as the model to be followed for longer, more complex tasks, and projects. Examples of these initial activities with high probabilities of success would include: (a) any think–pair–share task; (b) a lesson using pairs, in which student A describes a "thing" and student B draws a visual representation of it; and (c) a short "interview" in which student A is to discover (and then share) student B's response to something important.

In Closing

The construction of the teams can be a fascinating and complex part of a teacher's job. Over the course of a school year, use of the Dual Objective should make each student more willing *and* able to handle the demands of group work and to deal effectively with potential interpersonal conflicts. Getting the CL program off to a good start is an important factor in the management of classrooms and the first creation and use of teams should go a long way to setting the tone, clarifying the expectations, and promoting the necessary attitudes for year-long success.

Chapter 4 Big Ideas

1. Building of student teams should be done thoughtfully and intentionally and almost always should be done by the teacher. The most productive size for groupings is two, three, or four students.
2. Student teams should work together in every single class and should receive carefully derived feedback from the teacher and, potentially, teammates.
3. Diversities are strengths; thoughtful integration to balance factors such as gender, ethnicity, interests, experiences, and personality styles is a good idea.
4. Teachers should be careful about their talk publicly of the rationale behind specific team memberships and always stress the positives about individuals.
5. Having explicit roles for students is one way to increase engagement, but more important is the quality of the contributions to conversation during problem-solving or product creation.
6. Left to choose their own teammates, students will pick friends, isolate some class members, and are more likely to see the group work as a social event, not a learning activity or an opportunity to develop themselves personally.
7. Other factors that teachers might want to consider when building balanced and powerful teams include students' previous experience with CL, students who are transfers, fluency with the English language, and students with disabilities.
8. Students should not change teams daily; semi-permanence helps allow students to get to know each other more realistically and under differing task conditions.
9. Suggestions like using the tactic "three before me," opening with a quick clear task that is publicly assessed, and explicitly aligning teamwork with specific 21st-century skills would help smooth the transition from a large-group to small-group structure for both students and teachers.

References

Ambrose, S.A., Bridges, M.W., DiPietro, M.C., Lovett, M.K., & Norman, M.K. (2010). *How learning works: Seven research-based principles for smart teaching*. San Francisco, CA: Jossey-Bass.

Astin, A. (1993). *What matters in college: Four critical years revisited*. San Francisco, CA: Jossey-Bass.

Bennett, N., & Cass, A. (1988). The effects of group composition on group interactive process and pupil understanding. *British Educational Research Journal, 15*(1), 19–32.

Cohen, E. (1994). *Designing groupwork: Strategies for the heterogeneous classroom*. New York, NY: Teachers College Press.

Dweck, C. (2006). *Mindset: The new psychology of success*. New York, NY: Random House.

Gillies, R. (2006). Teachers' and students' verbal behaviors during cooperative and small group learning. *British Journal of Educational Psychology, 76*, 271–287.

Kahneman, D. (2011). *Thinking, fast and slow*. New York, NY: Farrar, Straus and Giroux.

Miller, N., & Harrington, H.J. (1992). Social categorization and intergroup acceptance: Principles for design and development of cooperative learning teams. In R. Hertz-Lazarowitz & N. Miller (Eds.), *Interaction in cooperative groups: The theoretical anatomy of group learning*. New York, NY: Cambridge University Press.

Mitchell, S.N., Reilly, R., Bramwell, F., Lilly, G., & Solonsky, A. (2004). Friendship and choosing groupmates: Preferences for teacher-selected vs. student-selected groupings in high school science classes. *Journal of Instructional Psychology, 31*(1), 20–32.

Myers, J., Bardsley, M., Vermette, P., & Kline, C. (2017). *Cooperative learning for the 21st century* (forthcoming).

Vermette, P. (1998). *Making cooperative learning work: Student teams in K–12 classrooms*. Upper Saddle River, NJ: Merrill/Prentice Hall.

Vogt, M., & Echevarria, J. (2007). *99 activities for teaching English language learners*. New York, NY: Pearson.

Webb, N.M., & Farivar, S. (1994). Promoting helping behaviors in cooperative small school groups in middle school mathematics. *American Educational Research Journal, 31*(2), 369–395.

5

What Does the Teacher Do While Students Work?

"From Well-Meaning and Intuitive to Systematic and Intentional"

Over the years, we have been in hundreds of classrooms in the U.S. and Canada. Adorning many walls of these classrooms are colorful posters, signs with inspiring quotations, visuals of great people, lists of desired behaviors or class rules, facsimiles of important documents like the Declaration of Independence or the U.S. Constitution (in Christian schools, the Ten Commandments are often visible), and newspaper clippings of heroic actions. When we ask teachers or administrators about the specific choices of these materials, we hear a varied set of answers. The following represent the most common themes we hear:

"Those tell the kids how life is supposed to be lived."
"Those provide models for students to reference."
"They promise greatness and set the ideal."
"I am not sure how they got there, but I sometimes refer to them during what I call a 'teachable moment'."
"They inspire the students to be their best."

We are going to do two things to open this very important chapter. First, we want to have you examine one illustration of the "teachable moment and inspiring sign" approach to dealing with important beliefs and actions. Second, we want to show you the shifts and modifications necessary to have "teachable moments" occur every day and which utilize the Dual Objective to make them intentionally productive for non-cognitive growth.

Understanding "Systematic and Intentional"

CASE: Mr. Gilmore's 9th-Grade ELA Class

To start first period class today, a 16-year veteran, Mr. Gilmore, displays four famous quotations:

- ◆ "90% of life is showing up" (Woody Allen)
- ◆ "Just do it" (Nike)
- ◆ "To be or not to be, that is the question" (Shakespeare)
- ◆ "So it goes" (Vonnegut).

He then calls on a student asking, "Yolanda, what does one of these mean?" which is met with a blank stare. He waits a moment and then asks, "Can anybody help her?" Two hands shoot up, one wildly waved by a boy in the back. "Marco, what do you think?" "Like, if you don't go to work, or go to practice, or come to school, then you lose . . ." he replies.

Just then, two boys walk into class late and head for seats up front as Mr. Gilmore points at them and says, "What about being late? Does Woody Allen suggest that, too?" The class laughs and the two boys look a bit bewildered. One, Steve, asks, "Do we need a pass?" Mr. Gilmore asks Yolanda to bring the new students up to speed. She does so quickly and accurately. He then remarks, "You know, this is pretty funny timing. Did Steve and Stan actually miss anything by being late?"

If you were to continue reading this description, what would you expect to happen next?

1. Students are asked to pair up and take one minute to make a list of things that Steve and Stan really missed by not showing up?
2. A few minutes of continued one-at-a-time classroom discussion of what Allen's quote means and how it applies?
3. A mini-lecture about the phrase "So it goes" as they prepare to read *Slaughterhouse-Five*?

Our Take

- ◆ Mr. Gilmore knows an opportunity when he sees one. He has not planned to talk much about the meaning of each of the first three quotes as his real focus is on the final one, but he decides to open up with the one from Woody Allen. He senses its value as a consequence of the "teachable moment" sparked by the two late students.
- ◆ For our prediction of his next step, we think that he'd probably choose the second option, and continue a large group, one-at-a-time discussion, feeling pleased that he could use the boys' lateness as an

immediate example. We'd prefer he choose the first option, involving everyone in an analysis of the consequences of lateness. However, he didn't plan for that activity and didn't anticipate the two late joiners: He wasn't ready so he scrambled to make something out of the opportunity given him. How he handled the situation was not a bad thing, it was just not as powerful as it could have been.

Furthermore, we wish to point out three things:

1. When Kline was first experimenting with the Dual Objective in her middle school Spanish classes, she coined the phrase "systematic and intentional" to explain to others that she was not doing "virtue of the month" or "using teachable moments"; instead, she was intentionally creating opportunities for kids to "study" and "practice" the desired affective skills they needed for life success. She would create a **formal opportunity for the students to examine and experience these explicit skills** and would give them feedback on their use of them.

2. Teachers almost universally know about and seek opportunities to use those "teachable moments," times when they can teach life skills, positive attitudes, and effective behaviors. In fact, many ELA teachers plan whole lessons around the study of such things as the effects of racism (*To Kill a Mockingbird*), prejudice (the poem "We and They" by Kipling), or bullying (*Thirteen Reasons Why*). *But,* and this is key, there is rarely an explicit expectation for the students to demonstrate affective competence in their comments and actions. These would include such things as requiring that the teens treat each other respectfully, use self-regulation in class, try hard, and use logic, evidence, and reasoning in their actions. Almost certainly, there is little systematic feedback on student behaviors unless they are gross violations of school rules.

   The Dual Objective turns the teachable moment upside down. It recognizes that the desired skills, be they Costa and Kallick's Habits of Mind, CASEL's Competencies, from the 21st Century Partnership's P21 Framework or Covey's seven traits, should be formal outcomes of school-based instruction. They should be treated as skills and competencies to develop during class, and they should be assessed regularly with feedback given.

   We also believe that a reporting out of affective and non-cognitive achievement on locally determined skills should be added to grade reporting. Non-cognitive skills are better predictors of college success and job success than are grades or SAT scores, so why not do so? Again, an example may help: A student, Ted, had a 96 percent average in math, scored a perfect 1600 on the SATs, and has been arrested four times for drug sales and twice for assault. How do you rate the effectiveness of that student's education and what do you predict for him over the next few years?

3. Some schools already have some kind of an "affective curriculum," but we haven't found many yet that have specific skills built into the scope and sequence, and which are formally taught and assessed. One of those that do such formal affective assessment are the famous KIPP schools, but we are not enamored with their seven-item set. The Ontario Ministry does have a province-wide reporting system for every student on six life skills: respect, organization, independent work, collaboration, initiative, and self-regulation. We like this set, but, at this time, there is little reliability for what a rating means on each of the six items across the province or even within schools. Often there is no clear evidence offered to support a particular score: The teacher ratings are not very reliable judgments. However, we do hold Ontario's model up as something of a success and worthy of your further examination.

After years of deliberation and investigation, we do not agree entirely on any single inventory of affective skills as superior to others. Each resource has its own unique flavor, feel, and intention. Although we may personally differ in our individual choices, we do, however, encourage the selection of a single source to structure implementation efforts. (This decision will sometimes be made by the district or school, but could be left to the individual teacher.)

It is important to recognize that many affective taxonomies are purposefully extensive (as a means of capturing the breadth of possibilities required to ready our youth for advanced schooling, life, and career), and will require narrowing in order to systematically focus classroom effort on designated skills. Using the example of the 16 Habits of Mind (Costa & Kallick, 2008), we have targeted eight that we think of as analogs to the important "keystone habits" that Charles Duhigg discussed in his award-winning book *The power of habit* (2014). (We will be focusing largely on these for analysis of the cases within this chapter.) See Figure 5.1 for the complete listing.

We suspect that you read the 16 Habits of Mind, evaluated them quickly, and are now predicting which ones we see as our "keystone" habits. We will tell you soon. We wish to note that in a very important article back in 2015, the inventor of "grit," Angela Duckworth and her research partner David Yaeger, suggested to the research audience that educators shouldn't seek to use standardized tests for affective skills *nor* do we wish a universally adopted set

Figure 5.1 Habits of Mind

1. Persisting Stick to it! Persevering in task through to completion; remaining focused. Looking for ways to reach your goal when stuck. Not giving up.	**2. Managing impulsivity** Take your time! Thinking before acting; remaining calm, thoughtful, and deliberative.
3. Listening with understanding and empathy Understand others! Devoting mental energy to another person's thoughts and ideas. Make an effort to perceive another's point of view and emotions.	**4. Thinking flexibly** Look at it another way! Being able to change perspectives, generate alternatives, and consider options.
5 Thinking about your thinking (metacognition) Know your knowing! Being aware of your own thoughts, strategies, feelings, and actions, and their effects on others.	**6. Striving for accuracy** Check it again! Always doing your best. Setting high standards. Checking and finding ways to improve constantly.
7. Questioning and problem-posing How do you know? Having a questioning attitude; knowing what data are needed and developing questioning strategies to produce those data. Finding problems to solve.	**8. Applying past knowledge to new situations** Use what you learn! Accessing prior knowledge; transferring knowledge beyond the situation in which it was learned.
9. Thinking and communicating with clarity and precision Be clear! Striving for accurate communication in both written and oral form; avoiding overgeneralizations, distortions, deletions, and exaggerations.	**10. Gather data through all senses** Use your natural pathways! Pay attention to the world around you. Gather data through all the senses: taste, touch, smell, hearing, and sight.
11. Creating, imagining, and innovating Try a different way! Generating new and novel ideas, fluency, originality.	**12. Responding with wonderment and awe** Have fun figuring it out! Finding the world awesome and mysterious, and being intrigued with phenomena and beauty.
13. Taking responsible risks Venture out! Being adventuresome; living on the edge of one's competence. Try new things constantly.	**14. Finding humor** Laugh a little! Finding the whimsical, incongruous, and unexpected. Being able to laugh at oneself.
15. Thinking interdependently Work together! Being able to work in and learn from others in reciprocal situations. Team work.	**16. Remaining open to continuous learning** I have so much more to learn! Having humility and pride when admitting we don't know; resisting complacency.

Modified from " Habits of Mind Across the Curriculum," Costa & Kallick (2008)

of items until far more work has been done. She also said that for local purposes (a particular school or particular teacher), the clear statement of affective expectations is all that is needed to begin the instruction and evaluation process. So, before the political and scholarly community makes a Common-Core-like decision about a mandated non-cognitive skills curriculum, we offer you a small sub-set of Habits (a starter kit if you will) that are universally applicable across the curriculum and vertically throughout secondary teaching:

- ◆ Persisting
- ◆ Managing impulsivity
- ◆ Listening with understanding and empathy
- ◆ Thinking flexibly
- ◆ Striving for accuracy
- ◆ Questioning and problem-posing
- ◆ Creating, imagining, and innovating
- ◆ Thinking interdependently

We suspect that secondary students who rate highly on these skills are high achievers and leaders who have strong relationships and a complex support network, apply a fine work ethic, see diversity as strength, inhabit a growth mindset, and have overcome failures. We anticipate a far more dismal record for those who are weak in these eight competencies.

CASE: Ms. Garcia's 8th-Grade Spanish Class

The teacher starts class with this set of directions:

"Today, you will be working in your assigned three-person team on your altar for Day of the Dead. Please remember the project total is worth 100 points. 50 points will be a group grade (the same grade for each member of the group) based on the altar rubric, 25 will be individual grades from your oral presentations, and 25 (also individual) from your teamwork evaluation form. You have all your resources available and we discussed the other details yesterday. As usual, I will be working the room, looking for three of our key skills: thinking interdependently, listening with understanding and empathy, and striving for accuracy, for which you will receive written feedback. The timeline is posted to help you track your work. Remember that your partners are your first resource, then another team, and finally me."

Our Take

- ◆ This class is a contrast to scenario one. The "teachable moment" becomes far more, as the affective objectives are well-structured and well-planned; this teacher cannot wait for spontaneous events to set up a life skills experience but has a plan to address and assess them from the beginning.

◆ The students are practicing three specific affective skills and know they are being assessed on them.

◆ Moreover, their individual part will include reflection on their and their teammates' contributions during group work (the team evaluation rubric), as well as their oral presentations. (There are two product rubrics, one for the oral presentation, and one for the group altar, which they have created previously to drive the quality of their work.)

This is the Dual Objective in action. The teacher has explicitly focused effort on affective skills (in addition to cognitive expectations), and is assessing these daily as students work on the assignment. Our associate, Emily Kaufman, frequently reminds us that school is part of the "real world" for youngsters, making this a "real-world" application! We suggest that working collaboratively in Ms. Garcia's class predicts their ability to do so in other real-world applications. With adult instruction, guidance and feedback, teens can increase their affective competence alongside learning "how to conjugate –ar verbs."

Student Team-Talk: Considering Interventions and Feedback

What we call "working the room" (Konkoski-Bates & Vermette, 2004) revolves around providing carefully considered *spontaneous interventions* (Flynn, Mesibov, Vermette, & Smith, 2004) as students work on task. These interventions provide feedback to team members about their ideas, plans, decisions, accuracy, and treatment of each other. Most teachers are used to commenting on academic accuracy and/or logical reasoning, but many have never carefully watched for the way students "practice" (actually incorporate) their various non-cognitive competencies: Student-to-student interaction makes all of this visible and audible and provides opportunities to scaffold improvement.

What do teachers do? In short, the answers to the title question of this chapter are as follows:

◆ assure that students are doing the work in an effective fashion and that each one is contributing;

◆ assess the quality of the thinking and the quality of the interactions with the purpose of preparing and delivering feedback on *both*;

◆ clarify and reinforce community norms and strengthen relationships to foster an effective learning environment.

With those ends in mind, and referencing the abbreviated Habits list (key items) offered earlier, read the following segments of four classroom conversations and plan your response to the students. We urge you to focus most heavily on how the *process of interaction* is going and how well the students are demonstrating the key Habits of Mind. Our commentary follows each.

CASE: Mr. Dinero's 11th-Grade Business Class

In his 11th-grade business class, Mr. Dinero has formed teams so that today students are creating an advertisement for a real product using the ideas they have explored in previous classes and in their reading. This is what he hears as he walks by a specific team:

Jude:	OK, listen up; we only have 15 minutes to get this ready to share. Are you two ready?
Maddie:	Sure, this'll be fun.
Clark:	Yeah sure, fun. Why doesn't he just babble on like other teachers?
Maddie:	Stop with that. Besides, Jude needs the plus that Smith offered for good ones and, don't forget, we all get the A if the one he calls on is good.
Clark:	OK, OK. I'll do it for you. What are we doing?
Jude:	In the envelope is the name of the product we have to design an advertising jingle for. We got "Pepsodent!" That's a toothpaste.
Clark:	I know, I know. I actually read about how they—one guy—made it a *huge* business success. I mean, Fucillo-HUGE! Hey, I never thought about it—does this stuff even still exist?
Maddie:	Yeah, we use it at my house. See how white my teeth are? (*She grins, lips pulled back.*)
Jude:	Uh— they're pretty white—except for the lettuce (*laughter*). Wait a minute, how about a slogan—like—"As White and Pure as Maddie?"
Maddie:	(*Shoving him a little with a good-natured push.*) Get serious—a slogan is not a jingle. But the "white teeth" and "smile" and "clean" all can be used. It also makes my mouth feel good—refreshed. That's why my mom brushes after smoking. What are some rhymes for those words?
Clark:	We should start with a tune—something popular like . . .
Jude:	Good. If we have the tune, and then the words, we're done.
Maddie:	We're also supposed to say why it may work to sell the product—but we can make that up later.

At this point, Mr. Dinero steps away from the group conversation and makes a decision about his own reaction. What do you suggest?

Our Take

◆ We are not sure how often this teacher uses the Dual Objective, or what has happened before, but we would urge him not to mention the comments about him (at the outset) or the playful joking the students engage in. He should note these actions, though, and follow through on observing for those behaviors next time.

◆ There is much to praise in these students' work. Generally, there is value to validating or noting successful contributions. Three examples of things we think are worth noting include the following: Each student is participating and contributing to the common good; the group made an effort to know exactly what their understanding of the task would mean; and, they listened to each other while trying to stick to their work expectations. These actions align nicely with "thinking interdependently" and "striving for accuracy" from our key Habits. If Mr. Dinero is using an affective assessment (teacher, team, or self), he could reference it here.

◆ We would want Mr. Dinero to take the time to ask two questions, address them to two different team members, and look for other people's reactions to the responses. First, we think he should ask Maddie about Clark's knowledge of Pepsodent to see if more of his past experience could be made relevant. Second, we think he should directly ask Jude how well the group was working together. Jude's answer to that question would open up a discussion about what he could look for in the next observation.

CASE: Mrs. Singh's 7th-Grade ELA Class

In this class, Mrs. Singh has created four-person teams to work together every day this month. They are looking at some poetry and thinking about how to best end the lines that they are interpreting. Students are given famous poems, with the last section of a line left blank. (This is a form of the "cloze" activity used in reading comprehension.)

Kyra:	OK—hey, get ready. We gotta do this now. She wants us to figure out what words go in the last place of some of the sentences.
Tyrone:	I think she calls them lines.
Kyra:	Whatever. Here's this poem; see with these blanks? Now let's get 'em done so we can relax. Yusuf?
Yusuf:	Why don't we just look the real poem up online, find the real word, and fill 'em in?
Anna:	Huh! Good idea—here's my phone.

Kyra:	Hey, put that away—you know the rules! *You* use the phone and *I* get a zero. No way. We'll get a B if we even try, *and* we get them all wrong—like if we stick in words like "green" or "dog" or "osmosis" or "typhoon" . . . *(gesturing to Tyrone)*.
Tyrone:	My name is Tyrone.
Kyra:	We aren't talking about you—well, now we are. Anyway, I think I should read it; we talk, get an idea, and just write it down.
Yusuf:	Hey, if we are gonna get a B for almost nothing, why not try a little bit and get the A for the daily grade? Maybe it'll be fun.
Kyra:	OK, you read. There are 10 we gotta do in 45 minutes.

At this point, Mrs. Singh has to decide how to respond. By the way, her choices do include ignoring this opportunity to give verbal feedback and waiting for another time, including walking away. Walking away *is* a decision. What do you suggest?

Our Take

◆ We suspect that this is a typical group of students that is trying to get the job done with as little effort as possible. One of the affective skills that pairs well with this activity is "creating, imagining, and innovating," which Mrs.Singh could rely on here for commentary. Furthermore, if "striving for accuracy" was a target skill for all of her classes, she could use the two in a powerful combination as she intervened. She might redirect as follows:

1. "Hey guys, by the way . . . thanks for putting the phones away . . . that shows that you are 'striving for accuracy' in your actions regarding rules. I can hardly wait to see what you come up with doing the same for your endings. I'll check back in a few . . ."

2. "Hey guys, I have to applaud you for putting those phones away. Obviously you are both innovative and creative, or you wouldn't have thought of them in the first place. So now, how about trying the same for the writing?"

3. "Hey guys, I know you can be creative, because you just showed me you are . . . (phones?) . . . try it now with your words. Can you guys put your minds together to come up with some really good answers? Do you need anything from me?"

◆ On the other hand, Mrs. Singh could just walk away, making notes about what she had observed for later reference. Her actions depend upon the presence and choice of affective competencies selected for the class. She should absolutely reinforce or redirect behavior as she works the room based on the affective and cognitive objectives previously determined. Doing so demonstrates to her students that she is paying attention to both affective displays as well as content quality, to guide their "whole" growth. If they do not have affective objectives, this potentially powerful exchange is limited to being a "teachable moment," which falls short of our goal of "systematically and intentionally" teaching affective competence in the CL environment.

CASE: Mr. Goldman's 7th-Grade Math Class

Mr. Goldman teaches the math class on the same teacher team as Mrs. Singh. The teachers work closely and, in fact, keep the students in the same teams in every subject each month. This means that the students get plenty of time working with familiar people and each teacher gets to observe and share insights with other faculty. Today in class, students are examining visuals to identify geometrical figures and realize how complex, and how interesting, math can be.

Tyrone:	OK, so we got this really complex drawing—all straight and crossing lines. But straight. He says that . . . wait, what'd he say?
Yusuf:	He says that we wouldn't be able to count the squares, even if we knew what they are. I did already. There are 48.
Kyra:	Say what? I counted, too—there are 56. OK, we're done.
Anna:	Can we put down both numbers?
Others:	(In unison) No way!
Anna:	Well, the average is around 52 . . .
Yusuf:	Seriously?
Anna:	OK (pause). How can you both get different answers? I'm sticking with 52.
Kyra:	I think Yusuf is wrong, but now I'm not sure. I have an idea. Why don't we count them together?
Tyrone:	Yeah, but one of us has to make sure that we don't count some square twice.
Anna:	You know I hate math, but I think that *this* and *this* are both squares (*she traces lines on the handout*), but together they make a rectangle. Aren't all squares rectangles?
Yusuf:	Yes, they are, and he said to count *rectangles*, not squares, and I counted a total of 114!
Kyra:	Wait, all squares are rectangles, but not all rectangles are squares?
Yusuf:	Yeah, you got it.
Tyrone:	Look at the board. It says count rectangles for handout #1 and squares for #2. Can we just start over?
Anna:	Guys, this stuff isn't that hard. Let's take figure A—let Tyrone count out loud and we check him.

Kyra:	Me, too. I wanna count.
Others:	(*In unison*) OK! (*They laugh*)
Tyrone & Kyra:	(*Tracing each rectangle and counting in unison.*) Here is one . . . two . . . three . . .

At this point, Mr. Goldman is deciding how to react to this conversation before he gets moving to observe other teams in the room. What do you suggest he say to them?

Our Take

◆ We suggest that Mr. Goldman comments on how they all seem to be comfortable working together: they argue, they laugh, and they share (thinking interdependently). Alternately, he could comment on how well they worked together to make sense of their initial confusion and come up with a way to find the answers together (persistence).

◆ To make maximum use of this valuable "working the room" time, every teacher needs some method for documenting his or her observations for each group. This becomes the evidence (data) that enables affective growth through objective feedback. Be it paper-based or digital, simple or complex, universal (for use with any activity), or subject-specific, **we encourage developing your own tool based on the affective objectives you have set**. We examine several formats later in this book, however one which requires virtually no prior attention to format includes recording commentary in a narrative-type set of notes taken during the observation (à la "running records" in literacy practice). For example, during this snippet, Goldman could have written:

Kyra:

◆ Way she argued was very appropriate; she was assertive and supportive at the same time.
◆ She seems to be very comfortable with each of the other three kids (*thinking interdependently*).

Tyrone:

◆ Important role in making group examine what they are doing.
◆ He is *persistent*.

(In a section below, we will show you another example of a teacher with a short, but formal checklist.)

CASE: Ms. Riddle's 9th-Grade Science Class

Today, Ms. Riddle is using class to introduce eight important science generalizations (from the textbook) and is seeking to observe how much prior knowledge the students, and teams, possess. The tactic in play is called "re-write in your own words."

Matt:	We should really *read* the directions.
Mark:	OK by me.
Ruby:	Whatever—this sounds hard.
John:	It is—that's why we should work together. *(To Ruby)* You're lucky to be—
Ruby:	*(Interrupting)* Don't go there yet. I don't even know you guys.
John:	You're new here. You'll get used to us . . .
Matt:	Let's get to work, we have a lot to do.
Mark:	*(To Ruby)* Don't worry about it— Besides, we need to be able to work together here if we are ever gonna do it "out there" like Riddle says.
John:	Agreed. Let's start with this one on page 87. It says, "The path of osmosis is never straight."
Ruby:	Sounds like a fortune cookie saying.
John:	Maybe we can write something like, "Water always flows crookedly during . . ." Can we use the word "osmosis"?
Ruby:	Why did you say "water"? It's air, too— right?
John:	I don't think we can use "osmosis," but we can stick in the definition from the text. Here it is *(pointing)*.
Matt:	It is just water, but we can say "fluids" or "moisture"; and I like the glossary idea. Keep going.
Mark:	Hey guys— I'm not sure that moisture is the same as water.

At this point, Ms. Riddle moves from where she was standing to a position right next to them. She sends them an obvious smile and gives her always-present "thumbs up" sign. (This is a very common occurrence.) She is deciding what to say to them. What do you suggest?

Our Take

◆ We want to make sure that Ms. Riddle knows that she has provided a constant positive intervention with her smile, her focused attention, and the "thumbs up." She might want to just jot down a couple of things and move on. She has given them feedback and a silent acknowledgement of their high-quality interaction.

◆ Assuming an affective goal of "thinking interdependently," if she were to ask one question to the group, we would urge her to ask about the progress they are making in involving everyone (considering Ruby's recent arrival). It would be interesting to have them share their insights; they would profit from the sharing of their private interpretations of the shared experience.

Two More Applications: Extending Transfer

We will now speak to two attempts to utilize the Dual Objective by teachers experimenting with it. Please read through both of them and select aspects of the scenarios that you like, aspects that you think deal effectively with affective growth and which utilize powerful "talking to learn" practices. Moreover, we have provided a set of elaboration and/or exploration questions to help you analyze the teaching. In the first case, we offer these questions at the end of the section as a review vehicle; in the second case, the questions are offered at the beginning in the hope of getting you prepared and focused. We have also added a few comments about the case, but have not directly provided an answer set to the questions we have asked.

CASE: Mr. Donoski's 8th-Grade Science Class

Mark Donoski, a 38-year-old who is in his third year of teaching at this school, is a former scientist who wanted to teach so that he could make a difference in kids' lives. He was hired during a time when the district (in rural West Virginia) was committing a huge effort to improve its work in STEM (which is now STEAM across the district) and it has spent a great deal of money on this initiative. In the grade 6–12 program, there are three science teachers and test scores have not been very good for a long time. Mr. Donoski feels pressure but is also excited about trying out the Dual Objective form of Cooperative Learning. He suspects that the adults in the district have lost many of the social and emotional skills and attitudes that they once had and that students need to think about them, embrace them, and get good at them if they are going to succeed in life after high school.

"Good afternoon," he says to greet the sixth-period students after lunch. "Today, we have only two things to worry about; whether I forgot what we're doing *or* whether you're going to just sit there in your chairs and not do anything." (*This is met with laughter.*) "No way I'd ever forget what we are going to do today and no way you'll just sit; so it looks like there's nothing left to worry about . . . why don't we get going?"

He almost always smiles and is encouraging to every student; he hopes that his enthusiasm and passion for scientific investigations will "rub off" on the young people, but he also knows that he needs to go beyond modeling and the teachable moment to get them to develop the skills of persistence, inquiry, respectful collaboration, and self-regulation that are the hallmarks of science and scientific inquiry.

"Today, we are going to begin our comparison of two hugely significant science words: 'demonstration' and 'experimentation.' We also know that both of these fit under the term 'investigation,' so I guess that one of our objectives is to describe what all three of these words mean. Our second objective today deals with more science words. By the end of the day, when you write your paragraph summary in your journals, I want you to correctly use these three terms as well: 'prediction,' 'hypothesis,' and 'evidence.'" (*All six words fill the large board over his desk.*)

"One more thing, as we do every day, I am watching your personal skills, your Habits. Today is going to be fun and a bit different. I want you to show some enthusiasm for what we're doing, to be captivated by some of the things that you may not know about science, and to encourage the same in your teammates. OK? Let's call that goal to have you 'react with awe and wonder at the world' . . . or better yet, why don't we just look for the 'awesomeness' of science?"

"Take out a blank paper and put your heading on it. Somebody help Roman out." (*He waits while a girl gets Roman some paper*). "Thanks, Bita. Now, I am going to show you three short films that show some neat science stuff and I'll stop them before you see the results of the demonstrations. You are going to predict how the demonstrations end and, yes, you can talk it over at your tables, but you do not have to agree with the other folks you talk to."

In the first video, a cup of water in a large glass beaker is put into a microwave. The machine is set for four minutes and turned on; a quick cut in the movie shows the bell ringing at the end of four minutes. "Guys, is the water at the same level, a lower level, or has it expanded into a higher level? Write down which and why."

Ninety seconds pass. There is some student-to-student verbal interaction.

"OK; our second example is very simple. It is about the weight of things and how they float. In this video you'll see a fish tank and eight objects. Each has been weighed and the first four weights will be shown. Please note if each item sinks or floats. Then you will see the other four, and be told their weights. You must predict whether they float or not, and jot your predictions on your sheet for each item. You can just put the item name and 'sink' or 'float' next to it."

He plays the short video and then waits 90 seconds. There is more conversation going on than after the first video.

"You have your predictions recorded, right? Our final video shows a flower in a pot in a dark room. Over 36 hours, the flower gets five minutes of bright light from its right side and half a cup of water from its left every hour. You will see that the growth is measured at various one-hour intervals. After 36 hours, you will see its overall progress and predict what happens if the same treatment is done over the next 36 hours. Just write a few words describing what you think will happen. Ready?"

He plays the video and waits 90 seconds. The room is quite loud with discussion during this time.

"OK, get your paper and a pen and find your other two assigned partners from yesterday. The names of team members are also displayed over on the wall. Each group has access to a computer and your own phones, of course. I am going to give you 25 minutes to do two jobs. First, find the real answer to each of the three problems we just saw in the videos. Your predictions could all be right and similar, but we scientists want outside experimental confirmation, not just a wild or even educated guess. Then, look at this list of 40 scientific demonstrations available on video that I got from the internet. I Googled, 'Cool science experiments' and got these demonstrations." (He shows them on his computer, which is displayed on the whiteboard in front.) "I want you to summarize the first five in two or three short sentences. If anyone wants to do more than five, feel free. I will consider extra points for your effort."

"Oh yeah—don't forget, treat each other well (collaborate thoughtfully), get the job done (stay on task), and our special goal for today, recognize how *awesome* science can be (respond with awe and wonder). I will call 'time' with about ten minutes left in class to give you time to write your reflections in your science log."

"One last thing, I should tell you that we are going to actually do a bunch of these demonstrations tomorrow. We could use the items listed on the side board, if you can bring in anything, please put your name next to it."

With that, students begin the process of following through on these challenges and Mr. Donoski begins working the room. He silently changes the display on the far wall so that it shows the daily affective rubric (Figure 5.2) that he is completing while working the room. During the student work period, he will circulate often and be able to assess half of the class. Tomorrow he will focus on the other half.

Figure 5.2 Daily Affective Rubric

Daily Affective Rubric
Group _____
Class Period _____

Name:			Date:
ELEMENT	LEVELS		
	Frequently	Usually	Seldom
Collaborates thoughtfully			
Stays on task			
Shows enthusiasm and wonder			
Comments about work effort:			

Questions for Analysis

1. Mr. Donoski is relying on technology for much of what he is doing today. What are three major concerns he should have before starting this lesson? What should he do about each?
2. While the students are in three-person teams that had met one time before, are they ready for a complex challenge? How can he assure individual accountability in such a unstructured environment? Does he give them too much choice? Is there too much work given?
3. How well did you think the first activity (the three predictions) helped set up the second, longer one?
4. Mr. Donoski really wants to be good at the Dual Objective and he knows his science. What did you think of his selection of non-cognitive competencies for this lesson?

5. Assume that the real purpose of the lesson is to develop a working knowledge of the six big concepts: prediction, hypothesis, experiment, demonstration, evidence, and investigation. How could he examine each student's level of understanding of the six terms at the end of two lessons?

Our Take

◆ We applaud this teacher for tackling what he calls the "lost" social and emotional (SEL) skills head-on. He sees his complex role as helping kids understand and appreciate science, helping students become better people, *and* making a positive difference in their lives. Many teachers have a fixed mindset (Dweck, 2006) when it comes to student attitudes and skills; adopting an "it is what it is" frame of mind, they view these attitudes and skills as unchangeable. Of course, we do know that teachers can be huge change agents for all kids if they make it a priority and use supportive interventions (Farrington et al., 2012). Everything Mr. Donoski chooses in this lesson reflects his understanding of students as capable, good people, naïve scientists, and those who matter. (We love teachers who think that teenagers actually matter and proceed accordingly.)

◆ We think that he has created many opportunities for students to stay on task and to work interdependently. Moreover, he has designed a plan that invites students to become enthusiastic about a science as a whole. If he is attentive, encouraging, and clear about his expectations, this learning segment may be a great experience for many in the room. However, we urge him to consider what happens if some groups actually do not succeed. Paul Tough (2012) suggests that reacting well to failure (thus turning it into an affective success *and* strengthening a growth mindset) is *central* to affective growth. We are reminded of a scene from a Hollywood movie in which young Bruce Wayne (later in life, Batman) falls into a pit; his loving, supportive, and wise father tells him that the reason we fall down is so that we can learn to get up. Failure per se is not a good thing until it develops into a good thing and that transformation often requires an outside agent. Teachers can be such agents of change for many teens. Mr. Donoski has to be ready to coach and support every student in the next few days.

◆ His use of technology seems relevant and contemporary. Moreover, unbeknownst to the students, he knows that they all have study hall last period, so it is possible for them to continue this lesson into that time (hence he offers the extra points for more investigation of the 40 demonstrations). Although he knows that he might suggest this idea later in class, he is confident that one of the students will recognize the opportunity and make the point for him; he would then be able to build off of a student suggestion. (He is literally planning a spontaneous intervention!) He is ready to challenge the students on their goals and on their persistence. He also knows that the large number of videos will invite concentrated effort and a need to stay on task, which he sees as aligned with Ericsson and Pool's thoughtful, purposeful, and deliberate practice (2016). He is not yet worried about grades and grading: those considerations will come later. While he hopes his students know that they matter to him and to each other, he is confident that they know that he values their efforts.

◆ We are not sure how he built the three-person teams, but he did have them work together yesterday. We do know that there are no single-sex groups. We certainly hope that they were thoughtfully created (see Chapter 4 again) like everything else he has carefully planned (materials, information sheets, technology, etc.). We also note that he has foreshadowed the next class and told the students that they will be designing and performing demonstrations. He has them very active and expects enthusiasm, so he is looking for positive experiences that he can build on when he "works the room."

◆ Finally, we appreciate his use of a checklist to document his observations. Notice that his rubric has three elements that mirror his expectations and which will be used many times during the year. Three rating levels for each element are enough to ensure that he observes an individual student for a sufficient time and can make an evidence-based judgment. His structure makes level two, called "usually," the default score (mid-point), thus offering most students an opportunity to score well every day. As he is a teacher who is comfortable with technology, he may choose a digital form for quick access and easy tabulations. Finally, this particular checklist can double as an instrument for student reflection or for team processing, putting the students into the powerful role of being responsible, honest, and (self) observant.

This is a bit of a wild, fascinating, and potentially powerful teamed learning experience for these youngsters.

Questions for Analysis

As you read through the following high school lesson, try to picture it actually happening (or envision it unfolding as a movie does). Please record your perceptions of the student–student interactions and try to visualize the teacher operating during these times.

1. Which affective skills is the teacher seeking to teach during the student–student interactions? Will the teacher have accumulated sufficient evidence upon which to make assessments and create useful feedback interventions?

2. This teacher has many steps in the lesson and has created interesting questions. Is this level of complexity for planning a lot to ask of busy teachers? Does it have too much detail, locking the teacher into following a script-like path? Do you think it is likely that this teacher will shorten or cut out the student interactions to make the lesson fit the given timeframe?

3. While we are more concerned with affective skill development, the schools rightfully worry about students actually learning history! Is there enough history learning in this plan or has the balance toward non-cognitive skills gone too far?

CASE: Ellen Johnston, Womanhood, and the Industrial Revolution

This is lesson #2 in a six-day unit in 10th-grade social studies—75 minutes in length.

Central focus of learning segment: Personal, cultural and economic changes sparked by the Industrial Revolution

Objectives/Learning targets:

Cognitive:

1. Students will be able to explain Johnston's life decisions in terms of the environment she faced.
2. Students will be able to interpret (with textual evidence) at least one passage from Johnston's poetry.
3. Students will be able to compare work options for females in the U.K. during the 1850s with those in the U.S. today.

Affective:

1. Students will listen to other people's interpretations with empathy and understanding.
2. Students will strive for accuracy in their work.

Standards: Determined locally.

Opening:

1. The teacher says "Hello," then points to objectives on the board and to the word wall.
2. The teacher reads a passage (below) as students read along. At the end of the reading, students will identify at least three sections worth discussing with others:

> The Thames flows by our open window, its purple sludge heaving . . . bouncing . . . one can actually see refuse as it floats atop the thick fluid. Worse, we could smell the river before we could see it: I cannot imagine washing in it, let alone cooking or drinking it. I will be in this framed building until the blistering sun sets at 9:00, again tonight . . . working, sweating and making money for Smith. At least I get something for my effort, unlike Charles whose broken leg means his family starves: He has been replaced by Robert, who at 12 will not know how to make pace. I do not hate my machine . . . which sits like a monster waiting for me to feed it and make it produce for the master. I cannot be idle any longer. I will record my thoughts and bitterness again later.
>
> Anonymous, 1857, London

3. Students will pair up and explain their reasons for their selections. After a minute or two, they will be asked to choose one of their choices and draw it visually on the paper provided.
4. Pairs will briefly share their drawings with another pair, again exchanging reasons; the teacher circulates, generally without comment.

Exploratory Phase (Step 1)

1. The teacher hands out three visuals related to the Industrial Revolution (not attached). The visual about farm life is quite graphic, involving an equipment accident. Students are asked to work in pairs to identify and discuss the implications of what they see in the visuals.
2. In debriefing, the teacher raises these questions:

   a. What was life like during the Industrial Revolution in the U.K.?
   b. Picture #2 represents Ellen Johnston, who we are about to study. What do you see there? What are you expecting when you read about her and from her? Females worked then—so what?
   c. How is farm life different than industrial life? How does industrial life in the 1850s compare to ours now?
   d. Why did conditions in the town and at work seem harsh? What did unions and the government do about these conditions?

Discovery Phase (Step 2)

1. Students work in pairs, reading the second and much longer passage (not attached, but can be found in Strayer & Nelson, 2016, in a section called "Zooming In," pp. 752–753). As students read and talk, they are seeking to make meaning and identify insights worth sharing. They are given about seven minutes to begin this task.
2. As part of that reading, student thinking will be aligned around the three cognitive objectives, which are now portrayed as questions to be answered by the pair, in writing. This will extend this section of class to about 16 minutes.
3. The teacher reminds students that they will be assessed on their two affective objectives and that while they read and work, he will be "working the room" and giving feedback. (He does this for the full 16 minutes.)
4. Class is stopped with 18 minutes to go. The teacher says, "This was a hard life for a girl back then, although she had time to write poetry. Do you agree (*pause*), Jill?" Jill responds with evidence, and the teacher asks Karl if he agrees. Then, three more students are randomly selected to offer their ideas about the various prompts. After each student offering, the teacher briefly probes for the evidence for the insight and then asks the students how their comments connect to what has already been said.
5. The teacher points to the document camera projection at the front of the room. Names on the board reveal new student pairings. Students are asked to match up accordingly and share their insights to the three cognitive objectives. The teacher then announces the individual quiz to be completed by end of class. When the bell rings, the teacher says, "Drop off today's notes—they count for a grade. I will return your quizzes next class. Please thank your partners and I thank you as well for your effort. Bring your phones tomorrow!"

Assessment—Quiz

Please answer these two questions as well as you can in the time allowed:

1. Briefly describe one change in life patterns for teenage females in London at the time of the Industrial Revolution.
2. You worked with several different partners during class today. Describe one time when you listened carefully to what s/he said. Be specific.

Accommodations, Modifications, and Adjustments

There is one IEP, a girl with ODD, who has a temper problem; her regular partner is a dear friend who helps her with self-regulation efforts, and when they work in larger groups they stay together. There is a student who lost his father in an industrial accident a few years ago, but he knows the content of the lesson, has seen the visuals, and wants to participate.

Next Class

1. Review what was written today in large group discussion and examine the feedback from the individual quiz.
2. More fully explore the real Ellen Johnston (using pairs of pairs). This will take the form of research and will utilize technological resources.
3. The new objective will be to validate how well the fictitious passage from Anonymous read today compares to actual primary source documents that do exist.
4. The students will be collaboratively writing the answers to these five questions and turning them in for the daily grade:

   a. Describe (using illustrations) the working conditions in a factory or mill in the U.K. during the 1850s.
   b. Create a more detailed (albeit fictional) diary entry of one part of Ellen Johnston's life.
   c. Invent a slogan to be used by the factory owner to inspire workers to more effort.
   d. Explain how working in an office today compares to working in a mill during the Industrial Revolution.
   e. Assume the role of the teacher, and explain which parts of these lessons he enjoys teaching.

Be honest with yourself and your teammates and assess your own thinking about this topic the past two days.

Our Take

◆ Among the most noteworthy aspects of this lesson plan is the fact that the teacher has many activities, with many opportunities to demonstrate 21st- century competencies, and has planned two different ways to assess the affective component. We note that the teacher has a checklist in hand and is keeping some written notes on each student. These will be shared on the following day and the individuals will be asked to respond in writing. Finally, we also are pleased that part of the next class will be a large discussion about both the content involved and the quality of student interactions.

◆ This teacher is utilizing technology, implementing Cooperative Learning, and tasking students to read for meaning. These provide a lot of avenues to success and the lesson offers a variety of ways to create deep understanding. Add in the explicit affective component and you have a 75-minute lesson that helps teens develop in many skill areas and across many varied contexts.

- We are not sure about the many "changing partners" component of the paired and teamed work. Generally, students need to work for extended periods across many challenges to develop trust and comfort in the team setting. We'd suggest that if the teacher likes the "mix and match 'em" approach, he should temper it with several units in which students work in stable, heterogeneous teams for an extended period of time.

- One danger in the CL approach is the concept of the "free rider," a student who just hangs with his or her team and never contributes. Generally, this practice works well for disengaged teens unless measures are taken to eliminate it as an option. This "free-rider" phenomenon is most common in settings where the teacher relies heavily on group grades, which, unfortunately, is common with novice users of CL. The Dual Objective stresses individual responsibility and accountability.

- We applaud this lesson for its attempt to develop a whole-class sense of community. (This may be why the teacher uses the "mix and match" tactic.) There is no senseless competition; positive interdependence is promoted by making students aware of each other and by requiring listening. There is no wasted time.

- The only other thing we would want to talk about with this teacher is his or her specific plans while "working the room." Lesson planning often does not ask the teacher to specify the plans for this rather large component of the day but relies on the wisdom of spontaneous interventions, which can be dangerously akin to the randomness of the "teachable moments" approach. Fortunately, this teacher has the five objectives guiding student work; they should focus his or her thinking, observing, and feedback.

In Closing

We wish we had a nickel for every time we have heard the complaint that "the teacher is just watching *not* teaching when kids are in groups." Believe us, the effective teacher is working very hard when students are doing their CL group work and is making hundreds of decisions every day. When students work in groups, the teacher analyzes, assesses, records, and intervenes on both affective and cognitive developments; he or she then observes and judges the impact of the interventions he or she implements. This is highly skilled work and gets better with multiple reflective experiences and with an attitude of persistence and deliberate/purposeful practice.

The interventions during group work are hugely important factors in effective instruction, and as we said earlier, we should be "systematic and intentional" in our efforts. When John Hattie (2012) says that feedback is most important to the teacher, this is the very point that he is suggesting. The group work itself is audible and visible data that gives teachers clear insight into the ideas and actions of their secondary students and becomes the data guiding teacher intervention. What students say and do *matters* in the Dual Objective.

In short: Working the room to reinforce the focus on both cognitive and affective objectives is the key to successful use of the Dual Objective.

Chapter 5 Big Ideas

1. While many teachers claim that they love those famous "teachable moments" when a spontaneous class discussion gets into important, relevant, confusing and fascinating topics that touch the students and their everyday lives, the use of the Dual Objective Model creates those opportunities in a way that is planned and anticipated.

2. The use of the Dual Objective Model takes the teacher from "well-meaning and intuitive to systematic and intentional," regarding students' affective growth. The teacher must be explicit about the affective skill(s) being used and clear in his or her feedback; most schools do not have a systematic framework.

3. The approach called Habits of Mind (Costa & Kallick, 2008, p. 14) provides an exemplary taxonomy of affective competencies that could be easily integrated into the Dual Objective Model.

4. As teachers "work the room" during group work, they must listen, assess, and decide on the content and timing of their interventions with each group. This feedback system for both affect and cognition is the essence of the Dual Objective.

5. Among the questions that teachers will be reflecting on as they "work the room" are the following: (a) Are the interactions and contributions of each member effective? (b) What does this student (or this group) need right now and/or in the future? (c) How productive is the environment within the team?

6. During group work, the teacher is in the perfect position to reinforce meta-cognitive and self-assessing student efforts. The actions involved in collaborating allow the teacher the chance to observe affective behavior both audibly and visibly for analysis and feedback.

7. Students must assess the team effectiveness regularly; this leads to goal formation and developing a realistic sense of self.
8. Teachers using the Dual Objective are in a very complex and stimulating environment most of the time; it is highly skilled instruction. Dealing with the many simultaneous interactions becomes a highly developed skill with extended and thoughtful experience.
9. "Working through" cases and sample situations helps clarify human thinking and decision-making as well as offering options and alternatives to existing behaviors.

References

Costa, A., & Kallick, B. (2008). *Habits of mind across the curriculum*. Alexandria, VA: ASCD.

Duckworth, A.L., & Yaeger, D.S. (2015). Measurement matters: Assessing personal qualities other than cognitive abilities for educational purposes. *Educational Researcher, 44*, 237–251.

Duhigg, C. (2014). *The power of habit: Why we do what we do in life and business*. New York, NY: Random House.

Dweck, C. (2006). *Mindset: The new psychology of success*. New York, NY: Random House.

Ericsson, A., & Pool, R. (2016). *Peak: Secrets from the new science of expertise*. New York, NY: Houghton-Mifflin Harcourt.

Farrington, C.A., Roderick, E., Nagaoka, J., Keyes, T.S., Johnson, D.W., and Beechum, N. (2012). *Teaching adolescents to become learners: The role of non-cognitive factors in shaping school performance*. Chicago, IL: Consortium on Chicago School Research.

Flynn, P., Mesibov, D., Vermette, P., & Smith, R.M. (2004). *Applying standards-based constructivism: A two-step guide for motivating middle and high school students*. Larchmont, NY: Eye-on-Education.

Hattie, J. (2012). *Visible learning for teachers: Maximizing impact on learning*. New York, NY: Routledge.

Konkoski-Bates, E., & Vermette, P. (2004). *Working the room: The key to cooperative learning success*. Presented at the Great Lakes Association for Cooperation in Education, Toronto, Ontario.

Strayer, R.W., & Nelson, W.W. (2016). *Ways of the world: A global history with sources* (3rd ed.). Boston, MA: Bedford/St. Martin's

Tough, P. (2012). *How children succeed: Grit, curiosity and the hidden power of character*. Boston, MA: Houghton-Mifflin.

6

How Does the Dual Objective Align to the World of Reform?

Connections and Commitments

Charles Dickens' famous dictum, "It was the best of times, it was the worst of times" certainly holds true for the current educational landscape (at the time of this writing). Society is divided on a host of issues and education is at the center of many social and economic analyses. A quick look at the previous week's newspapers might reveal stories on the Educational Reform Movement, low PISA scores, the opt-out (of standardized tests) movement, the Common Core, the creation of new charter schools, merit pay for teachers, new student-centered approaches to learning, the end of local control, "flipping" science teaching, the rise of MOOCs and on-line courses, the impact of income inequality on achievement and/or the need for high school courses on financial literacy or code-writing or second language. Any way you cut it, **education** is a very controversial and timely topic today, and will be tomorrow as well.

Given this context of deeply focused attention and a polarized population, it might be surprising to hear us say the following: "If the question is about an instructional problem, at least a part of the solution lies with the well-structured use of Cooperative Learning!" As we have pointed out in the previous chapters, the Dual Objective Model of CL has enormous power to systematically bridge differences, help individuals persist and practice new concepts, solve problems, and communicate effectively, promote healthy notions of self, and to develop skills needed for an unknown and rapidly changing future. In this chapter, we wish to take a small set of concerns or movements in education and demonstrate how the Dual Objective aligns with each one.

Globalization and the Common Core

During this generation, has any one word conjured up more meanings than "globalization"? In truth, the concept suffers from "too many cooks in the kitchen," but educators must recognize several internationally flavored factors that affect the next generation far more than previous ones. Let's agree for a moment that despite varying definitions and political maneuvering, globalization is really happening and it consists of the following factors:

- ◆ Closer interconnections are being made between nations on issues of commerce, trade, and business.
- ◆ Education is expected to bridge international gaps in understandings, language, and communication.
- ◆ Technology has shrunk the space between individuals and between institutions and organizations.
- ◆ Diversity is now perceived as a more natural and accepted part of the fabric of human social interaction and its impact is growing.

If we do agree on the rise of these four factors, then education must change, but perhaps not in the way that the Common Core Learning Standards (CCLS) suggest. CCLS is essentially a curriculum that promotes the teaching of powerful cognitive *skills*, including such things as using knowledge to form an argument, reading for meaning and comprehension, and assessing author text-based evidence. These are the thinking skills needed by really smart people in white-collar jobs, but they alone are not enough. Job and career success is predicated on the social and emotional skills developed by the use of the Dual Objective but are generally ignored in the Common Core intellectual context. From hotel maid to secretary of state, people benefit if they can see the global context of their job (and pay scale), communicate with people from non-local communities, utilize technology to advance their perspective or gain depth of understanding, and join forces with people who are demographically or attitudinally different from themselves.

Traditionally structured education lacks the experiential base that puts globalized learning in a relevant, personal, real, and individualized context. Reading about or studying people who are from "somewhere else" is different than chatting with them on-line or in a face-to-face team. Discovering similarities and differences in daily habits is often a noteworthy occasion for people working together: it is far more powerful than seeing it happen in a movie or on TV. Creating and performing a skit with school associates creates deeper processing and more emotional investment than does being part of a large-group, class-wide discussion on a canonical piece of literature. As the Earth flattens and shrinks, we will discover that we are far more all in this together than at any previous time in history. Communicative technology will not roll back nor disappear, immigration will not end (nor will refugees cease to exist), transportation avenues will not evaporate, and economics will not become more parochial any time soon. Education must be for the present lived reality and the future anticipated, not for a past that has expired.

The clothes we wear, the food we eat, the news and stories we digest, the tendencies we note, the prices we pay, the sports, movies, and celebrities we crave to know, and the choices we realistically face in our lives, are all *heavily* shaped by international, globalized forces. Young people will be far better prepared for these opportunities and challenges if they have developed a global, diverse, and complex attitude and accompanying skills set, one that has been experienced in their own learning activities and responsibilities in secondary school.

P21 Partnership for 21st Century Learning

P21 is an internationally recognized collaborative that sees its goal as preparing youngsters for the challenges that they will face in life and work in the 21st century. Their articulation is as follows:

> The Partnership for 21st Century Learning recognizes that all learners need educational experiences in school and beyond, from cradle to career, to build knowledge and skills for success in a globally and digitally interconnected world. P21 unites business, government and education leaders from the US and abroad to advance evidence-based education policy and practice and to make innovative teaching and learning a reality for all.

These challenges are remarkably similar to those highlighted above in the section on globalization. Moreover, having read that section, the reader knows that we have made the case for the development of adolescents' skills *beside*, and *in conjunction* with, Common Core-type academic abilities. As part of their 21st Century Framework, P21 chooses to call these affective competencies "learning and innovation skills" and "life and career" skills, in keeping with their mission. This is a phrasing that we particularly like and promote;

the skills are not *just* for career and college, they are also for citizenship and for living a productive life.

As part of their 21st Century Framework, P21 says that preparing youth for their futures involves a concern for the following demands that they will face:

◆ adapting to change;
◆ being flexible;
◆ managing goals and time;
◆ working independently;
◆ becoming self-directed;
◆ interacting effectively with others;
◆ working effectively in diverse teams;
◆ managing projects;
◆ producing results;
◆ guiding and leading others;
◆ being responsible to others.

To deconstruct the P21 vision for the daily work of a modern secondary teacher, here is a brief sampling of their student learning objectives/outcomes that can be met through judicious use of the Dual Objective Model of CL on a regular basis and across subjects (see Appendix 1 for the complete listing):

1. Work effectively in a climate of ambiguity and changing priorities.
2. Understand, negotiate, and balance diverse views and beliefs to reach workable solutions.
3. Monitor a task without direct oversight.
4. Know when it is appropriate to *listen* and when to *speak*.
5. Respect cultural differences.
6. Leverage social differences to create new ideas, increase innovation and quality of work.
7. Respond open-mindedly to different ideas and values.
8. Incorporate feedback effectively.
9. Reflect critically on past experiences (to inform future progress).
10. Adapt to varied roles and contexts.

In all honesty, we think that each of these ten objectives are directly linked to the well-planned operation of the Dual Objective Model of CL. Can you see them in the examples below?

TASK: P21 and Affective Behaviors during CL

Each of the exemplars below demonstrates positive affective behaviors while working in cooperative groups. Can you match the situation to its respective P21 outcome (affective goal) from above? (We think the linkages should be very clear; however the answers are offered beneath.)

_____ Because they use Jigsaw in Global History, 10th-grader Jose's job is to research and report to his team about the religious practices in Columbia. Other teammates are studying different aspects of the nation and the members trust each other to do a thorough job on their individual parts.

_____ The science teacher, Mr. Stratton, reminded the group that they were not enticing contributions from all members of their 6th-grade team. After he left the group, both Tom and Josh verbally suggested that they should try to do what was suggested; the others agreed.

_____ In the project on capital punishment, 11th-grader Marcia is often the lone "pro" voice heard. However, the others are willing to listen to her and are seeking a middle ground between polarized positions.

_____ The first day that his new team was asked to work together, 9th-grader Seth was stunned that he was placed with Mohammed, Avril, and Lisa. His first thought was, "Oh no! Three immigrants and two girls with scarves!" Today he laughs about it and recalls when Lisa told him that her first thought was, "Please . . . not the Jewish guy!" Three weeks later, they see similarities that unify and differences that enhance.

_____ Usama loved being the team leader for the first two days on the project in biology class. Now, on day three, Tunoush wanted to have him become "recorder" and shift the responsibilities of all four members to new roles. Realizing that these changes would create useful and productive experiences for everyone, he agreed, and the others followed suit. (This action made him proud of his leadership.)

_____ In his base group, Tony is often unsure of where his team is going during a project on child labor, but trusts that they will discuss their options and include everyone in the decisions being made.

_____ Before they shared their essays about how the team worked, Bika wrote about how she had felt slighted by the others; she felt that she was often ignored and not appreciated but she worried that the other 11th-graders would respond poorly and make the situation even worse if she said anything. However, she also realized that she had _not_ been very assertive about being heard and decided to offer ideas about her own role and her expectations from others when they did group processing.

———— Monica always wants to get her love of rap music into any project that her 6th-grade class is asked to do. Today, her partners include a violinist, a baseball player, and a dog lover and they have found a way to integrate all these passions into their short video for art class.

———— After he found that the first attempt at working through the sample exercises in AP Literature was a bit clumsy, Harold is conscious of his timing about when to contribute new ideas and when to actively listen to his teammates' ideas. (Listening carefully is relatively new to him: he was used to using that non-speaking time to create his own responses and rejoinders.)

———— Slowing down to overcome her initial doubt, Amber began to think that Ti's ideas about softening the tone of characters' language in the play about 9/11 that they were writing was a wise idea.

Answers: 3, 8, 2, 5, 10, 1, 9, 6, 4, 7

As we leave this section on the connection between the Dual Objective and the P21 Framework, we wish to make a suggestion. Students should often be reminded of why they are taking the courses they are taking, why they are completing the tasks they are assigned, *and* why the teacher is using CL. Sharing the P21 Framework with them would show the rationale behind a teacher's decision-making. Furthermore, showing students the P21 bulleted "demands" of adult life could help them serve as learning targets, behaviors, and attitudes that are linked to their future success. Finally, having students explain how each bullet is linked to the ten classroom examples may prove to be a powerful learning activity that could allow students to debate, discuss, analyze, and reflect on the expectations that they are facing in class today and in the world tomorrow.

Problem-Based Learning and Project-Based Learning

Note: This next section was originally drafted by two associates, a pair of superb new teachers, Ms. Emily Kaufman and Ms. Kimberly Alexander. They showed a deep interest in the relationship between problem-based and project-based systems, and the connections of each to the Dual Objective Model of Cooperative Learning. Moreover, their expectations are that secondary teaching is in the midst of a transition that will "force" the profession into more student-centered and inquiry-based investigations before they reach tenure.

Problem-Based Learning

Problem-based learning (PBL) is a student-centered pedagogical approach that facilitates the acquisition and long-term retention of knowledge by challenging students to determine viable solutions to real-world problems through self-directed and collaborative learning. As its name suggests, the *problem* in a problem-based learning task structures and focuses the learning experience. This method was first used in medical preparation programs in the 1960s and has steadily gained popularity. Responding to the concern that medical students were ill-prepared to adequately perform in the clinical environment because their preparation had called upon rote and decontextualized memorization of biological knowledge, medical schools began to renounce their traditionally lecture-centered programs in favor of a problem-based learning curriculum. Since then, various fields (including education at various levels) have adopted problem-based learning approaches. Today, many high-school programs have begun to look to PBL for alternatives to traditional teaching.

In practice, problem-based learning "is initiated by an authentic, ill-structured problem" (Hung, Jonassen, & Liu, 2008). In collaborative groups, students first interpret the teacher-provided scenario to determine the problem's source and brainstorm what is collectively known at the outset of the task. The problems that teachers design must be appropriately "messy" so that students cannot immediately offer a viable solution based on background knowledge alone. In their teams or base groups, students decide what they need to learn, where they might find the necessary information, and how research will be conducted. As part of the self-directed learning that is characteristic of the PBL method, students individually find, evaluate, and use sources to gather information that the group will use to propose a solution. Working cooperatively, students are expected to communicate their findings effectively, listen openly to their peers' remarks, and make group decisions. At the end of the task, students present their solutions, consider feedback, and participate in a teacher-led, full-class debriefing to reinforce and accommodate new knowledge.

Consider the following characteristics of PBL, which have made it a suitable alternative to traditional educational methods:

◆ *Learning is structured around a problem that provides a context and purpose for the learning experience.* During PBL, learning begins with a problem that focuses student thinking. For effective PBL tasks, many acceptable solutions to the problem must exist such that originality and critical thinking become hallmarks of the learning experience. Of course, the problem that students encounter must also be relevant and meaningful for the students. When students are excited about or intrigued by the problem, they become stakeholders in the process of finding a solution, thus facilitating lasting motivation and engagement.

◆ *Learning is student-centered. The students are seen as researchers while the teacher takes on the role of tutor.* What makes PBL such a distinct (and challenging) instructional method is how it redefines the roles of teacher and students. Unlike more traditional approaches, in PBL, students are the agents of knowledge production while the teacher serves as a resource, tutor, and model (Stepien & Gallagher, 1993). Teacher responsibilities include planning the learning task and designing the problem scenario, offering immediate feedback to student groups, and providing any necessary scaffolds students might need to complete the task. Teachers also model expected behaviors and effective questioning techniques that will help drive student research.

◆ *The learning task emphasizes knowledge acquisition and skill development through the process of inquiry.* The goals of PBL are threefold: students acquire content knowledge, develop skills related to effective inquiry, and when PBL is part of a collaborative environment, improve social-emotional and communication skills. By considering multiple perspectives from their peers, finding and evaluating source materials, and synthesizing information from multiple disciplines, students democratically craft rich solutions to complex problems.

◆ *Student learning is self-directed and self-regulated.* One of the benefits of PBL is that students become active learners. Because of the agency that PBL affords, students take ownership of their learning in ways that deviate substantially from traditional teacher-centered models of education.

◆ *Individual research conducted by each student informs group decision-making.* Students are expected to make individual and group decisions throughout the problem-solving process. Students are therefore held accountable, individually and collectively, for their efforts. At the end of the learning experience, students reflect on the group's performance and their own contributions by evaluating content-based decisions (i.e. the strengths and weaknesses of the proposed solution) as well how well the group worked together to make those decisions.

Project-Based Learning

Project-based learning is often confused with problem-based learning. Though both approaches stem from developments in cognitive psychology (specifically the science of learning), the two methods are not as similar as their shared acronym may suggest. Project-based learning is a teaching method that engages students in applying knowledge in real-world activities that emulate the kinds of problems and situations with which experts engage. While the focus of problem-based learning is the *problem* that structures the learning experience, in project-based learning, the focus is on the *project* that students create and which is often made public. Like problem-based learning, project-based learning involves a guiding question that serves as a prompt for student projects. Students work in collaborative groups to create a product that responds to or explores the guiding question. Therefore, in contrast to problem-based learning, project-based learning is product-driven and focused on outcomes. Students are expected to *apply* their new knowledge in novel ways as part of a "learn by doing" experience.

It is probably not surprising that project-based learning developed in response to an apparent lack of student engagement and has flourished during the rise of constructivism. The primary goal, then, is to motivate and engage students in their learning. When implemented strategically, both problem-based and project-based learning have the potential to provide meaningful contexts for learning and engage students, increase knowledge retention, facilitate deeper conceptual understanding, and encourage the transfer of knowledge to new situations.

A crucial difference, however, is the role of the teacher. In project-based learning, teachers provide more direction, acting as instructors or guides who offer suggestions for creating better products. Teachers also coordinate the involvement of outside entities and experts. Learning occurs during the process of creating this product and can last for a sustained period.

PBL Connections and Comparisons

To clarify, while problem-based learning has a greater focus on knowledge acquisition through the process of inquiry, project-based learning emphasizes the application of knowledge through the creation of meaningful projects. It's worth noting, however, that both approaches can be used together. A model, designed by Barron et al. (1998), shows how a unit of study can shift focus from problem-based learning to project-based learning, although there are certainly many ways that the two can be integrated.

Although problem-based learning and project-based learning should be viewed as two distinct pedagogical approaches, both forms of PBL are closely aligned with CL, and specifically, the Dual Objective Model of CL. Recall that the Dual Objective involves the inclusion of dual educational objectives incorporating both content knowledge and non-academic skills. Any PBL assignment by its collaborative structure, naturally requires (and affords practice of) non-academic skills into the content-specific problem or project, and is therefore aligned with the Dual Objective. In particular, there are three main ways either form of PBL is connected to these types of non-academic skills: (1) Both forms of PBL *promote students' social and emotional learning*, as each is conducted in Cooperative Learning groups. If created properly, these groups should be diverse and students should be expected to hone a potential myriad of collaborative skills. (2) Both forms of PBL are expected to be connected to real-world problems and applications, which means that students will *strengthen their 21st-century skills*, both as they research the problem/project and as they develop realistic solutions. (3) Both forms of PBL are meant to challenge students to synthesize new, often interdisciplinary, information. As such, both PBL processes are in-depth studies that ultimately serve as a test of *persistence, flexibility, adaptability, project-management skills (and a myriad of others)*, promoting both determination and the *growth mindset* in students.

What do problem-based learning and project-based learning tasks look like in the classroom? We encourage you to work through this next task to get a glimpse.

TASK: Identifying Affective Skills Within PBL

Following are a number of problem-based and project-based classroom scenarios. As you read each, consider either the P21 student outcomes or the Habits of Mind that could be at play. Remember, as these are PBL, there are vast possibilities, limited only by your perspective. We have provided one possibility after each.

◆ 12th-Grade physics: Problem-based learning. The teacher asks the students what factors affect the period of a pendulum. Students work their way through an inquiry-based laboratory to design their own experiments to determine an answer to the question. Each group selects its own variables to test and then conducts an experiment to determine which variables affect the period of the pendulum. (Thinking interdependently.)

◆ 9th-Grade English: Problem-based learning. Students are reading Harper Lee's *To kill a mockingbird*. Before reading the verdict of the trial scene, students are asked to predict whether Tom Robinson, a black man accused of raping a white woman, will be convicted of the crime brought against him. Working in groups, students will consider what they know about the characters, setting, and plot thus far and conduct additional research related to the time period; the societal prejudices against black men, the fear of miscegenation, and the probabilities of conviction based on historical precedent, to offer a viable prediction. Student groups prepare to defend their predictions and engage in a full-class debate before reading on. (Listening with empathy and understanding.)

◆ 8th-Grade social studies: Problem-based learning. Students are asked to determine similarities and differences between the current presidential election and previous significant election years by comparing economic policies, social justice issues, international relations, and the public's perception of government. Each group is assigned an important election year and must research this election as well as the current one to determine any similarities and differences. Students are expected to use this information to make logical predictions about possible impacts to the current election. (Persistence.)

◆ 9th-Grade biology: Project-based learning. Students are working in cooperative learning groups that were assigned based on the results of a learning style quiz such that each group has an auditory, tactile, and visual learner present. Groups are tasked with designing a genetically modified species that will benefit the human species in some way. They are required to present their findings to the class at the end of the unit in any format that they choose. Their presentation must consider the possible genetic engineering methods that could be used to create this new species as well as a cost-benefit analysis of the benefits and risks of such a project. (Creating, imagining, and innovating.)

◆ 10th-Grade mathematics: Project-based learning. Working in their CL groups, students are asked to create a design for a defined green space on campus. They must determine the appropriate dimensions of all components of their design as well as the cost of materials needed. Students have five weeks to complete the project, during which time they will also be learning about geometric calculations such as area and volume. They are required to present their proposals to the class at the end of the five-week study as if they were presenting their plans to a local developer. (Striving for accuracy.)

Finally, please note that as presently construed, each of the preceding vignettes includes well-structured CL, and is rigorous, challenging, and demands complex student conversation and thought. Traditionally, both forms of PBL have not been very attentive to formally recognizing the affective skills essential to making these models work (Davidson and Major, 2014) but they could be made to do so. As you can see, we have easily matched an affective objective which is directly aligned to the work being done in each of the classes. These skills represent crucial variables impacting the quality of both the group interactions (process) as well as the quality of the tangible (products). Adopting the Dual Objective Model with PBL delivers this structural missing link, providing systematic and intentional support for the important affective skills that enable completion of these more complex tasks.

Culturally Relevant Teaching

In a great book by Gloria Ladson-Billings (2009 [1994]) called *Dreamkeepers*, the author described her three-year investigation into what makes some teachers highly effective in a situation that the majority of others have failed at: reaching and teaching inner-city students from under-represented groups (in this case, African Americans). What resulted was an approach to teaching that she named Culturally Relevant Teaching (CRT). Culturally Relevant Teaching is a term that has undergone modifications over time, but its basic tenets have remained the same for 20 years and it is now a highly respected approach to quality schooling.

Ladson-Billing's conception of CRT includes several key factors that are clearly linked to the Dual Objective:

◆ *Sense of community.* The feeling within the classroom (often called class climate) is collaborative, friendly, and safe, and the environment is laden with a sense of community. Students work as teams and as a "family"; competition, a simple fixed hierarchal status structure, and inequality are downplayed (or non-existent), while cooperation, a complex fluid status structure, and equity are fostered. Central to the development of community is the notion that students must assist, help, and nurture each other, and that everyone's individual success is predicated upon the success of everyone else's contributions. (This is Johnson and Johnson's notion of positive interdependence at work.) Moreover, Tough (2016), building on Farrington et al. (2012), suggests that we cannot over-emphasize the importance of a student feeling that she or he belongs in a particular academic community at any specific point in time.

◆ *Knowledge is continuously recreated, recycled, and shared.* Contrary to a positivist view of knowledge as a static entity (to be transmitted as such), CRT recognizes the truth of the constructivist notion of knowledge as internal and unique to the individual (and that each person has to learn/create her own version of it). Discussions, interpretations, mental representations, and meanings are all tentative and worthy of examination by groups of students working together. In the well-structured Dual Objective classroom, these meanings extend to the affective domain as well and students are encouraged to reconsider their decisions, their insights, their beliefs, their interaction patterns, and their past experiences in light of new ideas or considerations.

◆ *The teacher helps students make connections amongst their various identities.* Despite efforts by some educators to promote an academic or objective stance to ideas; anything that engages students to think deeply has emotional aspects. Teachers want students to feel engaged (maybe even in "flow") in the entire educational enterprise and *not* just offer a superficial, cognitively based attempt to reply or participate. Thus, encouraging students to think about the social contexts of school content, as desired by CRT, calls for respectful interaction and a student–student commitment to listening to each other. Moreover, this third CRT factor urges educators to seek issues of local interest and/or personal involvement as a springboard for deep and meaningful learning experiences.

CRT and the Dual Objective in Practice

Interestingly, much that has been written about applying CRT has not explicitly recognized the central role that student–student connections and collaborations play in its success, as the emphases have been more often on student–teacher relationships. Let's take a look at two scenarios that show how the CRT approach benefits from conscious use of the Dual Objective.

CASE: Middle School Math in an Urban District

During the bell-work for today's lesson, Mr. Bagda gives his students a set of three problems to solve using their prior knowledge. Here is problem #2:

> Jose, 17, is trying to decide whether to buy a weekly bus pass that costs $16.00 or simply to pay the one-trip fare of $1.50 every time he travels. Which is the better deal?

At the close of the "solving time," Mr. Bagda announces, "If the bus costs $1.50 each way to school, then 10 trips a week costs $15.00, which is less than the weekly rate of $16.00, and therefore . . ." But immediately hands go up all over the room, students are shouting out ideas, and a bit of chaos falls upon the usual math boredom. This was not perceived by class as a simple "math problem to solve"; rather, it was a *cultural question*. What questions might the students have (which should be acknowledged) *before* they can solve it?

Our Take

- We anticipate some of the following questions may arise: (a) Does Jose use the bus for school? (b) Does Jose use the bus for work, and how many work trips does he usually make? (c) Does Jose ever go anywhere by bus on weekends? (d) Is the weekly pass "transferable?" (e) How does he pay for and receive a weekly pass? (f) If he buys a weekly pass and doesn't use up all the money, can he use it the next week? (g) What are his friends choosing to do? (h) How come the bus costs so much when Jose is not making very much money at his job? There are many more.

◆ Now, if Mr. Bagda is paying attention to his students, he is ready for these questions and, in the spirit of CRT and "ambitious math teaching" (Lampert, 2001), he will spend time handling these ideas as he moves his students toward the "rational" choice of the two alternatives offered.

◆ Despite the Common Core's intention to make everyone automatically academic, much of education (as this problem shows) cannot be divorced from the reality of the individuals and groups being taught and their prior emotional experiences. However, Mr. Bagda could have chosen to let the students work in small groups (think–pair–share: Lyman, 1981) before he opened up the large-group discussion. Doing so would have flushed out all of the mentioned questions (and many more); empowered students to speak their minds and take ownership of the problem; allowed students to practice their listening and conversational skills; and to explicitly grasp the social context of the item. Having them work in groups first would have also provided feedback for some of the computation aspects of this math problem.

◆ In general, sharing in small groups *before* large-group conversation is a very good idea. When both cognitive and affective goals are in play, it is almost a mandate. As promoted by Vygotskian theory, true dialogue helps both parties, and in the classroom context prepares them for the large-group exchanges.

CASE: High School U.S. History in a Suburban District

The class is engaged in a large-group discussion about securing the vote for different groups throughout history. A large chart is on the board: The columns are labeled "Group," "Year," and "Reason," and the teacher is about to call on individuals to pull data from their homework assignment to complete the chart.

As this process develops, a quiet student in the back raises his hand and asks, "Why didn't we start with *why* people were originally *excluded*, not when they were *included*? Oh, and my cousin, Liam, is a felon, and he'll never be allowed to vote. Where does he go on this chart?" Many of the class members scowled and grunted at these comments and were clearly negative about them; moreover, the teacher ignored the whole thing and continued. What could the teacher have done differently if a proponent of CRT? Should he have anticipated this question?

Our Take

◆ This is an interesting scenario: It shows that certain comments, questions, and insights are not welcomed by class members and that rudeness to the speaker was an acceptable response in the face of a potential controversy. Both of these violate the tenets of the Dual Objective and CRT. Students are expected to provide ideas, insights, and challenges, and be able to have them treated as legitimate inquiries.

◆ The teacher could have anticipated the situation and had them work in small groups first, as suggested in the last case. He also could have used the response by the crowd as a discussion point about decision-making, individual freedoms, and democracy at a particular point in time. Clearly, he didn't expect the comments to be made as the chart was being completed and his lack of preparation combined with the whole-class structure created this tenuous situation.

◆ In both of these scenarios, the teacher's vision of whole-class teaching that is focused on specific cognitive outcomes limited the opportunities to make the educational process more meaningful and interesting and devalued the insights and experiences of students. Both of these classes would have developed differently if the teacher saw the Dual Objective as the desired structure of the classroom environment.

New York State Teaching Standards and Danielson's Framework for Teaching

In the modern world, the word "standards" invokes all kinds of emotions and thoughts in the minds of different people. In fact, the authors tend to believe that it is one of the most misconstrued academic terms used today across various social and political contexts.

Put aside for a moment any thoughts *you* might have about the word "standards" that conjure up the universe of standardized testing, Common Core, etc., and instead let the image of standards as "goal statements" float across your mind. Also, let us clarify between "learning standards" that drive curricula vs. "teaching standards" that drive pedagogy and professional practice. (The two are often confused outside of academia.) Herein we wish to present the latter, goal statements for good teaching.

New York State Teaching Standards

In this section, we wish to show you a sampling of what we think is a collection of teaching expectations that is the finest ever produced by a governmental agency or a ministry of education. These are called the New York State Teaching Standards (2011) and they are great for many reasons. In short, they spell out a vision of good teaching that is research based, within the capabilities of all competent teachers, reasonable, (largely) observable and measureable. The set is comprised of seven broad standard areas broken into 39 elements. These 39 elements have been further delineated into well over 100 performance indicators; it is at this level, the level of the performance indicator, that the document becomes most helpful.

We wish to provide you a sample of these indicators (a.k.a. "expectations" within the teaching job) and to show their alignment with the Dual Objective. Interestingly, the state cannot mandate how teachers teach, yet a quick look at the ten items in the following activity surely sends the message that Cooperative Learning is expected to be used, and that teachers should be teaching for affective gains as well as cognitive (the two fundamental goals that drive the Dual Objective). To get you thinking about your prior experience in these areas, please complete the following activity.

TASK: The Role of Teacher

Peruse the following selection of performance indicators (taken from the New York State Teaching Standards), and thinking about a specific instructional situation that you know well (i.e. yourself as teacher, a colleague, or a teacher you had in a class) "rate" the teacher on his/her demonstration of the following skills (choice of scale is yours):

———— 1.2.c Teachers explain instructional decisions citing current research.

———— 2.2.c Teachers provide opportunities for students to engage in collaborative critical thinking and problem-solving.

———— 2.2.d Teachers model and encourage effective use of interpersonal communication skills.

———— 3.1.c Students are actively and cognitively engaged through teacher facilitation of student-student interactions.

———— 3.5.b Students work effectively with others, including those from diverse groups and with opposing points of view.

———— 4.1.c Teachers recognize and reinforce positive interactions among students.

———— 4.1.e Teachers create an environment where students show responsibility to, and for, one another.

———— 4.3.c Teachers facilitate instructional groupings to maximize student participation, cooperation and learning.

———— 6.2.c Teachers share information and best practices with colleagues to improve practice.

———— 7.3.b Teachers participate actively as part of an instructional team to improve professional practice.

Without taking each of the ten individually, let's look at the overall meaning of the set:

◆ Students are expected to be in groups on a regular basis, to talk directly to, and with, each other, to effectively interact with people who are different than themselves, and to solve problems with classmates.

◆ Students are expected to be responsible for each other! We see this indicator as a revolutionary notion in a society that promotes individuality as strongly as the U.S. does. Outside of class, adolescents often find themselves in formal groups and are told that they "are all in this together": picture football teams, musical groups, social clubs, yearbook staffs, and debate teams. It appears that the people who wrote the standards are well aware of the research support for CL and accept an idea of the school as a place for teens to develop non-cognitive skills (Tough, 2012).

◆ Finally, it is clear that teachers' jobs have changed; they are expected to follow research and utilize research-supported strategies *and* they are supposed to continue to **grow as collaborative professionals**. Moreover, they are expected to **model the skills being taught** to students.

Danielson's Framework for Teaching

While it is clear that we are enamored with the New York State Teaching Standards, we also wish to briefly mention Charlotte Danielson's (2013) now well-known Framework for Teaching. When she first brought her ideas to light in 1997, we hailed her in the way of a conquering heroine: Here, in one book, was the best description of good teaching that was research based, meticulously constructed, clear, and useful for teacher assessment! Today there are other plausible models, but hers still ranks at the apex of such documents. We would choose New York's teaching standards as a job description over Danielson's framework, but we are not unhappy with hers and its acceptance by many districts as the basis for teacher evaluation.

Briefly, there are several aspects of the Danielson framework that align nicely with the Dual Objective.

◆ *Domain 2a—Creating an Environment of Respect and Rapport.* The most prestigious level ("Distinguished") calls for student–student respectfulness, no "put-downs" or ridicule, and constructive feedback from student to student. Certainly, this is consistent with the

Dual Objective. But we are troubled that "proficient" teaching allows for hesitancy in these interactions. We find this disturbing because it appears as if teachers can keep their positive self-image without creating the environment necessary for student success.

◆ *Domain 2b—Establishing a Culture for Learning.* The criterion stating that "students assist their classmates" is reserved for "distinguished" and not "proficient" ratings. We feel that this student behavior should be the norm in all classrooms, not just those of the exemplary. Moreover, this section reminds us that student-assisting behavior cannot be taken for granted; it is not an input, but rather an *output* (or *outcome*) of working through the Dual Objective Model of CL. Students need to learn how to support each other and recognize why doing so is important: These are both central to the Dual Objective.

◆ *Domain 2c—Managing Classroom Procedures.* For the "proficient" rating, students are supposed to be "productively engaged in small-group work," which clearly supports the notion that the Danielson vision includes Cooperative Learning as a normal part of everyday instruction.

◆ *Domain 3b—Using Questioning and Discussion Techniques and 3c— Engaging Students in Learning.* Both 3b and 3c show expectations of students' ability to work together. Specific language includes "invite comments from classmates and challenge one another's thinking." She suggests that "students may serve as resources for one another," and that "groupings of students should be appropriate to the activities," which certainly suggests a vision of students taking over their own learning, using teammates to clarify and extend ideas, and being collegial in the form and tone of their interactions.

In these two powerful descriptions of good teaching, the New York State Teaching Standards and Danielson's Framework for Teaching, there is supportive evidence for the use of Cooperative Learning and an expectation that social and emotional skills are to be developed and used within that CL framework. Again, the Dual Objective provides the model for those skills to be developed systematically and intentionally in all adolescents.

Developmentally Appropriate Practice

As we mentioned at the outset, modern education provides a contentious forum for parents, the media, politicians, policy-makers, industrialists, and the public in general. In the furious debates over Common Core, teacher tenure, charter schools, test scores, and the impact of poverty, among others, one important consideration seems to have been left out of the planning and decision-making: What are the best developmental experiences for children and adolescents as complete human beings?

For 40 years the answer to that question has been the beautiful phrase "developmentally appropriate education," or in other words, schooling built on the real needs, real abilities, and real growth patterns of real adolescents. Educators have responded to the thoughts of Dewey, Vygostky, Bruner, Piaget, Gardner, and notably, recent work by Siegel and from Steinberg about human development. However, like everything else, this too has become the center of focused attention. (In fact, this notion of developmentally appropriate content was largely ignored by the creators of the Common Core, leading to the need for recent revisions in both ELA and math standards for New York State.) You should know up front that we favor the developmentally appropriate approach and consider the Dual Objective the perfect structure to promote its practices.

TASK: Developmentally Appropriate?

To explore Developmentally Appropriate Practice and its converse, standardization of achievement, we will begin by having you compare and contrast the comments and academic vocabulary of two educators in the same school.

Teacher Brown: Our scores put us way behind other schools of our size around the state. We need more rigor, more homework, and maybe a re-alignment of our implementation plan.

Teacher Black: You know our kids: they need to flourish as individuals, not data points. We are faced with so many blocks to growth that the important things like persistence, creativity, ownership, and maturation are lost in the shuffle.

Teacher Brown: There is no shuffle and no time for these frills. If we wait on our targets, we will face the consequences. Everything boils down to accountability you know. Students should do what we need them to do, when we tell them.

Teacher Black: Adolescence is also an age of incredible conflict and social disruption. We should be giving them an education that is meaningful and relevant and one that is geared to their uniqueness, their developmental pathways, and that nurtures their individuality and their ability to interact with others.

That is enough: You know that these two may never get to compromise, but if they conduct this debate in a mature manner, they may start to develop deeper understanding and more respect for the two polarized positions represented. To us, the historical commitment to Developmentally Appropriate

Practice puts us on the side of Teacher Black but we understand that Teacher Brown speaks truths that cannot be ignored.

An expert in this field, Thomas Armstrong (2006), has developed an approach to examine these two conflicting philosophies in a book he titled *The best schools*. Below is a sampling of his "laundry list" of practices that middle and high school students *need* to fully develop as workers, citizens, family members, students, and friends. Let's see how these connect to secondary teaching and the Dual Objective.

TASK: Conditions for Student Success and the Dual Objective

1. Consider each of the following classroom practices and see if you can determine which three Armstrong aligns with the high school experience, and the six he connects with middle school.
2. In addition, check those that have been mentioned thus far in your reading as aligned with the Dual Objective.
3. Do you agree with your tentative middle vs. high school categorization?

_____ *Democratic (small learning & collaborative) communities*
_____ Emotionally meaningful curriculum and instruction
_____ Respect for student voices in classroom interaction
_____ *Entrepreneurial enterprises*
_____ Metacognitive activities built into classroom activities
_____ Safe climate
_____ *Internships/projects and reflection*
_____ Small learning communities
_____ Emphasis on social and emotional growth

Our Take

◆ Yes, it's not surprising, those in italics Armstrong includes as high school practices and the others, middle school. Now the authors respect Armstrong's work, but beg to differ that many of those listed as appropriate for middle school are also appropriate for high school. Having taught both levels, deeply entrenched in the culture of social–emotional learning and living the Dual Objective, we see tremendous crossover and great benefit for application throughout the secondary experience.

◆ By the way, did you check any . . . most . . . all, as aligned with the Dual Objective Model? We believe all have been either directly referenced, or one could easily infer their connection to the quality learning that occurs when well-structured CL follows the Dual

Objective Model. In short, successful implementation of the Dual Objective meets what Armstrong feels are the developmental needs of adolescents and does so with the benefit of high academic achievement as well: These are the best of both worlds.

We must also comment on two recent books: Dan Siegel's *Brainstorm* (2014) and Laurence Steinberg's *The age of opportunity* (2014). Both authors individually discuss changes in the brain discovered by rather recent scholarship that serve to mark adolescence as a time for physical and psychological change and development and a time that screams out for healthy connections with concerned adults and for meaningful experiences.

Siegel argues for the importance of four things that traditional academic schooling rarely provides: novelty, emotional intensity, social interaction, and creativity. The design of the Dual Objective provides each of these on a regular basis. The projects and tasks students engage in are largely controlled by the team itself, so they are novel in structure and creative in nature. Working together in diverse groups provides novelty, too, but it often means there is an emotionally intense aura surrounding the learning experience; certainly the Dual Objective offers social engagement and interaction as a fundamental structure. A school or a classroom set up by Siegel would likely mirror the structures of the Dual Objective.

Finally Steinberg, a long-time and well-respected scholar, is an advocate of what he calls "the new science of adolescence." He emphasizes two notions that secondary teachers should think about carefully.

First, he makes a strong case for self-regulation (self-management, managing impulsivity) as the key factor in individual life success. Adolescence is a time when this can be experienced in many forms and over many years, and with the help of guiding, caring adults, in conjunction with other adolescents, good decisions can be made, implemented, and validated. In this regard, he sees schools and teachers as partners with (not replacement for) parents in raising young people who can manage themselves and contribute to the common good.

Second, we offer a potentially surprising finding. A school system that publicizes the powerful capacities of character, teamwork, perseverance, motivation (and the like) through an inspirational poster and "virtue-of-the-month" approach, should expect to be *no more* effective in spawning internalization of these competencies in their youth than sister schools that don't bring such attention. Steinberg says that self-control development requires something other than "parables, slogans, banners and encouragement": It needs a systematic and coherent plan of action, reflection, and adjustment. Again, the development of self-control and/or self-regulation requires students' implementation and examination of the skill during an actual experience in a specific context. Kline refers to this as being "systematic and intentional" about the planning of shared learning experiences, and she uses the Dual Objective Model to do so.

We wish to note that there are national programs that foster such implementations, like those which the Collaborative for Academic Social and Emotional Learning (CASEL, 2015) has identified as meeting its specifications. CASEL refers to successful research-based programs with the acronym SAFE: These programs are **S**equenced logically, **A**ctively practiced, **F**ocused upon as an integrated aspect of learning activities, and **E**xplicitly identified. While CASEL has focused on school-wide implementation, we suggest that individual teachers can systematically implement a SAFE-like structure that promotes affective development using the Dual Objective. Such a classroom program should be sequenced, involve active implementation and examination, focus on specific skills, and explicitly teach and assess those specific skills.

In Closing

This brief tour highlighting alignments of the Dual Objective with some of the major movements in education has revealed that Cooperative Learning has become an acceptable and desirable strategy in the toolbox of secondary teachers. It is recognized as a routine part of everyday practice; it aligns with models of effective practice in a globalized context; it is culturally and developmentally appropriate; it promotes the honing of 21st-century college and career skills; and it increases students' conceptual understanding. (More than likely, the student engagement sparked by the thinking, interaction, support, and commitment will also increase test scores.) No matter what, a positive classroom environment (supported by use of the Dual Objective) will lead to many students having greater overall life success, a point consistent with a finding from a study by Jackson (2014).

In summary, serious attention is now being paid to the affective side of student growth and development. From James Heckman's concern for non-cognitive skill development to Angela Duckworth's discovery of the power of "grit" have come a recognition that education is for the whole person *not* just the cognitive abilities of that person. We believe that the Dual Objective offers a structure, a process, and a feedback mechanism to help assist affective improvement while maintaining an academic focus on achievement. These structures and practices are aligned with the important movements in modern education detailed in this chapter. Many teachers claim that they work on these so-called "soft skills," usually in the form of a reaction to an unplanned, spontaneous "teachable moment," but rarely is it done in in a well-structured way. To reiterate a point from the previous chapter, one of the authors (Kline) has coined the phrase "from well-meaning and intuitive to systematic and intentional" to describe the shift from a teacher who is providential to one who is planned and organized. We think the Dual Objective is a structure that maximizes the intentional concern for affect and we believe that an organized and sequenced approach holds more promise than does a hope for providence.

Chapter 6 Big Ideas

1. Education is facing a huge set of societal changes and suggested reforms; many educators are overwhelmed by all of these innovations and disruptions.
2. Well-structured implementation of the Dual Objective Model aligns well with key education initiatives and movements including:

   a. globalization, which stresses embracing diversity, understanding differences, and a commitment to the Common Core-type of upper-level skills that collaboration fosters;
   b. the Partnership for 21st Century Learning's P21 Framework, which demands that students develop a host of social and emotional skills as a regular part of education. These include: creativity and innovation, critical thinking and problem-solving, communication and collaboration, flexibility and adaptability, initiative and self-direction, social and cross-cultural skills, productivity and accountability, and leadership and responsibility, each of which enables contemporary life and career success;
   c. problem-based and project-based learning, which demands collaborative interaction and teamwork and requires original thinking;
   d. Culturally Relevant Teaching, which suggests that students benefit from collaboration and community;
   e. the Danielson Framework for Learning and the New York State Teaching Standards, which suggest that good teaching utilizes and improves student–student interaction on a regular basis;
   f. Developmentally Appropriate Practice and recent findings of adolescent research, which require that students collaborate and work in small learning communities to reap the benefits of their explicit focus on social/emotional development.

3. Research (from Jackson, 2014) shows that success in developing affective skills will benefit students across their lives more than a rise in test scores. The sense of community sparked by an emphasis on classroom climate and fostered by the Dual Objective will develop these skills (Tough, 2016).

References

Armstrong, T. (2006). *The best schools: How human development research should inform practice.* Alexandria, VA: ASCD.

Barron, J.S., Schwartz, D.L., Vye, N., Moore, A., Petrosino, A., Zech, L., & Bransford, J.D. (1998). Doing with understanding: Lessons from research on problem-based and project-based learning. *Journal of the Learning Sciences, 73*(3–4), 271–311.

CASEL (2015). *2015 CASEL guide: Effective social and emotional learning programs—middle and high school edition.* Retrieved January 31, 2017, from http://www.casel.org/middle-and-high-school-edition-casel-guide/

Danielson, C. (2013). *Enhancing professional practice: A framework for teaching.* Alexandria, VA: ASCD.

Davidson, N., & Major, C.H. (2014). Boundary crossings: Cooperative learning, collaborative learning and problem-based learning. *Journal on Excellence in College Teaching, 25*(3–4), 7–55.

Farrington, C.A., Roderick, E., Nagaoka, J., Keyes, T.S., Johnson, D.W., & Beechum, N. (2012). *Teaching adolescents to become learners: The role of non-cognitive factors in shaping school performance.* Chicago, IL: Consortium on Chicago School Research.

Hung, W., Jonassen, D.H., & Liu, R. (2008). Problem-based learning. In J.M. Spector, M.D. Merrill, J. van Merrienboer and M.P. Driscoll (Eds.), *Handbook of research on educational communications and technology* (3rd ed.), pp. 485–506. New York, NY: Routledge.

Jackson, K. (2014, revision). *Non-cognitive ability, test scores, and teacher quality: Evidence from 9th grade teachers.* NEBR Working Paper 18624. Cambridge, MA: National Bureau of Economic Research.

Ladson-Billings, G. (2009). *Dreamkeepers: Successful teachers of African-American children.* San Francisco, CA: Jossey-Bass.

Lampert, M. (2001). *Teaching problems and the problems of teaching.* New Haven, CT: Yale University Press.

Lyman, F.T. (1981). *The responsive classroom discussion: The inclusion of all students.* In A. Anderson (Ed.), *Mainstreaming Digest* (pp. 109–113). College Park, MD: University of Maryland Press.

New York State Teaching Standards. (2011, January 1). Retrieved January 31, 2017, from https://www.engageny.org/resource/new-york-state-teaching-standards

Siegel, D.J. (2014). *Brainstorm: The power and purpose of the teenage brain*. New York, NY: Tarcher Penguin.

Steinberg, L. (2014). *The age of opportunity: Lessons from the new science of adolescence*. New York, NY: Houghton-Mifflin.

Stepien, W., & Gallagher, S. (1993). Problem-based learning: As authentic as it gets. *Educational Leadership, 50*(7), 25–28.

Tough, P. (2012). *How children succeed: Grit, curiosity and the hidden power of character*. Boston, MA: Houghton-Mifflin.

Tough, P. (2016). *Helping children succeed: What works and why*. New York, NY: Houghton-Mifflin.

How Does the Dual Objective Look in Practice?

Examining Examples and Exploring Challenges

Introduction: Cases and Examples to Examine

This final chapter has been designed to accomplish three things:

1. We wish to provide you with examples and cases for you to work through to deepen and develop your ability to use the Dual Objective in many situations.
2. We wish for you to experience the necessity of using many varied applications to deepen your own mental representation of the Dual Objective in action in long-term memory (Ericsson & Pool, 2016). Thus, this chapter offers numerous opportunities for you to apply *deliberate (or purposeful) practice* to extend your learning about the Dual Objective and effective Cooperative Learning: Don't cheat yourself by skimming it or ignoring it;
3. We wish for you to see the diverse ways that teachers can try to implement the Dual Objective Model while being creative, using favored content or activities, and maintaining fidelity to the approach. Our examples and cases are varied and take advantage of the concept called "interleaving," which is now being closely examined in educational practice (Brown, Roediger III, & McDaniel, 2014).

The structure is as follows: first, we will offer three opening activities that could be borrowed or modified for your own implementation. Each of these field-tested activities is powerful, easy to use, and perfect for the first day of school or modified for the first use of Cooperative Learning. We offer some thought-provoking focus questions for you to reflect on (or, preferably, to discuss with a partner) *but* we do *not* provide our own answers to these items. We will also address the reader as "you," hoping to personalize our suggestions as much as possible.

Second, we offer a set of classroom lesson descriptions that feature a teacher attempting to use the Dual Objective. We ask that you critique them and use them to both challenge and broaden your own understanding. Again, we provide focus questions but, in this section, we *do* offer our brief reactions to the teacher's instruction (while not directly answering our own questions). We do have a fanciful idea that small groups of teachers will take these cases and their matching analysis questions into productive discussions. Professional Learning Communities (PLC) and book clubs have shown the power to generate and sustain changes in practice (largely because they mirror the power of Cooperative Learning).

We ask you to recognize that the applications and analyses we ask for in this section amount to a test of your understanding (albeit without a grade). As such, they will work to your benefit by way of the "testing effect" (a.k.a. "retrieval effect"), another highly regarded learning tactic being closely examined at the present time (Brown et al., 2014).

In the final section, we offer a set of frequently asked questions to help synthesize your understanding of the Dual Objective Model. Posed as potentially problematic issues or concerns, we hope to close the book on a very practical note. We anticipate that readers may have personally generated many of these questions and ask that you peruse them with an eye for utilizing the ideas as you implement the Dual Objective in your work.

Three Opening Activities: Starting Strong, Showing Potential, and Realizing Success

As mentioned above, we offer three examples of ways to get Cooperative Learning and the Dual Objective started. We always want the first exposure of something new to be successful from a student's perspective, so we offer you strategies with very high probabilities of success. Please note that each of the three is preceded by focus questions. Try to use them to guide you as you do the reading and to consolidate your reactions afterwards.

TASK: The Venn Diagram: Who Are We?

Focus Questions

As you read this next section, try to answer the following questions:

1. Envision this activity happening in your room. How would this Venn diagram tactic work in each of your classes? What could cause difficulties that would prevent the perfect application shown here?
2. If you tried the strategy exactly as described, would troublesome partner-pairs be created? If so, how can that be avoided?
3. Some teenagers might not be impressed with finding their commonalities with others, yet they might notice that others in the room are impressed. How can you emphasize the importance of this task to everyone?

Description

This is a very easy tactic to use and can be repeated every time group membership is changed (although we love it as the overall opener in our own work). A simple pair of circles that overlap by about 70 percent (the most common Venn diagram) are provided to students who are then asked to turn and find a partner who is close. Do this quickly and watch for many groups of three being developed as students try to "friend up" and choose to be comfortable with familiar folks. Break up the threes as best you can (maybe even assuring that this is short and fun).

Students are then given 60 seconds to talk and discover and *list* (in writing on the Venn diagram) ten or more commonalities that they share. Don't give them hints but do anticipate confusion: Some items that may come up include number of siblings, religion, countries visited, favorite things, why school is bad, favorite foods, and pets. Try to have all pairs work for the full 60 seconds, and work the room encouraging urgency.

At the end of the allotted time, have a few students read their lists to the entire class and then give them all another 60 seconds to bring the list to 16 (random choice), the gist is to have them continue interacting. After this additional conversation and documentation, pairs have discovered many commonalities that they share. Moreover, students are actually interviewing, listening, documenting, sharing, clarifying, and often empathizing with "strangers"; these are always respectful interactions and cross-cultural in nature. This entire procedure, which can be done well in eight minutes or so, allows the teacher to confidently announce, "You have just found out that you and another person, maybe even someone you didn't even know, have much in common. This should convince you to have a little trust in working with him or her and to start expecting to have commonalities with many folks. Most of you seemed to enjoy the sharing and the talking. Hopefully you will also enjoy working in teams as we start to do the real work of class."

Our Take

◆ This tactic is often used as an opening before the students engage in a more difficult and complex task; using it creates a successful experience to build on.

◆ We have found that the "commonalities" are important in breaking the ice between people and often result in bemused smiles and laughter. Moreover, the important differences that do shine through became relegated to a later time: **Do not have students record the differences they discover**. We believe that **trust follows a successful sharing of commonalities** and that the differences will arise naturally in discussion and will prove to be beneficial in particular situations. Diversities extend us, enrich us, and make us better, but we must be open to letting them happen "naturally." At the end of this segment, teachers can tell students that "we are both alike *and* different; we need differences to grow and we need commonalities to feel a sense of community."

TASK: "The Gronk": (A teaches and B draws)

Focus Questions

As you read this section, please try to answer the following questions:

1. Using "The Gronk" (or a suitable replacement paragraph) requires that the students "follow the rules." What disobediences and/or confusions do you anticipate and how will you handle these classroom management challenges?
2. The learning from one another strategy, "A teaches and B draws" can be used almost every day for different content. In our experience, students never tire of it. However, to make it work, students must read, draw, discuss, and give feedback while listening with empathy and understanding (a keystone Habit of Mind, of course). How much detail will you share before they start the "teaching-drawing" segment?
3. How would you react personally to being asked to do this activity at the start of a professional development workshop? Would you be willing to share your take on doing the tactic with your own students? (Note: This tactic uses pairs but understands that that there could be one extra student. Perhaps you could serve as the "teacher" of that student! If you personally do work as part of a pair, the student involved will have a slightly altered status in the eyes of others. Positive or negative, your direct involvement will be noticed.)

Description

A personal favorite, "The Gronk" learning experience has been used by the authors on a regular basis for as long as we can remember. (It was described in a 2004 book by Flynn, Mesibov, Vermette & Smith, but was already a decade old then.)

We wish to make several points about the implementation of "the Gronk". First, the overall notion is that students will learn from each other in a semi-structured way.

This idea was loosely based on some of the work by Donald Dansereau (1987) on paired student interaction. Students are moved to pairs and asked to get ready do an important task and to follow directions (a social skill). Student A will read and "teach" (explain) a written passage of five to seven sentences in length while Student B is to draw the thing being described without looking at the written passage. We use the thing called the Gronk, a mythical beast that has worked perfectly in our experience, but you can choose any paragraph from any text in your course. We urge you to be a little careful about your choice, though, as vocabulary and complexity matters. The paragraph should be something easily visualized.

Second, the actual steps follow this line of action. Students are placed in pairs and one (Student A) is given the reading passage and is asked to **hide it** from the other student. You announce that the person with the reading is going to teach the content to Student B and he or she is going to draw a visual of it. (Please promise that these drawings will be seen by all.) The reader **may not** show the passage to the drawer but can do anything else to help the learning partner. Both parties should try hard and be respectful to the partner (these are the emotional skills being utilized). After the teacher announces that there will be a "public test at the end," the students are given three and a half minutes to get it done.

Third, as students make sense of the task, engage in it and complete it, you should work the room to make sure that they are on task, being respectful, and doing the drawing as required. You will find some students taking notes first, some just reading slowly, and some giving feedback as the drawings are created. We suggest that you find one from a pair who will be comfortable in front of the room. Ask the one who drew (Student B) if he or she could share the drawing with everyone, and after you get approval, take it in your hands. He or she will think you really liked the drawing, thus giving a positive emotional twist to the public test.

Finally, when time is up, ask the drawer (Student B) from the selected pair to come to the front and hold up the visual so all can see (or use a document camera if available). Commend her and thank her for being willing to share, then hide the drawing momentarily. Chat a bit about how nicely everyone worked in the activity and what good attempts there were. Ask the selected Student B about her experience working with her partner. (How did Student A show respect during the exchange? There will be an answer suggesting the Dual Objective is at work!) Then, **have her turn so she can no longer see the visual (but show everyone else)**. Having "wasted" three or four minutes, ask her the following "test" question: "Tell us five things about the Gronk, please." This is often met with a laugh and smile, a bit of stammering, and then a cascade of right answers. When it stops, you can announce, "Well, it looks like you had fun, practiced being respectful, and learned everything. Not bad for three-and-a-half minutes. Wait . . . who taught you about this Gronk?" After 15 years, we still laugh when we hear that the answer is "My partner, Bob." We, of course, disagree. "*No*, we taught it; through Cooperative Learning by having you work with Bob (and he did a fine job). Moreover, it worked so well that we will probably use CL a lot more during the coming year. You are a good learner and obviously he is a good teacher, so we might as well take advantage of these factors."

Our Take

◆ The nicest thing about "The Gronk," where Student A teaches and Student B draws, is that it is engaging, meaningful, and really requires high levels of **positive interdependence** (Johnson & Johnson, 2009).

◆ Interestingly, "The Gronk" as an activity always works. In a short time, every person we have done this with can detail the Gronk and describe the paired experience. This public test confirms its power as a learning experience and often sparks a flurry of questions or comments. It is both smooth and convincing in its demonstration of teamed effort leading to achievement for all.

TASK: Establishing Rules by Which we Learn

Focus Questions

We present this third idea as a case study. As you read this section, please try to answer the following questions.

1. This tactic takes planning and structuring: Where will you get the time, materials, information and room access to make this happen for multiple classes on day one? What modifications could you make to have it fit into your specific situation?
2. This tactic both teaches about and uses affective skills. Essentially, the teacher is teaching about the important purpose of his rules. If you don't follow his approach, how do you inform students about the rules for your class and their purpose? Please compare your approach with his.
3. Truthfully, the tasks in this approach could be done by students working alone, but the teacher chooses to take advantage of CL by putting the students together. What are three advantages of his decision to have them do the required work together?

Description: Tim Miller's Class Rules

The scene is an 800-student middle school in suburban Georgia. It is a new, air-conditioned building and it is the first day of school for the 7th-and 8th-graders. At 7:55 a.m., Tim Miller starts the first day of his 7th-grade math class in this fashion:

As the bell rings, Tim announces to his class that they are going to start every day on time. He also makes sure that all of his students are in their proper seats. There are names and a packet at each. Within a minute, he says, "Good morning . . . On the board, you will see there are six rules. These are the expectations that we are going to live by in our math class, and you will be graded on them every day!"

Groans and comments fill the room, but he says, "No—easy—easy. Eyes up here and please listen." He waits a moment and then continues. "We have to decide what these rules mean, so look closely. There is a paper and a pencil in the packet in front of you that you can use as we continue."

He points and reads each rule in a loud but friendly tone.
Mr. Miller's Class Rules

1. You must be respectful to every other person in this class at all times.
2. You must be on time and stay to the end of class.
3. You must try hard, especially on difficult tasks.
4. You must contribute to other people's success.
5. You must think about how you are managing yourself.
6. Promises are made to be kept so get in the habit of doing so!

On the other wall is more block printing. Tim points out a short list of four items that read:
My Promises to You

1. I promise that you will be safe in this classroom at all times.
2. I promise that you will be respected by me and by all others.
3. I promise to always do my best to help you learn, help you grow, and help you develop as a young man or young woman.
4. I promise that I will never lie to you and will believe what you tell me.

"Now choose the two of the six rules that you find *most* important to you. Please jot them down on the scrap paper." He waits (smiling) patiently as they struggle with this challenge and begin shuffling through the packets. He also doesn't say anything when several students begin talking and gesturing.

"OK; let's see what we've got. 24 students × 2 each; we have a total of 48 selections. As I read each number, raise your hand if you've selected that rule as one of the most important. Number 1?" He continues through all six and posts the results of the sum of "the most important rules":

#1 20 votes
#2 9 votes
#3 13 votes
#4 3 votes
#5 2 votes
#6 1 vote

"OK, we have interesting data here. Please take two minutes and write a summary sentence for what this data says. I am going to read everything you write! Please get started . . . and yes, you can help each other. By the way, you should also know that there will be an outslip assigned every night and you can share ideas with each other on those tasks, too."

After two minutes, during which he intently observes student behaviors, Mr. Miller gets attention and calls on three students to stand and read their sentences. After each one reads, he claps and asks others in the room to applaud as well; they do. He doesn't challenge any of their interpretations, but offers a synthesis of the three in his own words: "We as a class have decided that each of the six expectations is important and that the most important ones are being respectful and trying hard. Hey . . . we should follow these! They would make us a better community and smarter. *But*, we have another situation to consider. In your packet is a sheet with your name and the names of three others. Find those folks and introduce yourself in a professional manner. You will need to develop the ability to shake hands and say 'hello' for the rest of your life, so start now. You will be working with the other three for the next five minutes. Go quickly and be respectful."

Chaos erupts and movement fills the air; the classroom shrinks and sweats, as if a beast had come alive. After a minute Tim says, "OK, please be seated to do the following task. Here is a chart (he shows an item from his packet) that needs to be filled in by the combined work of your group. For four of the six rules, please state three reasons why it is a good idea for either adults at work or students at school to follow it. In the next column, state what the results might be if the rule is broken. (Think of people not following the rule.) In the last column, tell what a person should do to avoid breaking the rule. Each person has to submit his or her own sheet and I want you to listen to each other carefully and respectfully while you work. Start now, please."

A few minutes later, Tim calls time and debriefs the task.

While this process takes up most of the first class, Tim is establishing that his classroom management system is the same thing as his affective agenda. He expects his students to have *integrity* and to improve their abilities to be *respectful, punctual/responsible, gritty/persistent, helpful and collaborative*, and *self-regulative*. These are what he considers the six most important affective skills for his students and they will utilize and be assessed on each one every day. Moreover, when he debriefs this latest task (the reasons behind the rules), the reasons for the affective skills will be recognized and better accepted by the students. Students will have discovered reasons for the rules, identified consequences of the rules not being followed, and have discussed possible interventions for people trying to self-regulate themselves into staying within community expectations. (Maybe one day the rules will be internalized by all students.) Furthermore, Tim plans to start tomorrow with the sharing of the outslip data for a few minutes and will be asking the students to assess him on how well he is keeping his promises. He wants them to see that what he calls SEL skills are good for adults and students.

Tim uses the last eight minutes of class to provide three math problems, stating, "These are like the ones you will get all year. Please work together on them with your team mates until the bell rings. The other sheet in your packet is your short homework called an 'outslip'—just a few completion statements about this, our first meeting. Both are due tomorrow. Get to work, please."

Tim works the room until the bell rings, making sure that every student found the homework, which takes the form of these completion items:

1. The thing I liked best about today was . . .
2. My team mates are named . . .
3. We decided on our rules and they will help me learn math by . . .
4. I kept myself working hard by . . .
5. Working in teams in math means that . . .

Our Take

- ◆ Tim's is a powerful opening and links cognitive growth to effort and affective skill in an explicit and measureable way. His expectations (or, if you prefer, rules) are both *clear* and *powerful* and they have become his agenda in the Dual Objective Model.
- ◆ We offer what we see as the three advantages of having students work together instead of alone (question #3 at the top of the Miller scenario). These are:

   a. The teacher establishes that sharing is a normal procedure and that he sees the class as a community, not as an assortment of isolated individuals. Humans collaborating accomplish far more than individuals do alone; positive habits are reinforced in community settings (Duhigg, 2014).

   b. The students themselves find areas of enjoyment when they share ideas and get feedback: If the students agree, they are validated, and, if they disagree, they learn that it is safe and normal to have different ideas. All of this is done on very safe subject matter grounds (the conversation seems to be about math not about personal beliefs) and thus any potential argument is about "content," not about "person." Differences don't have to become divisive.

   c. Examine the six-item outslip. Three items require working with others. Answering those items draws attention to the importance of student use of names, explores the implications of teamwork for math learning, and offers a nod to building a sense of community by the use of "we." These are *not* minor or superficial factors: They explicitly support the power and meaning of the Dual Objective.

Cases and Lessons to Examine

In this section, we offer several mini case studies for you to critique and think deeply about. This is your chance to synthesize your understanding of both good teaching *and* the Dual Objective (which we see as heavily overlapping concepts) and to consider options or modifications to your own practice. While each of the examples has a slightly different structure, they can be used to spark discussions with colleagues of vastly different backgrounds and experiences resulting in "growth for both."

CASE: Mr. Maloa's 10th-Grade Social Studies Class

Miquel Maloa, a 26-year-old, third-year Global History teacher at Margaret Sanger High School (a city school in a Michigan district), is starting his first unit of the year, the French Revolution, with his 27 10th-graders. (This is 10th period, so it is his fifth time teaching this lesson today.)

After the bell rings, Mr. Maloa finishes taking the class count. He has 27 bodies in the room and 27 on the list, so he starts: "Good afternoon: it is hot—perfect for exploring what was once the hottest event on Earth! Please take out a piece of paper and put your heading on it. You must turn this in at the end of class, one, so I'll know that you were here, and two, so I can read your thoughts and justify giving you a full ten points for the day. You will be graded every day, as you might expect, but now know."

So let's get started: "Please number your paper from one to eight. Hurry—that's not complicated. Now, you have one minute—60 seconds—to jot down **descriptors** about your ideas of revolution. No questions; no talking. Ready? . . . Go!"

The minute seems to last forever. Some students never seem to get started, some are writing furiously, and some appear to be sort of trying. At the end of minute, Mr. Maloa says loudly, "OK, now continue numbering your papers 9 through 14. You have another three minutes to mill around and ask others politely for one of their responses. When they give you one, write it down and put his or her name next to it. Let me show you an example."

Mr. Maloa turns to Rialdo and asks, "Rialdo, what is one thing on your list?"

"Ugh, well, ugh—lots of dead people," is the reply.

"OK, so I would put 'lots of dead people—Rialdo' on my paper (he shows this on the front board). I want you talking to a few people so only take one idea from any one other classmate. Hurry—I want everybody to have 14 considerations listed on his or her paper (no duplicates) when I call time."

After three minutes, he calls time. "Tracia, please go the board. I am going to call on students and they are going to tell us their ideas. Would you please record them? Thanks. Let's start with Jose."

It takes a few minutes, but a total of 22 offerings make it onto the board. Students are encouraged to take a photo of the lists with their phones: most do. Mr. Maloa then says, "OK, get into your assigned teams—and captains, make sure three things happen while you guys do the next three tasks: (1) make sure everybody contributes, (2) make sure that your recorder documents all of the ideas correctly, and (3) make sure that you follow the leadership style we learned about last week.

"Here are the three tasks (displaying for all via the document camera):

1. Write a statement that explains how violent the French Revolution was and how historians come to those conclusions.
2. Revolutions are usually in a format of Group A vs. Group B: one group facing off against another. It seems that France in 1798 had three groups: what gives? How come they have three, not two? Be ready to show us a visual that

represents these three groups and be prepared to share any related reasoning for there being three.

3. Design four plausible newspaper headlines for different dates during the Revolution and be ready to explain each one.

You can use any resources in the room, laptops, tablets and your phones, but you cannot leave, and you must all reach consensus on the answers. You have 25 minutes. Please try to be inclusive of everyone in your team's ideas and respectful of their contributions. Gatekeepers stay aware of each person, OK?" The class goes to work.

With 11 minutes left in class, he calls the class to order, using his arm held high (the signal to listen). Quiet does follow. "OK, I know that every team has at least two tasks done. Remember, for full credit today, you have to have all three—right? So let's take a minute to examine what we have and then get you back to finish. Marcos, what did you guys do for the violence item?"

Marcos stands up proudly, holds his paper out firmly and says, "We couldn't find an exact number, but there was a lot of killing and a lot had to do with the head chop-er-off-er (class laughs), which was a form of capital punishment. They even got the King and Queen."

Mr. Maloa probes: "Why are hard numbers difficult to locate? How would historians figure these things out?"

Many hands shoot up across the room. "Hmm, Marcos, would you please call on someone to offer his or her opinion and be ready to comment on whatever he or she says."

He chooses Jody, who says, "A historian from France around 1850 wrote that he estimated 3,000 dead in the first year by looking at death certificates—it's a kind of ratio thing—both rich and poor were killed but only rich kept records."

Mr. Maloa asks Marcos for his take. He responds: "I think that Jody did OK, but how accurate is it if only the rich kept records?"

Mr. Maloa knew a teachable moment when he felt one. "Good question Marcos, and Jody, before you answer—everybody, take three minutes to search materials and resources to try to answer this: 'Why do we believe what we have read in the books about French Revolution?' Go."

Instantly, noises erupted from the teens—phones went on, books were paged through, five students jumped on the computers. Essentially, research was happening (even though several students did nothing; they just sat).

After a bit of time, Mr. Maloa raises his arm and announces, "Two minutes to go. Quickly—John (one of the sitting students), please ask Jody what she just found and be ready to paraphrase it for rest of class. Jody?"

A moment later, the bell rings, ending class and further disrupting this digression. As students leave, he shouts, "We pick up tomorrow where we left off here."

Questions for Reflection

1. How important were the three considerations (everyone contributes, the recorder documents well, and a specific leadership style is followed) that students were following in their teamwork? Are these considerations primarily just for social studies teachers, or are they valuable for teachers of other subjects *and* for parents?

2. Miquel believes that he is using the Dual Objective: if so, what are his objectives, both affective and cognitive?

3. Think for a minute about this unit culminating in a complex project done by the student teams *during* class. Perhaps examine the "100 Products" offered earlier in the book for some suggestions (i.e. design a Hollywood movie, write a book of poetry, create the hypothetical journals of several people for each of 30 days of the revolution). What Habits of Mind and/or 21st-century affective skills would you stress for how the students interact during their project work?

4. Quickly chart the things you liked and didn't like about this lesson (create a T-bar). Then, give it an overall evaluation rating and compare your rating with that of a colleague.

Our Take

◆ In our minds a T-bar would show a preponderance of positives. We think that Mr. Maloa's questions and tasks were rigorous, challenging, and potentially interesting to a critical mass of students. He also provides feedback, much of it in the form of probing, thought-provoking challenges. Moreover, his structure entices students to build directly on each other's ideas, thus supporting the notion of a classroom as an organic community and downplaying divisive competition.

◆ We applaud his opener, which involves tapping into each student's prior knowledge and enhances class-wide student interaction. This also sets up an expectation that students will be actively learning and thinking at high levels throughout class.

◆ We also note that he utilizes Johnson and Johnson's (1987) suggestion to use assigned roles within teams to make each student responsible and accountable. He has a captain, a recorder, and a gatekeeper; however, we have no evidence that he has taught the skills involved in these roles, nor do we have evidence that students get feedback on their handling of the jobs.

◆ On the other side of our T-bar, we are not happy with bringing a student out of her team mix to write on the board unless this was an intentional strategy to help that student. Way too often, a "board recorder" is relieved of having to pay attention and think: he or she becomes a simple scribe. This whole process of capturing and tabulating ideas can also be aided by the use of technology, which they seem to have. We would suggest he investigate options to expand his repertoire throughout the year. This effort connects directly to assuring 21st-century readiness for students.

◆ Regarding assessment of both cognitive and affective skills, we are unclear of what criteria this teacher will use to assess student learning on this day. There is nothing wrong with "grading every student every day" as long as it is backed up with criteria and evidence. Social studies is one of the easiest disciplines for targeting affective development, and had Mr. Maloa used any of the popular taxonomies, he would have provided needed structure to evaluate the **process of learning** that occurred within his student groups.

◆ Our last point deals with the pace of the class. This is a demanding, fast, and highly structured session and reflects a clear sense of urgency. We assume that this is intentional. However, we do hope that the teacher monitors the effects of this pacing and slows down when necessary. His idea of "picking this up tomorrow" suggests that either he underestimated execution or student response time, or he saw this as more than a one-day learning experience from the start, and they will continue in their teams to complete the balance next class.

Furthermore, many students process ideas very slowly and deliberately and working in teams often allows them to slow the pace down to one they can handle—this is one way for students to learn to account for individual differences. Please note that there is no research behind the idea that slowing down the pace during the teamwork damages the learning of the faster students. Moreover, Cain (2012) has argued against Cooperative Learning because "too much talk" bothers introverts; this is not sustained by scholarly work (as noted by Davidson, 2015) and Cain herself ends her book by calling for introverts to adjust to a team-oriented world. She is right to do that.

CASE: Mrs. Niam's 9th-Grade Math Class

Mrs. Niam is a 27 year old in her third year at this school, having started here after a year of subbing elsewhere. Their building is 9–12 and she is one of three teachers in the math department.
RIINNNNGGGGGG!

Mrs. Niam enters the room just as the bell rings starting first period on a cold Monday morning in March. She waves, smiles, and tells the 23 Math 9 students to get to their seats and get out *both* parts of their homework.

About three minutes later, she leaves the chair and moves to the front of her desk. "Good morning, let's take a look at the practice items. Anyone want to do number 1?"

In the front row, Richard barks out, "I got this one. The answer is b—23.7."

Mrs. Niam nods and says, "Good job. Class, are we OK with this answer?" Three quiet seconds pass. "Richard, would you please do the next one?"

"Sure: 2 is c, 3 is d, 4 is a, 5 is a . . ." She cuts him off. "Not so fast. Let's take these one at a time. Margie, could you explain why number 3 is d?"

Margie looks up, her eyes widened and her mouth in a frown. She stutters a bit, and then offers, "Well, that one is tough. I think, if you use . . . if you use the formula, you get 94.01, which is d."

Mrs. Niam's face softens. "I think we should change up for a minute. For the next five minutes, work with anybody you want to that is here in class, and make sure you know *how* to answer each of the 15 questions. Then we'll continue going over the homework."

As she retreats to her desk, several students move to sit with others, four put their heads down, one leaves through the back door, and Richard takes out his chemistry book.

When she looks up from her paperwork, Mrs. Niam rises and begins walking around the room. As she does this, she urges students to really try on some sample questions (they are from old Regents Exams) and talks quietly with those folks who have their heads down.

"OK, you've had a couple of minutes. When I call on you, I'd like you to explain how you attacked the problem and how you arrived at your answer. Number 5—Jonie?"

For the next six minutes, students attempt to explain their answers and she makes notes on the board. Her face is mostly set in an encouraging smile, and only when one student's answer takes the form of "Huh?" does she show a bit of anger. This section of class ends with her saying, "And please do the next 15 tonight. Now take out part two of the assignment."

About ten students arrange papers in front of them while the others try not to be seen by the teacher. "OK, we are trying this 'flipping' thing, so I hope you watched the video last night. Bob, did you like the way Kahn explained the theorem?"

Richard groans loudly as Bob nods *yes*. "Why?" Bob has no clear answer for that, so Mrs. Niam asks, "Guys who actually *did* watch the video and took notes? Would those folks please pair up, compare notes, and be ready to tell one good thing you liked."

Again, she retreats to her desk chair as students slowly shift positions. (A few are actually in pairs, each of which is same gender: there are no cross-gender pairings in the room for these few minutes.)

It is now about ten minutes before the end of class. She speaks from the chair: "Take a look at the board. I am going to walk us through the same problem that Kahn showed on the video. Then, if we have time left, we'll do some applications problems. I ask that you do not watch the next video as was planned. We have to master this stuff first, OK?"

Questions for Reflection

1. This is a badly taught math class and the teacher is struggling to hold attention and to get students engaged. (It reminds us of the math lessons featured in the book by Stigler & Hiebert, 1999:

Japanese lessons are marked by analysis and discussion while American lessons feature students watching, listening, and trying simple practice.) Mrs. Niam flirts with some Cooperative Learning, but does so without structure or intention. Moreover, she ignores the affective domain completely, which is odd since the CCSS in math requires teaching "persistence." With all that said, here is the question: Why is she so controlling?

2. Her use of the Khan video is intriguing: How could she have incorporated Cooperative Learning into its showing?

3. What we see suggests that she is trying to "stamp in" math knowledge rather than trying to get students to use what they *do* know in a complex and collaborative fashion. Is this a major reason why so many students dislike math and tell everyone that "they are just naturally weak" in math? Which specific Habits of Mind would help her students improve?

4. We have described four important purposes of student talk back in Chapter 3. Which of those purposes are applicable in this situation?

Our Take

◆ Mrs. Niam has a glimpse of students working in pairs in her vision, but she does it very poorly. We would suggest she consider think–pair–share as a structure. There are many places where partners could share insights. Instead of bell work, she could implement the retrieval effect by giving one or two *new* example problems whose formats are closely aligned to the actual homework. Students could work together and be called on individually. This tactic could also be used to open the discussion of the Khan video.

◆ We'd urge her to assign partners and offer bonuses if both do well *and* focus on two specific Habits of Mind. First, we should accept the Common Core and teach students how to persist in math (see Farrington et al., 2012 for more about the importance of *academic persistence*). Second, thinking interdependently would help these learners: If the pairs are mixed on math achievement, there would be great opportunities for student explanation and challenge in the paired conversations (factors that predict cognitive gain). We also think that should she do these things, she would help students gain a deeper practical understanding of empathy and respect for others.

Note: The following case was crafted by Mrs. Jade Bloom, a new teacher of French in a school in Toronto, Ontario, Canada and a graduate of the Niagara University secondary program.

CASE: Madame Bloom's 8th-Grade French Class

Madame Bloom is a new teacher who works in an all-girls school. The students in her Grade 8 Extended French class are currently studying health-related vocabulary. While the textbook they use focuses primarily on physical health (healthy eating, working out, etc.), Madame Bloom has decided to create a lesson on mental health, and more specifically, on building self-esteem, in hopes that it would have a positive effect on the students' persistence and their treatment of each other.

Madame Bloom begins the lesson by asking students for the definition of self-esteem in English. She puts up a picture on the Smart Board of a cat that looks into a mirror and sees a lion to help prompt the students. Once she has heard some definitions from her students, she puts her own definition up on the board for the students to see.

She then asks her students to reflect on their own level of self-esteem. She asks them all to stand up and gather in the middle of the classroom. There are two whiteboards at either end of the room: on one is written the word "true," and on the other is written the word "false." She tells the students that she will read a list of statements that can help them determine their own level of self-esteem. She asks them to be honest as they respond by walking to one side of the room, thereby judging the statement to be true or false. Once she finishes reading the statements, she asks the students to reflect, once again, on their level of self-esteem. She explains that building self-esteem is like building a muscle—it takes time and effort.

Madame Bloom then hands the students an article about ways that individuals can build self-esteem. She divides the students into heterogeneously mixed groups of four, which were created ahead of time based on the students' personalities, backgrounds, and needs. The students are asked to read the article and put together a summary for the class. She asks each group to assign one role to each of the students in the group: (1) the vocabulary searcher, (2) the strategy locator, (3) the example creator, and (4) the artist. All students are asked to read the text once through, as a group, and are then given time to work on their own task.

- ◆ **The vocabulary searcher** must identify ten new vocabulary words from the text and provide a French definition and an English translation for each word.
- ◆ **The strategy locator** must locate and choose his or her favourite five strategies from the text and summarize them in her own words.
- ◆ **The example creator** must provide one example for each of the five strategies chosen that shows how the strategy can be applied to her life.
- ◆ **The artist** must create a visual representation of the text in the middle of a piece of chart paper.

Once the artist has created her visual representation of the text, the other group members are asked to add their information to the chart paper. One at a time, the groups come up to present their chart paper. These large pieces of paper are then taped to the wall as a constant reminder of the new vocabulary related to the unit, as well as the ways in which the girls can build their self-esteem.

Questions for Reflection

1. What were the teacher's expectations for how members would act in the second part of the lesson? How could Madame Bloom have assessed the students' work habits and interpersonal skills while they worked on the project?

2. Madame Bloom likes heterogeneous groups. What were some factors that could be considered in building mixed teams, especially in a single-sex classroom?

3. She is a superb teacher but lacks experience. Where in the lesson could management problems arise and how should she be prepared to handle them? How does this question about classroom management align with the implementation of the Dual Objective?

Mme Bloom's Commentary

◆ The first part of the lesson is designed to catch the students' attention. However, it is not until the second part of the lesson that the Dual Objective Model is put into action. First, the students are put into groups; they do not pick their own. By building the groups herself, Madame Bloom gives her students the opportunity to work with peers that they may not have worked with otherwise, while pairing students whose strengths complement other students' weaknesses.

◆ The activity was designed with both a cognitive and affective goal in mind. In terms of cognitive growth, the students learn about vocabulary related to health while developing their reading comprehension and writing skills in French. With respect to affective growth, students are given the opportunity to work interdependently, enabling them to develop listening and negotiation skills as they learn to think flexibly and remain open to new learning.

◆ By giving the students a different role within the group and a different task to accomplish, each group member gains a sense of accountability and responsibility. Since each student is responsible for a different task, he or she has no choice but to rely on his or her group members to successfully complete the whole project. This type of collaboration helps to create a sense of community between students who might not have interacted otherwise. As students discuss the information they put together (which is part of their task), they develop a better understanding of what they learned. This type of discussion creates a deeper learning experience that will most likely result in long-term retention of knowledge.

Our Take

◆ Madame Bloom has taken an important step in that she has recognized the role that affect plays in the class and has actually used a great deal of class time to improve student understanding of the notion of self-esteem. (Again, the work of Farrington et al., 2012, suggests that how a teen sees herself as belonging to a specific learning community matters greatly.) Moreover, she trusts the power of collaboration across the whole class. This lesson is exceedingly complex but does demand that students listen intently to each other and be responsible for specific work. Johnson and Johnson (1989) are famous for giving every team member a job that they must do for the team to be successful: they call it positive interdependence.

◆ Because we can read Madame Bloom's rationale, we can see how she uses two steps in the lesson (Flynn et al., 2004). One step is to gain attention, tap into prior knowledge, and create a shared common experience; the second step involves getting students to work on a learning activity and using the Dual Objective. Because she has this lesson thoroughly planned she can answer the familiar question, "Why do we have to do this?" with a *good* answer. Many times, teachers resent that question: They reply with some version of "because I said so," angering the student and shutting down an opportunity. We suggest that the teacher just answer it honestly. We urge you to complete each of the following four possible replies that Madame Bloom could better use in response to this common question:

   a. We all are in this classroom community together and how we treat each other matters, so you . . .
   b. To learn French and get high grades, we will be needing each other, so today . . .
   c. Almost all of you will be at work with others someday, and you need experience . . .
   d. I want you to figure out how different people's skills complement each other so I . . .

   We are sure that however you complete the replies, they are far more effective to stimulate understanding than "because I told you." We are often reminded how powerful a good answer to that challenging question is for helping adolescents see the purposes of what we do in school.

◆ If successful on this first attempt, Madame Bloom can use a variety of other strategies to help teens examine the purposes of working together and the skills in doing so. This is a very good start and we offer three follow-up suggestions:

a. Let teams study together briefly before the first vocabulary quiz. If each team member meets a particular score, give *each* member a bonus. ("If everybody in your team gets 70 percent or higher, I will give everyone on the team, even the 100 percent folks, an eight-point bonus. You have ten minutes to get each other ready.") By the way, this team bonus option results in bright kids caring about low achievers in class and helping them learn.

b. We suggest that she use an outslip; then she can create stems like this:

    ◆ Something new I discovered today was . . .
    ◆ One way that I helped my team mates today was . . .
    ◆ French is about communication and listening. To that end, using partners in class means . . .

c. As we have mentioned before, the use of an instrument helps. A checklist aligned to the affective goals from the lesson could include things like:

    _____ Works interdependently
    _____ Listens carefully
    _____ Thinks flexibly
    _____ Is open to learning

    Such a checklist could be used quickly and with many students in the class during a brief activity.

Note: The following case was drafted by Ms. Kim Alexander and is based closely on a lesson she planned and taught in spring 2016. Kim is the co-author, along with Ms. Emily Kaufman, of the section on Problem-Based Learning (PBL) in Chapter 6. Other aspects of the science unit that this case is drawn from are also featured in Myers, Bardsley, Vermette, and Kline (2017).

CASE: Ms. Alexander's 9th-Grade Science Narrative

Food Chains and Food Webs, Living Environment, Grade 9

Objectives:

A. Cognitive

1. I can identify producers as well as primary, secondary, and tertiary consumers in a food chain or food web.

2. I can predict how a change in one population will affect the population size of other species in the same food chain or food web.

3. I can create a food chain that illustrates the flow of energy in an ecosystem.

B. Affective

4. I can work effectively in groups to achieve a common goal.

DESCRIPTION

9:00 a.m.

As the bell rings, Ms. Alexander welcomes her 9th-grade living environment class and asks students to take their seats. She excitedly tells them this is her favorite lesson of the year and she hopes the students will enjoy it too. She then tells the class that they'll begin with challenge questions (which is a familiar opening "bell-ringer" activity for her students). Ms. Alexander puts the first challenge question on the board and asks students to independently jot down their ideas on scrap paper or in their notes. After a moment she poses the second question and gives students time to record ideas. Then, she tells the class that they have 47 seconds to consult with a partner and be ready to answer either question aloud. Students are aware that they are not always expected to get challenge questions right, but they are expected to have ideas ready to share. After about two minutes, she calls the class back together and then asks a few students to share what they thought about each question.

9:06 a.m.

Ms. Alexander tells the class they'll be watching the "coolest YouTube video ever made" (she challenges them to find a cooler one, but assures them they won't). She tells students that they are not being asked to take any notes, but that they should pay attention to the video as they'll be working with examples from it for the remainder of class. As the four-and-a-half-minute video on trophic cascades plays, Ms. Alexander watches along, and walks through the room to ask students to focus if they appear distracted. When the video closes, she passes out a notes sheet with an example food web diagram at the top. For the next ten minutes, she works through the vocabulary words with the students, identifying examples of each vocabulary word in the example web as they go. Students record definitions of the words and label the food web.

9:22 a.m.

Ms. Alexander shows a final slide that explains the discovery activity. She tells students that they will be working in their base groups to solve a "case study" food web problem. They will need to identify and label the species in the food web according to their new vocabulary words and then they will need to identify how each species in the web will be affected by the disturbance presented in the case study. As students work, Ms. Alexander circulates through the groups. She chats with each group (multiple times) to be sure that they understand both components of the case study and that each group member is actively contributing.

9:33 a.m.

Ms. Alexander calls the class back together. She then asks a few groups to share their findings. She commends the class on their work on the case studies and passes out their exit slips. She tells the students that they are free to use their notes to assist them, but that they must do the exit slips independently. The exit slip has six questions: two check students' understanding (one thing they've learned and one lingering question), two ask for feedback on the lesson (positive and negative), one addresses non-academic skills, and one asks students to create their own food web. Students turn these slips into Ms. Alexander at the door on their way out, as she thanks them for their hard work and wishes them all a good day.

Questions for Reflection

1. Ms. Alexander is moving toward the practical and daily use of the Dual Objective. However, she could work to hasten that development. For example, it would help if she were clearer about the specific social and emotional skills that she wants students to utilize during "cooperation." Her intention to make them work effectively in groups is correct, but it can be broken down into discrete skills such as thinking interdependently, listening with empathy and understanding, or simply encouraging the contributions of others. What are some other examples of specific skills that could be integrated into this lesson?

2. How could Ms. Alexander get more evidence of the students' demonstration of mastering the various objectives?

3. If you could offer her a short list of things to note while she worked the room, what would be included? Would your list change drastically from lesson to lesson or could it be used as a stable base instrument across all lessons of a unit or a marking period?

Ms. Alexander's Commentary

◆ Three components of the preceding lesson were explicitly connected to the Dual Objective. Relationship-building was fostered in the opening activity. Students were encouraged to work effectively in their Cooperative Learning groups as the teacher walked throughout the room during the discovery activity, and the exit slip formally assessed students' social and emotional learning (non-cognitive skills), which also serves as an authentic assessment. An analysis of the linkage between each of these three components of the lesson and the Dual Objective follows.

◆ The first connection this lesson made to the Dual Objective occurred during the opening activity. The challenge questions encouraged students to recall information from a previous lesson and apply it in a new way. They also foreshadowed the coming lesson and served as an inquiry-based opening. It was the use of the think–pair–share method, in conjunction with these challenge questions, however, that best illustrates the Dual Objective. When they are given the opportunity to share with a neighbor, students strengthen their relationships with one another. This not only fosters community, but also provides students an opportunity to practice their interpersonal skills of cooperation. In this way, Ms. Alexander asked students to practice their non-cognitive skills as they discussed living environment ideas.

◆ The Dual Objective was also apparent during the discovery portion of the lesson as students worked in their base groups on the case study. The base groups are "home base" groups that students work in periodically throughout the year. Ms. Alexander carefully arranged these groups at the beginning of the year. They are structured to be heterogeneous in terms of gender, ethnicity, and personal qualities (preferences). By having students work in diverse groupings, Ms. Alexander again promoted community and interpersonal skills among her students. Additionally, as Ms. Alexander circulated through the groups, she monitored students' understanding of the content as well as students' ability to work as team players. This was connected to her fourth objective for this lesson as well, which stated that students would be able to work effectively in groups.

◆ Finally, the Dual Objective was exemplified in the students' exit slips, specifically in the fifth question. The question read: "One way that I helped someone today . . . **or** . . . One act of kindness that I will perform today is . . ." Students' exit slips were collected as formative assessments, and were graded (for participation points) out of five points. Students received one point for supplying a reasonable answer to this question. This question allowed Ms. Alexander to formally assess students' social and emotional learning, consistent with the practice of the Dual Objective.

Our Take

◆ In a thoroughly modern learning experience, this teacher has the students using content, hearing other people's insights, and showing their understanding. Simply put, she has featured important content, led the students into examining and elaborating on it, and enticed them to work respectfully with others. That is a lot of good things all happening at the same time for all students.

◆ The video plays a subtle but important role in the students' knowledge development. Moreover, she gives them a specific direction for watching: they will be using examples later. She also tells them that this will be an emotionally positive viewing: if it is, she will have gained great credibility with them.

◆ She does collect outslips (she calls them exit slips) with evidence of students' personal thoughts about the entire experience including non-cognitive aspects. She will be using this feedback in future classes, thus building on Glasser's call for inviting and investing in student influence, which he sees as their use of the motivator called "power."

◆ Importantly, this lesson met our highest standard for engagement: the students and their thinking were at the heart of the lesson. She could not have taught this lesson without students. This may sound simple, but it is profound. When students are essential and at the heart of the lesson, they matter and the lesson is far more meaningful. Far too many classes are currently taught without any connection to student thinking or input and therefore are only about content and not about students' thinking about the content.

◆ In her post-observation narrative, Ms. Alexander describes several positive things: she clearly had planned to work the room, seeking opportunities to give feedback; she had built heterogeneous groups and had a "theory of the team" in mind; and she made smart use of think–pair–share (Lyman, 1981) in the way that modern teachers often do. However, her use was not just a brief tactic but part of a well-structured, intentionally designed plan.

◆ We wish to make a comment about task timing and its impact on positive student perceptions. During the lesson, Ms. Alexander offers a time of "47 seconds" for students to collaborate, and then waits two minutes before moving forward. Two things here: The mention of an odd time like 47 seconds may distract students trying to concentrate deeply in both content and following directions, causing "overload" with the potential for shutdown. In addition, unrealistic timeframes have the capacity to make slower processing students feel like failures if they don't complete in time. Our suggestion is that if two minutes are required to complete the transaction with quality, then we suggest using that time, perhaps with a 30-seconds-left reminder as she works the room. Once she gets a feel for the pace of completion she can make subsequent alterations.

CASE: Mrs. Hightower's 11th-Grade Social Studies Class

Mrs. Hightower is a 34-year-old teacher from New York State. She has graduated from a secondary teaching program and has just started a job as a global studies teacher in a village in northern Louisiana. At Huey Long High, she teaches all 10th- and 11th-graders and has one section of psychology. First period is her smallest group: seven students, a mix of high and low achievers, poor and working class, four boys and three girls. One student (Jaden) is severely autistic. This is the third day of the two-week unit on the American Revolution and she is pleased with the progress of this class and both of her other (larger) classes.

Mrs. Hightower begins: "Today, guys take out your essays about one of the causes of the Revolution. We are going to work on them for about ten minutes. I am going to come around and give individual feedback based on what I saw and read yesterday. If you have written more, or made changes, please show me."

The students start to work and she gestures to the rubric on the board. The elements of the rubric are as follows: (1) strong thesis statement, (2) evidence/support, (3) use of writing conventions, and (4) clear closing.

During the work time (which she extends to 15 minutes because every student was working), she does talk to each student individually. She spends longer with Jaden than with anyone else.

"OK, stop please. Take a look. You have cause #1, cause #2, or cause #3 printed on the top of the sheet? For the next eight minutes, you have to find the other person with that same cause, and do some peer editing. Remember the rules for peer editing; we showed them on day one and they are on the wall there (pointing to a huge poster with huge writing on it). I want to see how well you can listen carefully, wait your turn, and accept feedback; that last one is a tough one. Go find your partners."

She waits patiently to watch how the students will react to working directly with Jaden. Nothing out of the norm happens when two students discover they share cause #3 on their paper, as does Jaden. One student even says "OK, with three here it might be tougher to edit that way, but we can do it. Mrs. Hightower always reminds us about being flexible . . ."

Mrs. Hightower watches the peer editing from the desk behind Jaden and doesn't speak for the entire time. She does smile, though.

At the end of the work time, everyone seemed ready to move on. However, she says, "OK, now write two sentences for me, please. One is about what major advice you received from your partner and the second is how you reacted to the advice."

The students get this task done quickly. "Kenny?"

Kenny replies, "It looks like Maggie thought my thesis statement was pretty OK. People had all different amounts of money, just like we do. Well, that caused lots of 'anger and resentment' and people were 'bitter and hateful.' So people said, 'What the _____,' and revolted, started killing and oh yeah, I think because she liked it, I took her suggestions, even though she told me to change some of my words."

A little confused, Mrs. Hightower replied: "Kenny, was Maggie right? What did you change?"

"Well, she thought I should use 'anger and resentment' from the vocab sheet instead of what I had, and 'bitter and hateful' because the words I had were I guess . . . ah . . . bad. It's better now."

Mrs. Hightower debriefed the other two groups in the same way: by probing the answers until she was sure that students were meta-cognitively aware of how the process was supposed to work.

She then announced, "Well, we have about 12 minutes left. Let's start tomorrow's work right now. OK? Here are four questions: please compare, examine, and evaluate them. In short, what do you think of them? Please work by yourself and be ready to share:

1. What are the dates of the American Revolution?
2. How did people try to protect themselves amidst all the violence?
3. Imagine a new movie about the Revolution. What are four scenes that must be included?
4. What long-term effects from this event impact our lives in the U.S. today?"

The students sat and thought (or daydreamed). No work was shown on paper or in talk. After one minute, she says, "OK, please get with your partner and share anything you've just thought about." This goes well, but now there are only two minutes left. She starts again: "Tomorrow, I am going to ask you to write five *more* questions to ask me about the American Revolution. First, we are going to examine this set again and then, second, you create yours. Then, I am going to answer them. It will be 'challenge the teacher day,' OK?"

The bell rings. Mrs. Hightower smiles and waves the students out the door. She escorts Jaden, who moves more slowly than others. As he leaves the doorway, she realizes that Kenny is making his way back. He offers her a fist bump and says, "Really good class Mrs. H. I'll have good questions for you tomorrow." She smiles, knowing that she has struck a chord with him and because she expects the students to be able to answer their own questions as well.

Questions for Reflection

1. What do you think were some consequences of Kenny and Maggie doing the peer editing of each other's work? Were they ready to have their work seen by somebody else in class?
2. What did you think of the quality of Mrs. Hightower's questions and tasks?
3. Assume the Dual Objective. What were the teacher's two objectives today? What evidence did she collect to assess student achievement and growth?
4. What part of this class is most likely to leave a student unhappy? Explain your reasoning.

5. A case could be made that the use of choice results in each student only being exposed to some of the content required them to be taught (by state law). What are some things Mrs. Hightower could make in the next few days to rectify those potential gaps in some students' knowledge base?

6. Imagine you are Jaden. Keep a "mental journal" of the events in this class from his perspective. Briefly tell some of the things that went through his mind throughout the lesson. Predict whether he liked or disliked this experience.

Our Take

◆ In general, we appreciate what the teacher is trying to do in this class. The students are expected to be actively engaged, respectful to each other, and to feel like part of a larger community. She also spreads the content across groups, setting up a potential jigsaw and dealing with a great amount of subject matter quickly.

◆ She has integrated peer editing into the learning process and is very careful about Jaden (although we don't know why). She works the room thoughtfully and calls on students to "go public" with their experiences and thoughts. This is clearly a class that builds on students' thoughts and is totally student-centered.

◆ She subtly identifies both *listening* and *accepting criticism* as affective objectives for the day. Moreover, she uses her large-group time to examine these in the context of the actual class. She expects the students to use important affective skills to make cognitive gains.

A Final Q&A: Overcoming Commonly Perceived Obstacles and Resolving Hesitations

In this final section of the book, we have decided to use the format again of frequently asked questions encompassing both theory and application of Cooperative Learning in the form of the Dual Objective Model. We assume that you've been reading carefully, visualizing applications to your classrooms, evaluating many suggestions, and even experimenting with your students. If so, you now have a better working conception/mental representation of the Dual Objective Model than you had 100 pages ago. With each attempt at transfer, your conceptual understanding gets deeper, richer, and clearer. In layman's terms, "Once is not enough!"

TASK: Wrapping it all up

To guide you to the metaphorical "finish line" for employing group work that works, we suggest the following:

1. Read through each of the questions that follow.
2. Then, based on your own interest level, classify each of the queries using one of these three responses:

   N = need to read **Now**
   T = will go back and read **Tomorrow**
   S = too busy right now, but **Soon**

3. As priority, time and interest dictate, read each question, and create your own written response.
4. Compare your responses to those which follow under Our Take.

   _____ 1. Some of my students just refuse to work together. What can I do?

   _____ 2. My principal is a strong leader and boss manager and sees attention to "soft skills" as a waste of time. Do you have any suggestions about how to convince him of their value?

   _____ 3. I have one (7th-grade) student; let's call him Donald. Everyone hates Donald and no one wants to work with him. Should I just let him work alone?

   _____ 4. All of my current assessments (tests) are multiple choice. I would rather not have to redo all of them to better assess group learning. What can be done?

   _____ 5. I do not feel like I am really teaching while students are completing teamwork and when I am "working the room." I am also concerned that some students, parents, and administrators may feel the same. What can be done to make group work seem like a more normal expectation for schooling?

   _____ 6. Most of my colleagues have been putting our ELL students into their own separate groups in the regular classroom. This practice contradicts the benefits of heterogeneous groupings, and may be simply more convenient than effective. What can I say to them to defend my own decisions and to help these students excel, especially since there are many such students heading our way?

   _____ 7. Our 7–12 building sees itself as cutting edge and progressive. We advertise that we use "personalized learning," follow "project-based learning approaches," and that "blended learning" is common. This means that technology dominates our self-image. Yet, you say business and other organizations want team players who can work on ill-structured problems and leverage diversity. Are we all on the same page?

8. Technically, there are many ways to do Cooperative Learning: Jigsaw, think–pair–share, four corners, group investigation, complex instruction, STAD, constructive controversy, problem-based learning, Dansereau's dyads, reciprocal teaching, and others. I want to do more and more group work, but where does the Dual Objective fit into this set?

9. Paul Tough (2016), has recently published a book that seems to suggest that one cannot teach non-cognitive skills explicitly—the way schools teach reading or addition. Doesn't this make the Dual Objective's focus on affective skills a waste of time?

Our Take

1. Some of my students just refuse to work together. What can I do?

We are very troubled by this for several reasons, especially in the senior year of high school. Twelfth-graders are the students closest to leaving the developmental environment of schooling and entering a far more judgmental world. As they take a job, enter the military, and/or start college, they will be judged by their ability to (a) embrace diversity, (b) work effectively in all kinds of collaborative situations, (c) self-regulate, (d) persist, and (e) communicate (listen and talk), among numerous other affective expectations. Although applicable at all levels, students approaching their graduation year should, and *need* to be, the best at working together and having a positive work ethic. To facilitate such at any level, we suggest several things:

a. Tell your students that they have to be able to do CL if they wish to have any sense of success "next year"; have an open discussion, but if you believe that this is a true and important factor in their future, stick to your guns and proceed.

b. Also let your administrative leaders and the students' parents know about your intention to use the Dual Objective, and explain why.

c. Introduce CL with quick and easy tactics, such as those described earlier in this chapter and/or provide bonuses for effective teamwork. Make your plans visible to students.

d. One of the authors got great mileage out of this practice. Kline brought in examples of letters of reference instruments and evaluation forms used by businesses locally. It didn't take the students very long to discover that both of these assessments were much more interested in social and emotional habits than in more cognitive abilities. For example, the question, "Does the candidate display punctuality?" is more common than "Assess the candidate's understanding of mitosis." Another, "How well does the candidate interact with different kinds of people?" is more common than "How well does the candidate apply the Pythagorean theorem?" Finally, "How well does the employee display the Starbuck's pledge to be a positive force for the customer?" could be compared with "How does the employee apply statistical techniques in assessing his or her effectiveness?" We urge you to share these kinds of performance evaluations (and recommendation instruments) with those high school seniors who are graduating soon. Kline has done so in middle school with great success.

e. Start a dialogue with colleagues about your plans and attempt to get them to begin implementing well-structured CL in lower grades so that students have success experiences *before* they get to their final years. You can use some of the many scenarios we have offered you to get conversation going and/or look to the district mission statement for wording that supports your efforts.

2. My principal is a strong leader and boss manager and sees attention to "soft skills" as a waste of time. Do you have any suggestions about how to convince him of their value?

We have written this book so you could show administrators (and others) a source of your commitment: buy him or her a copy or drop a note offering your summary. Moreover, we always like to have people look at their own mission statements, so that may help. One other approach is to spark a conversation with him or her about why some students are failing: inevitably, the discussion will focus on things like "doesn't work hard enough," "high absenteeism," "thinks school is irrelevant," and "doesn't feel accepted by school community." When this happens, the principal recognizes the importance of "soft skills" and the need to formally approach them has already been established.

3. I have one (7th-grade) student; let's call him Donald. Everyone hates Donald and no one wants to work with him. Should I just let him work alone?

No . . . at least not initially.

Making this work can be tricky, and there is always a reason for poor behavior. Assuming that you have conferred with school guidance counselors and/or social workers concerning potential issues, in the classroom he must still participate. Your job is to teach, and his is to learn, without negative impact to the balance of your classroom community. We have several suggestions:

a. Our first suggestion is to help Donald and all of your students to see the deep and purposeful connections between expectations in your classroom and expectations in outside society. Donald is one of a community, just like the outside world, and he must work with classroom norms and expectations, in the same way that we all live under societal law and norms. You will establish a solid foundation and proactively address these and similar issues by being unwavering here.

b.   Be certain that all students are aware of and understand the affective skill targets that have been chosen for attention in class, and how these impact success for all. Involve them in creation or selection whenever possible.

c.   Start slowly, perhaps in interdependent pairs in which Student A needs to report what Student B thinks and says. Donald then matters to at least one other student in class. (This is a version of Cohen's "equal status" strategy.)

d.   If you know some of Donald's strengths, you can create a group product that takes advantage of those abilities: he will then be a contributor to a team effort. Do not give up easily on this student, even though you may want to.

e.   Always be honest in your feedback to his (and others') group efforts. One advantage of the Dual Objective is that the behavior students show to each other and to their responsibilities *is* part of the curriculum.

f.   Plan time to discuss his behavior privately, building on the concept of the growth mindset: The question to Donald is not "**Why** aren't you nicer to others?" but could be, "**When** will you start to show others the respect that they are due?"

The options for addressing Donald and similar students are nearly unlimited, and start with knowing who they are as people. The above suggestions are a few simple things which may apply. Please recognize that when you have tried multiple interventions, there does come a time when the option to remove the student from the collaborative process should be considered. Detriment to the community is neither acceptable nor productive.

4. All of my current assessments (tests really) are multiple choice. I would rather not have to redo all of them to better assess group learning. What can be done?

First, your questions are about only half of the Dual Objective Model—the cognitive. Although we do not encourage hefty use of multiple-choice assessments as evidence of learning, we do recognize their place. That being said, since this book is not about cognitive assessment but is about Cooperative

Learning we suggest that you utilize cooperative structures for developing understanding and that you choose other cooperative alternatives over or in addition to M/C testing.

To move in that direction, we offer the following "quick" solution. First, you have to know your students and build solid teams; then you have to design (or borrow from the "100 Products") some appropriate learning activities (options to the M/C test). Given this approach, we suggest that you also keep your multiple-choice component, but incorporate a team-based bonus that affects each member: that'll drive high achievers to share their knowledge with lower, even if it is for selfish purposes.

To guide your grading efforts we offer one last hint. Teachers new to Cooperative Learning often misuse the idea of group grading. Group grading is one of the huge (fatal?) flaws in teachers' unstructured group work. We suggest that the product, the project, the tangible representation of the group's efforts, could be group graded, but perhaps only for 40 percent or 50 percent of the overall grade. Give one of your multiple-choice tests for the other 50 or 60 points. Some students may scream "unfair," but this is a reasonable facsimile of the real world: some of our success is individual achievement but some of it is linked to the groups we are part of. This is true in all team sports, so many students will recognize and accept it. Moreover, there are few working adults whose achievement level is not influenced by the actions of other members of the organization.

Please understand that this answer addresses your question, but does not present anything about the affective focus of the Dual Objective. You must be ready to change much more in your practice for your students to reap the benefits of affective growth. When you are ready to do so, come back for another read.

5. **I do not feel like I am really teaching while students are completing teamwork and when I am "working the room." I am also concerned that some students, parents, and administrators may feel the same way. What can be done to make group work seem like a more normal expectation for schooling?**

Like much of our advice, the answer lies in communicating with others, especially students (who talk to their parents). Many modern jobs expect employees to "work well under conditions of minimal supervision," which is true of how the Dual Objective operates. However, picture a room in which Cooperative Learning is in operation: while groups A, B, C, and D are working, you are assessing group E, which means that you are working and actually in a position to provide feedback, which everybody knows is important for learning. As you move from group to group, you will be continuing to meet student learning needs.

By the way, the more often students experience CL, the more that working in teams on well-structured tasks will be seen as the "norm." Right now, CL can sometimes (incorrectly) be seen as "fringe" pedagogy, or as a simple break from routine. In fact, Tough (2016) seems somewhat surprised when he learns of a thing called "Cooperative Learning, a pedagogical approach that promoted student engagement in the learning process" (p. 92) being used at a highly rated urban school. We talk more of Tough in an item below, but we do wish to mention his commitment to building powerfully supportive classroom environments to promote affective growth in teens. His general acknowledgement of the place for Cooperative Learning (and maybe the Dual Objective in particular) in "helping students succeed" is noteworthy.

6. Most of my colleagues have been putting all of our ELL students into their own separate groups in the regular classroom. This practice contradicts the benefits of heterogeneous groupings, and may be simply more convenient than effective. What can I say to them to defend my own decisions and to help these students excel, especially since there are many such students heading our way?

One factor in success with ELLs is their frequent, routinized usage of *English* in their daily lives. By placing these students in supportive, heterogeneous teams whose members spend half of their class time talking to each other, they will develop fluency *and* content knowledge faster. Research also suggests that they will be recognized and accepted socially far more quickly this way. Segregating them from more fluent English speakers is not a good idea and cannot be supported by anything other than a weak comment about "familiarity."

7. Our 7–12 building sees itself as cutting edge and progressive. We advertise that we use "personalized learning," follow "project-based learning approaches," and that "blended learning" is common. This means that technology dominates our self-image. Yet, you say business and other organizations want team players who can work on ill-structured problems and leverage diversity. Are we all on the same page?

Please note that some of the examples you have examined in this text have shown teachers using technology in all kinds of ways. It is part of the normal classroom routine, as are projects and extended service; learning is not limited to listening to teachers talk and completing worksheets. The use of technology, or project-based learning, or service learning, does not preclude the use of the Dual Objective as the internal structure of the class; they are enhanced by it. Instead of 24 students in Math 11, the teacher could have 12 pairs, eight groups of three, or six groups of four, and proceed by including emphasis on particular affective skills beneficial to the learning activity and teaching strategy employed. In many situations the availability of technology for executing CL is crucial to student engagement outside the classroom as access to such expands the physical classroom to the world stage for additional authentic work.

This expanded view not only needs, but absolutely requires affective skills to enable academic action. The master teacher employing such strategies would be wise to incorporate the formal structure of the Dual Objective to assure that the affective skills needed for positive digital citizenship, responsible decision making and problem solving (among others) are included in the learning activity.

8. **Technically, there are many ways to do Cooperative Learning: Jigsaw, think–pair–share, four corners, group investigation, complex instruction, STAD, constructive controversy, problem-based learning, Dansereau's dyads, reciprocal teaching, and others. I want to do more and more group work, but where does the Dual Objective fit into this set?**

This is the easiest question to answer of this entire section. Each of the models mentioned has a proven track record of success for improving achievement (or cognitive gain). If one of those approaches is chosen as a structure for a year, a unit, or a lesson, we are fine with it. However, none of them has the systematic and intentional call for affective concerns in the way that the Dual Objective does. So, we suggest that if you choose one of these strategies that you make sure to add the affective feedback element as described in the Dual Objective Model. Sneak a peek at Chapter 2 again in order to review the graphic of the Dual Objective Model we provide.

9. **Paul Tough (2016), has recently published a book that seems to suggest that one cannot teach non-cognitive skills explicitly—the way schools teach reading or addition. Doesn't this make the Dual Objective's focus on affective skills a waste of time?**

This is an astute question and one with many implications. In short, the answer is *no*, but it is a bit complex. First, in his two most recent books, Tough has convinced much of the world that non-cognitive factors, no matter what we call them, are critically important to life success and that they can be improved. While he doesn't like to think of them as "skills," we accept Goleman's (1995) assertion that they are indeed skills and can be developed by intentional practice. This generalization is reflected in every parental attempt to influence a child's behavior and attitude and in every coach's attempt to get players to "play for the team and/or work hard on every play". These skills are also inherently part of any teacher's set of rules or expectations. Moreover, work by Brackett and Kremeitzer (2011) stresses the importance of being able to label these skills and emotions ("mean" is different than "arrogant" and "empathy" is different than "sympathy") and to talk about them in context. Tough cites the case of a great chess teacher who never uses the words "grit" or "self-regulation," yet we are sure she values and promotes these notions. We don't think that it would hurt her players to be aware of these terms or concepts and recognize their value to chess players. He concludes that it is the overall "classroom environment" of strong relationships and support by teacher and peers that matters so much. This is exactly the approach that we envision with the Dual Objective.

Second, he cites research by Jackson (2014) that shows that teachers who have excellent records in helping students develop "life skills" are indeed doing something different than their counterparts who concentrate solely on test scores. This commitment to non-cognitive learning yields positive long-term affective growth in students, enabling the development of constructive adult behaviors. Again, Tough attributes these gains to a great classroom environment and we wish to note that in secondary schools, this requires both teacher–student *and* student–student support. We interpret these findings to ardently support our expectations for the Dual Objective classroom.

Chapter 7 Big Ideas

1. Carefully planned "first uses" of the Dual Objective will help ease transition from previous practice.
2. Three powerful first uses include (a) the Venn diagram, (b) A teaches, B draws (The Gronk), and (c) "Let's examine the class rules."
3. Students drive the success of Cooperative Learning and teachers design the conditions that make it so.
4. Students need to talk and listen to diverse others, think deeply, show teamwork skills (in problem-solving), be accountable for their own learning, and recognize the importance of this kind of activity in their lives now and in the future.
5. Questions and tasks that call for extended reflection are very powerful learning devices and can be used quite often with teenagers to build affective competence.
6. Classroom management strategies, class rules, and "community" expectations are the de facto affective agenda of any teacher. Teachers often just try to enforce them; it would be beneficial if students

got to discuss them, examine them, and assess them so they could better internalize them.

7. Teachers never get enough opportunities to examine other people's practice thoughtfully. Using these opportunities prepares teachers for better decision-making.

8. Technology can and should be integrated into cooperative classroom learning experiences whenever possible to mirror real world collaborative practices.

9. A teacher's continuous improvement is almost totally controlled by his or her effort; self-assessment, goal setting and thoughtful practice all work to make teachers more effective.

In Closing

We wish to thank you for reading and thinking through this text. Getting this far means that you have shown persistence and grit. If you are going to try out some of these ideas, you may well be showing a growth mindset; and if you have done the embedded activities and had discussions with colleagues, you are clearly engaged in deliberate/purposeful practice. These are the three major theories that support our approach to teacher instructional development and which were introduced in the prologue (please check back).

We also wish to mention that our support of "continuous improvement" means that none of us is done right now: We can each get better, wiser, and more experienced. We wish you luck as you reflect on your attempts at implementing the Dual Objective Model of Cooperative Learning and helping your students become smarter, better people and better members of the local and global communities to which they belong and help shape. We also offer one author's e-mail address, pjv@niagara.edu, and urge you to feel free to write to us with feedback in the form of comments, stories, complaints, questions or, if need be, praise.

Thanks.

References

Brackett, M.A., & Kremeitzer, J.P. (2011). *Creating the emotionally literate classroom: An introduction to the RULER approach to social and emotional learning*. Port Chester, NY: National Professional Resources.

Brown, P.C., Roediger III, H.L., & McDaniel, M.A. (2014). *Make it stick: The science of successful learning*. Cambridge, MA: The Belknap Press of Harvard University Press.

Cain, L. (2012). *Quiet: The power of introverts in a world that can't stop talking.* New York, NY: Crown Publishing.

Dansereau, D.F. (1987). Transfer from cooperative to individual studying. *Journal of Reading, 30,* 614–616.

Davidson, N. (2015, Nov.). *Cooperative and collaborative learning: How are they alike, how are they different?* Presentation at the International Lilly Conference on College Teaching, Miami University, Oxford, Ohio.

Duhigg, C. (2014). *The power of habit: Why we do what we do in life and business.* New York, NY: Random House.

Ericsson, A. & Pool, R. (2016). *Peak: Secrets from the new science of expertise.* New York, NY: Houghton-Mifflin Harcourt.

Farrington, C.A., Roderick, E., Nagaoka, J., Keyes, T.S., Johnson, D.W., & Beechum, N. (2012). *Teaching adolescents to become learners: The role of non-cognitive factors in shaping school performance.* Chicago, IL: Consortium on Chicago School Research.

Flynn, P., Mesibov, D., Vermette, P., & Smith, R.M. (2004). *Applying standards-based constructivism: A two-step guide for motivating middle and high school students.* Larchmont, NY: Eye-on-Education.

Goleman, D. (1995). *Emotional intelligence.* New York, NY: Bantam Books.

Jackson, K. (2014, revision). Non-cognitive ability, test scores, and teacher quality: Evidence from 9th grade teachers. NEBR Working paper 18624. Cambridge, MA: National Bureau of Economic Research.

Johnson, D.W., & Johnson, R.W. (1987). *Learning together and alone.* Englewood Cliffs, NJ: Prentice Hall.

Johnson, D.W., & Johnson, R.W. (1989). *Cooperation and competition: Theory and research.* Edina, MN: Interaction Book Company.

Johnson D.W., & Johnson, R.W. (2009). An educational psychology success story: Social interdependence theory and cooperative learning. *Educational Researcher, 38*(5), 365–379.

Lyman, F.T. (1981). The responsive classroom discussion: The inclusion of all students. In A. Anderson (Ed.), *Mainstreaming Digest* (pp. 109–113). College Park, MD: University of Maryland Press.

Myers, J., Bardsley, M., Vermette, P., & Kline, C. (2017). *Cooperative learning for the 21st century* (forthcoming).

Stigler, J.W., & Hiebert, J. (1999). *The teaching gap.* New York, NY: Free Press.

Tough, P. (2016). *Helping children succeed: What works and why.* New York, NY: Houghton-Mifflin.

Appendix 1
Taxonomies of Affective Skills

Introduction

In this section, we want to offer you a chance to examine closely a brief set of available taxonomies that schools could use to structure their **affective curriculum**. (These are called by a variety of names including "soft skills," non-cognitive skills, dispositions, and social-emotional competencies etc., and have been recognized officially as critically important for learning and life success in a report delivered from the U.S. Department of Education in 2013.) We have already shared Habits of Mind (Costa & Kallick, 2014, 2008), in Chapter 2 alongside the P21 Framework skills from the Partnership for 21st Century Learning, and in their entirety in Chapter 5. In that same chapter, we mentioned that the Province of Ontario (Canada) has a set of six Work Habits and Learning Skills that are explicitly assessed for every student in every grade (1–12) four times a year. We have included their inventory herein. In Chapter 6, we delved more deeply into the use of the P21 Framework skills with a still-partial list. Herein you will find a more complete listing, including performance indicators (objectives), which are shared by a large set of influential organizations in the U.S. and abroad.

In addition to those referenced above, in this space we will share with you several others that may serve well in your search for appropriate affective focus in implementing the Dual Objective Model of Cooperative Learning. If you are interested, each can be easily found online and each has its own "story" to tell.

1. Collaborative for Academic, Social, and Emotional Learning (CASEL's) Core SEL Competencies
2. P21 Framework Skills from the Partnership for 21st Century Learning
3. Tony Wagner's Seven Survival Skills
4. Steven Covey's Seven Habits of Highly Effective People
5. KIPP Schools' Seven Character Strengths
6. Character First's 49 Traits
7. Ontario Canada's Learning Skills and Work Habits for Grades 1–12

The Collaborative for Academic, Social, and Emotional Learning (CASEL's) Core SEL Competencies

SEL is widely known today because of the efforts of this organization. They have organized a mountain of data and information and their website is a regular attraction to professionals who are committed to the education of the "whole child." They see five fundamental "core" competencies, each of which are shown below. For more, visit: http://www.casel.org/social-and-emotional-learning/core-competencies/ (retrieved 01/31/17).

◆ **Self-Awareness**	◆ **Self-Management**	◆ **Social Awareness**
◆ Identifying emotions	◆ Impulse control	◆ Perspective-taking
◆ Accurate self-perception	◆ Stress management	◆ Empathy
◆ Recognizing strengths	◆ Self-discipline	◆ Appreciating diversity
◆ Self-confidence	◆ Self-motivation	◆ Respect for others
◆ Self-efficacy	◆ Goal-setting	
	◆ Organizational skills	
◆ **Relationship Skills**	◆ **Responsible Decision-Making**	
◆ Communication	◆ Identifying problems	
◆ Social engagement	◆ Analyzing situations	
◆ Relationship-building	◆ Solving problems	
◆ Teamwork	◆ Evaluating	
	◆ Reflecting	
	◆ Ethical responsibility	

P21 Framework Skills from the Partnership for 21st Century Learning

The Partnership for 21st Century Learning in their P21 Framework incorporates four interconnected elements essential to successful 21st-century teaching and learning. Among those (and the focus here) are two, Learning and Innovation Skills and Life and Career Skills, which include performance objectives. When seeking affective skills for implementation within the Dual Objective Model approach to CL, there are none better. For more, visit: http://www.p21.org/storage/documents/P21_Framework_Definitions.pdf (retrieved 01/31/17).

LEARNING AND INNOVATION SKILLS

1. Creativity and Innovation

Think Creatively

◆ Use a wide range of idea creation techniques (such as brainstorming).
◆ Create new and worthwhile ideas (both incremental and radical concepts).

Work Creatively with Others

◆ Develop, implement, and communicate new ideas to others effectively.
◆ Be open and responsive to new and diverse perspectives; incorporate group input and feedback into the work.

◆ Elaborate, refine, analyze, and evaluate their own ideas in order to improve and maximize creative efforts.

Implement Innovations

◆ Act on creative ideas to make a tangible and useful contribution to the field in which the innovation will occur.

◆ Demonstrate originality and inventiveness in work and understand the real-world limits to adopting new ideas.

◆ View failure as an opportunity to learn; understand that creativity and innovation is a long-term, cyclical process of small successes and frequent mistakes.

2. Critical Thinking and Problem-Solving

Reason Effectively

◆ Use various types of reasoning (inductive, deductive, etc.) as appropriate to the situation.

Solve Problems

◆ Solve different kinds of non-familiar problems in both conventional and innovative ways.

◆ Identify and ask significant questions that clarify various points of view and lead to better solutions.

Use Systems Thinking

◆ Analyze how parts of a whole interact with each other to produce overall outcomes in complex systems.

Make Judgments and Decisions

◆ Effectively analyze and evaluate evidence, arguments, claims, and beliefs.

◆ Analyze and evaluate major alternative points of view.

◆ Synthesize and make connections between information and arguments.

◆ Interpret information and draw conclusions based on the best analysis.

◆ Reflect critically on learning experiences and processes.

3. Communication and Collaboration

Communicate Clearly

◆ Articulate thoughts and ideas effectively using oral, written, and nonverbal communication skills in a variety of forms and contexts.

◆ Listen effectively to decipher meaning, including knowledge, values, attitudes, and intentions.

◆ Use communication for a range of purposes (e.g. to inform, instruct, motivate, and persuade).

◆ Utilize multiple media and technologies, and know how to judge their effectiveness a priori as well as assess their impact.

◆ Communicate effectively in diverse environments (including multi-lingual).

Collaborate with Others

◆ Demonstrate ability to work effectively and respectfully with diverse teams.

◆ Exercise flexibility and willingness to be helpful in making necessary compromises to accomplish a common goal.

◆ Assume shared responsibility for collaborative work, and value the individual contributions made by each team member.

LIFE AND CAREER SKILLS

4. Flexibility and Adaptability

Adapt to Change

◆ Adapt to varied roles, jobs responsibilities, schedules, and contexts.

◆ Work effectively in a climate of ambiguity and changing priorities.

Be Flexible

◆ Incorporate feedback effectively.

◆ Deal positively with praise, setbacks, and criticism. Understand, negotiate, and balance diverse views and beliefs to reach workable solutions, particularly in multi-cultural environments.

(Continued)

(Continued)

5. Initiative and Self-Direction

Be Self-Directed Learners

- Go beyond basic mastery of skills and/or curriculum to explore and expand one's own learning and opportunities to gain expertise.
- Demonstrate initiative to advance skill levels towards a professional level.
- Demonstrate commitment to learning as a lifelong process.
- Reflect critically on past experiences in order to inform future progress.

Manage Goals and Time

- Set goals with tangible and intangible success criteria.
- Balance tactical (short-term) and strategic (long-term) goals.
- Utilize time and manage workload efficiently.

Work Independently

- Monitor, define, prioritize, and complete tasks without direct oversight.

6. Social and Cross-Cultural Skills

Interact Effectively with Others

- Know when it is appropriate to listen and when to speak.
- Conduct themselves in a respectable, professional manner.

Work Effectively in Diverse Teams

- Respect cultural differences and work effectively with people from a range of social and cultural backgrounds.
- Respond open-mindedly to different ideas and values.
- Leverage social and cultural differences to create new ideas and increase both innovation and quality of work.

7. Productivity and Accountability

Produce Results

- Demonstrate additional attributes associated with producing high quality products, including the abilities to:
  ◇ work positively and ethically;
  ◇ manage time and projects effectively;
  ◇ multi-task;
  ◇ participate actively, as well as be reliable and punctual;
  ◇ present oneself professionally and with proper etiquette;
  ◇ collaborate and cooperate effectively with teams;
  ◇ respect and appreciate team diversity;
  ◇ be accountable for results.

Manage Projects

- Set and meet goals, even in the face of obstacles and competing pressures.
- Prioritize, plan, and manage work to achieve the intended result.

8. Leadership and Responsibility

Be Responsible to Others

- Act responsibly with the interests of the larger community in mind.

Guide and Lead Others

- Use interpersonal and problem-solving skills to influence and guide others toward a goal.
- Leverage strengths of others to accomplish a common goal.
- Inspire others to reach their best via example and selflessness.
- Demonstrate integrity and ethics in using influence and power.

Tony Wagner's Seven Survival Skills

Tony Wagner's superb book, *The global achievement gap*, was meant to be a wake-up call for all U.S. schools. He suggests that even really good schools with really good standardized test scores are not effectively imbuing their graduates with the right skills to survive, flourish, and prosper in the coming diverse society and globalized economy of the near future. He would like schools and teachers to integrate and promote the following capacities:

1. Critical thinking and problem-solving
2. Collaboration across networks and leading by influence
3. Agility and adaptability
4. Initiative (entrepreneurship)
5. Effective oral and written communication skills
6. Accessing and analyzing information
7. Curiosity and imagination.

Steven Covey's Seven Habits of Highly Effective People

The Coveys have become a brand of sorts. They have sold millions of copies of books that tell about the importance of these affective traits . . . and how to do them. Their "leader in me" approach seeks to infuse young people with the right set of affective tools (they call them "Habits") for success. Their list includes the following:

1. Be proactive
2. Begin with the end in mind
3. Put first things first
4. Think "Win–Win"
5. Seek first to understand, then to be understood
6. Synergy matters (connect, collaborate, incorporate)
7. "Sharpen the saw" (seek to improve)

KIPP Schools' Seven Character Strengths

KIPP became more famous through focus on their model in Paul Tough's 2012 book. Importantly, their motto, "Work Hard, Be Nice," is expected to be followed every day by every member of the school community. They also strive to have students talk about "character" on a regular basis. They actually suggest the following steps to incorporating it often: (a) model it,

(b) name it, (c) find it, (d) feel it, (e) integrate it, (f) encourage it, and (g) track it. For more visit: http://www.kipp.org/our-approach/character (retrieved 11/28/16).

The Seven Character Strengths are as follows:

1. Gratitude
2. Social Intelligence
3. Optimism
4. Self-control
5. Zest
6. Curiosity
7. Grit

Character First's 49 Traits

Character First is a national organization dedicated to the promotion of a huge set of socially and morally desirable personality traits in educational and commercial endeavors. Some critics have stayed away from the use of the phrasing of "character" because it carries undertones of religiously based values (note the inclusion of "faith" and "meekness" in the list), yet we see significant overlap with the less morally charged language of other taxonomies. In our experience, this approach is often used by schools on a very limited basis, a sort of "virtue of the month": this month is a brief acknowledgement of "sincerity," but next month might be "compassion." Used this way, there is no structure to the importance, integration, or demonstration of the items. It is left entirely up to the teacher to determine how these should/could not only be promoted, but truly incorporated into learning. They do provide a most fascinating list for educators to examine:

1. Alertness	2. Attentiveness	3. Availability	4. Benevolence	5. Boldness
6. Cautiousness	7. Compassion	8. Contentment	9. Creativity	10. Decisiveness
11. Deference	12. Dependability	13. Determination	14. Diligence	15. Discernment
16. Discretion	17. Endurance	18. Enthusiasm	19. Faith	20. Flexibility
21. Forgiveness	22. Generosity	23. Gentleness	24. Gratefulness	25. Honor
26. Hospitality	27. Humility	28. Initiative	29. Joyfulness	30. Justice
31. Loyalty	32. Meekness	33. Obedience	34. Orderliness	35. Patience
36. Persuasiveness	37. Punctuality	38. Resourcefulness	39. Responsibility	40. Security
41. Self-control	42. Sensitivity	43. Sincerity	44. Thoroughness	45. Thriftiness
46. Tolerance	47. Truthfulness	48. Virtue	49. Wisdom	

For more on Character First's 49 Traits, visit: http://www.characterfirst.com/assets/CFDefinitions.pdf (retrieved 01/31/17).

Ontario Canada's Learning Skills and Work Habits for Grades 1–12

In 2010, the Ontario's Ministry of Education published a document entitled "Growing Success" outlining policy regarding the assessment and evaluation of students across the province. Drawing on their own research, that of the Conference Board of Canada, the Organization for Economic Cooperation and Development (OECD), various international organizations, and (not surprisingly) the work of Costa and Kallick, they created the Learning Skills and Work Habits for Grades 1–12 as a means of helping students succeed in school and throughout their lives. Below is their listing including exemplar objectives which are intended to be modified as developmentally appropriate. For more, visit: http://www.edu.gov.on.ca/eng/policyfunding/growSuccess.pdf (retrieved 01/31/17).

Responsibility

The student:
◆ fulfils responsibilities and commitments within the learning environment;
◆ completes and submits class work, homework, and assignments according to agreed-upon timelines;
◆ takes responsibility for and manages own behavior.

Collaboration

The student:
◆ accepts various roles and an equitable share of work in a group;
◆ responds positively to the ideas, opinions, values, and traditions of others;
◆ builds healthy peer-to-peer relationships through personal and media-assisted interactions;
◆ works with others to resolve conflicts and build consensus to achieve group goals;
◆ shares information, resources, and expertise and promotes critical thinking to solve problems and make decisions.

Organization

The student:
◆ devises and follows a plan and process for completing work and tasks;
◆ establishes priorities and manages time to complete tasks and achieve goals;
◆ identifies, gathers, evaluates, and uses information, technology, and resources to complete tasks.

Initiative

The student:
◆ looks for and acts on new ideas and opportunities for learning;
◆ demonstrates the capacity for innovation and a willingness to take risks;
◆ demonstrates curiosity and interest in learning;
◆ approaches new tasks with a positive attitude;
◆ recognizes and advocates appropriately for the rights of self and others.

Independent Work

The student:
◆ independently monitors, assesses, and revises plans to complete tasks and meet goals;

Self-regulation

The student:
◆ sets own individual goals and monitors progress towards achieving them;
◆ seeks clarification or assistance when needed;

(Continued)

(Continued)

◆ uses class time appropriately to complete tasks; ◆ follows instructions with minimal supervision.	◆ assesses and reflects critically on own strengths, needs, and interests; ◆ identifies learning opportunities, choices, and strategies to meet personal needs and achieve goals; ◆ perseveres and makes an effort when responding to challenges.

Habits of Mind

Visit: http://habitsofmind.org/ (retrieved 01/31/17).

Appendix 2
Kagan's Structural Approach

For many years, Spencer Kagan's work has been a mainstay in elementary school teaching in the U.S. and Canada, where teachers are looking for quick, simple, powerful and enjoyable "learning activities." Often, when people find out we are "interested" in Cooperative Learning, they immediately talk about their great experiences with Kagan's many "structures" (The Structural Approach to Cooperative Learning: http://www.ascd.org/ASCD/pdf/jour nals/ed_lead/el_198912_kagan.pdf [retrieved 01/31/17]). (Rarely do they mention Slavin's TGT or STAD, Johnson and Johnson's LT, Aronson's Jigsaw, and never do they mention the work of Sharan on Group Investigation.)

While more complete information on all of his many options is easily available, we thought we'd provide a little detail on four of his most frequently valued structures. Although teacher reliance on traditional practice or tech-based individual work has really limited the opportunities for teens to optimize growth intellectually, emotionally, or socially through Cooperative Learning, these group-based tactics are entirely appropriate for secondary education, and fit beautifully into the Dual Objective repertoire.

1. For **class-building,** the practice of **Corners** is offered.

   In this tactic, students are asked to identify their positions on an issue, usually with four options available. Students think about their reasons for support and then are moved to four different locations (i.e. corners) of the room with like-minded classmates. In the corners, they converse and build their arguments for their position, examining, sharing, and elaborating on the expressed evidence. Frequently this activity is closed with two additional steps. First, the corner groups report out their position to the whole class. Questions during the debrief may or may not be added. Second, after all evidence is presented, students are given an opportunity to change locations; that is, they can move to the corner representing a position different from their original if the others' arguments have been persuasive. Debriefings of the activity vary from teacher to teacher.

2. For **concept development** the practice of the **Three-Step Interview** is offered.

   In this tactic, groups of four are divided in half, with paired students facing each other (near the other pair). A one-way interview (on a given topic) is then held between opposing partners with, note-taking expected. Students then reverse roles and a second interview is conducted. Finally, a "round robin" occurs in which all four students take turns sharing the insights and ideas examined in the interviews. (Note: This is a "group within a group" approach and is meant to engage everyone actively.)

3. For **mastery of content,** the practice of **Numbered Heads** is offered.

   While reviewing material that students have been exposed to, the traditional large group Q&A (recitation) has been changed. All students in the groups are given a number between one and four and, after a question has been asked, wait-time is allowed so members of the group can "put their heads together" and discuss the question before any one is called to answer. (OK, what is the equation for energy? . . . Talk it over . . . OK, let's choose a number two, Myron?)

4. For **multiple purposes,** Kagan offers us the practice of **Inside– Outside Circle**.

   In this tactic, which teens will see as a form of "speed dating," the class is structured around two concentric circles, each student is thus facing another. Students are then questioned or challenged and they are allowed to collaborate with their facing partner before being called on. Each teacher challenge/question is followed by a rotation (inside circle step to the right!) so that partners only last for one question.